The Imagined Moment

FRONTIERS OF NARRATIVE

SERIES EDITOR: David Herman

Ohio State University

The Imagined Moment

Time, Narrative, and Computation

INDERJEET MANI

University of Nebraska Press ¦ Lincoln and London

Library of Congress
Cataloging-in-Publication Data
Mani, Inderjeet.
The imagined moment: time,
narrative, and computation /
Inderjeet Mani.
p.   cm.—(Frontiers of narrative)
Includes bibliographical references
and index.
ISBN 978-0-8032-2977-8
(cloth: alk. paper)
1. Time in literature. 2. Fiction—
History and criticism. I. Title.
PN3352.T5M35   2010
809.3'933—dc22
2009049418

Set in Minion Pro and Meta by
Bob Reitz.
Designed by A. Shahan.

CONTENTS

ILLUSTRATIONS

TABLES

ACKNOWLEDGMENTS

I am deeply grateful to the following scholars for their extensive comments on earlier drafts of the manuscript: David Herman, Ohio State University; Birte Lönneker-Rodman, University of Hamburg; Nick Montfort, MIT; and James Pustejovsky, Brandeis University. David Elson at Columbia University also provided valuable feedback. Thanks are also due to the helpful staff at the Lauinger Library at Harvard University and the Hayden Library at MIT. I would also like to thank my editor at the University of Nebraska Press, Kristen Elias Rowley, for many helpful suggestions. My copyeditor, Barb Wojhoski, also deserves thanks for her careful scrutiny of the manuscript. Any errors remaining are entirely my own doing.

The Imagined | Moment

Introduction

Stories inform our lives. The prince who renounces his kingdom to seek the meaning of life; the warrior who returns home after many travails and is reunited with his faithful wife; the ingénue who learns to find her way in a corrupt world; and the valet who rescues his master from embarrassments and entanglements—these stories live on in our imagination, long after the author has disappeared; they make their presence felt in books, movies, speeches, excuses for war, campaigns for peace, and moments when we throw away the cares of life and seek humorous relief.

How is it that a few strokes of a pen or taps of a key can summon up entire worlds, immersing us in the triumphs and traumas of various characters, and even suggesting how exemplary lives should or should not be led? My book attempts to answer this question, focusing on one key slice of narrative: time.

I examine time in narrative primarily from the perspective of recent developments in linguistics and the computational sciences. I try to account for some of the delight we feel in reading, in particular explaining our identification with narrative characters and their journeys in time. I do this with the help of computer models.

Computers have had a long history of use in analysis of literary works, the best-known area being authorship identification. Recent successes have included the unmasking of the journalist Joe Klein as the anonymous author of the roman à clef *Primary Colors*. (What gave Klein away was his relatively frequent use of adjectives ending in "inous," like "vertiginous," and his hyperactive use of prefixes such as "hyper," "mega," and "quasi.") Almost all of this literary forensics work has been focused on vocabulary, spelling, and grammar, aided by statistical analyses.[1] These methods are very useful in revealing the style and personal stamp of the author. However, computer science today can dig much deeper. I hope to convince the reader that recent developments allow us to posit a richly textured, even scientific account of what it means to understand the flow of time in literary stories.

As everyone knows, new developments in computer technology have made it possible for anyone to publish content in a variety of new media and to search and communicate almost instantaneously. Children use these tools of our age to tell stories. All sorts of stories in a variety of languages can be found today on the Web, manifested in e-mails, travel blogs, newsgroups, text messages, medical forums, even the dossiers of human rights tribunals; the variety seems almost endless. Much attention has been paid in the news media to the ways in which one can get noticed online and to the many new communication styles and brogues that can be found in text messaging, chat, and blogs. However, there has been relatively little discussion of what the technologies for sifting through information in human language on the Web can tell us about the way stories are put together.

News about some of this sifting has surfaced in the media now and then, mostly under the rubric of "data mining" and "surveillance" technologies that can crunch through reams of data to keep tabs on people's behavior. The newsworthiness of these technologies has so far been mainly related to fears about the further rupturing of the few remaining shreds of privacy we still cling to in our hyper-networked and highly surveillance-oriented society. However, the underlying techniques for processing data, particularly data in human languages, are of considerable relevance for narrative understanding. The main goal of this book is to show how these techniques can be of value beyond their use by Big Brother and Big Business, in particular, as applied to understanding how stories make use of time.

Although these techniques were aimed originally at applications favored by the military-industrial complex, the goals of this book are entirely humanistic, in the broad sense of seeking to enrich our literary culture, which is concerned, ultimately, with human self-expression and freedom. Such a humanistic approach can hardly be avoided when the subject is time.

We think of time as an additional dimension offered by the brilliant conceptual lens through which we view life. This dimension speaks to us of incessant change, of epochs and eras, of trajectories marked by beginnings and endings, births and extinctions. In addition to this rather somber message, time is also a harbinger of freedom, allowing us to escape from the eternal present, to resurrect a past that includes victory and failure, pleasure and suffering, and also giving us the wherewithal to prepare for and envision a better future. These twin characteristics of finitude and escape can be viewed as being in opposition, the first representing the heavy tug of reality, the second representing a flight toward freedom. Thus, many of our narratives of life, the stories we tell one another, reflect the uniquely human qualities of this tension. The computational theory I propose illuminates these very human aspects of timelines, allowing us to track characters filled with lofty or insidious goals, experiencing events that unfold along a timeline, reacting with pleasure or sadness, reconstructing a past and gazing out into a future.

I hope the book will not only alert lovers of literature to the power and promise of our tools today but also excite the interest of those who might want to encourage the further development of these models. To make the book interesting to the general reader, the ideas are presented here without any mathematical notation, using pictures to illustrate technical points.

THE THEORY IN A NUTSHELL

In order to understand how time is used in narrative, one needs a computational model of how time is used in language. My perspective on narrative is informed by research in computational linguistics. Developments in this field have resulted in systems that can answer questions as to when particular events in a text narrative are purported to happen. These systems create arbitrarily complex timelines that track mentions of events and times in any given document. Such systems, which can represent hypothetical past or future events, can anchor and order events in time, determining when an event happens, or whether one event occurs before another, irrespective of the order in which events are narrated.

Given this background, this book explores a computational theory of time in fictional narratives. I begin with a characterization of the timelines of literary texts. Here one must take into account not only the ordering and anchoring of events in time, but the embedding of stories within stories, and correspondences between entities of differing fictive status, such as events or times that are stated to occur or are merely remembered or imagined. These timelines can capture more than the succession of events: they can also represent their durations, and their distances from one another and from the time of narration, when such information is available. Given that such information is often not available, the model is still able to detect when the cloak of vagueness is present. All in all, this first layer is able to answer the question, given any text from Aesop's fables to the *nouveau roman*, of when something happened.

Narratives usually are more than an ordered list of events: they involve a story line that establishes a connection between the events. A reader can hazard a guess as to the motives behind the actions of particular characters and the outcomes and ramifications of those actions. However, there are many sequences of events in a person's life, such as my morning rituals of lifting the cap off the toothpaste tube and then brushing my teeth, that even if explained thoroughly in terms of when and why and whereof, are of no interest whatsoever (a point that some of today's bloggers seem not to have grasped). An event in a story is only significant if it means something, in a fundamental sense. And what it means, I believe, is tied to theories of what is good, desirable, avoidable, bad, and so forth in our thoughts and actions. A man may be a devoted father but a tyrannical ruler, and those behaviors could alter as the narrative evolves. A character might be uninteresting at the beginning but may grow in complexity. These are judgments that the reader makes, and these judgments can evolve over the course of a narrative. A layer is needed, therefore, to track, over the course of a narrative, changes in our emotional reactions to particular characters. Following Aristotle, I characterize the (idealized) reader's emotion only in terms of sympathy for or antipathy toward a character's situation. This layer, therefore, addresses the question of how a character evolves over time in the eyes of the actual reader. The actual reader is a member of what Peter Rabinowitz calls the "actual audience," namely, the "flesh-and-blood people who read the book" (1988, 20).[2] As Rabinowitz argues, each member of the actual audience can differ in the way she interprets a given work; clearly, interpretation can vary due to many factors, including the reader's class, ethnicity, historical period, familiarity with the work and its author, and so on. However, I argue that it is possible to arrive at generalizations about members of the actual audience based on comparing the reactions of one reader with another.

My theory thus characterizes the manner in which time is used in narrative to help characters construct and evolve identities that readers are happy to pass judgment on. The theory does not require that the interpretation of a text be completely determined, or even that there be a single interpretation. Of course, there is interpretation, and much can be learned that is of literary value from the study of the hermeneutic process of interpretation.

These two layers do not exhaustively cover the role that time plays in narrative. As the phenomenological philosopher Paul Ricoeur has argued, time and narrative can be viewed as intrinsically linked: "Time becomes human time to the extent that it is organized after the manner of a narrative; narrative, in turn, is meaningful to the extent that it portrays the features of temporal experience" (1984, 3). In Ricoeur's theory this linking of time and narrative occurs at three levels, tied to a theory of narrative as mimesis, the "imitation of action." Narrative comes (is "prefigured") with a variety of capabilities allowing for expression of aspects of action, including who did what to (or what happened to) whom; the agents, events, and entities involved; and the temporal order of actions. This level feeds into a second level of "imaginative configuration" of those action-related elements into a coherent structure by means of plot, providing an explanation for why things happen in the narrative, and allowing for considerable flexibility in the temporal locations, orders, and tempos in terms of which chronologies can be expressed. Finally, this level is mapped to a third level of "refiguration," which allows the reader to interpret the text in terms of his or her own experience — "the final indicator of the refiguring of the world of action under the sign of the plot" (77).

My account, while stopping short of any grand, all-encompassing theory, addresses aspects of these three levels within a computational framework. In terms of prefiguration, I delve into how computational tools can compute a basic level of linguistic analysis of the meaning of sentences in a narrative, one that covers the events, participants, their times, and places, and that provides a basic timeline for the text. In terms of configuration, my analysis includes the ability to detect various kinds of orders in which events are narrated, as well as their tempos.

Although I certainly believe that plot is crucial to any theory of narrative, I sidestep the modeling of plot, because more foundational research must be done in the field of artificial intelligence before one can effectively compute plots. Finally, regarding refiguration, I focus on a single aspect of the reader's interpretation of the narrative: her evaluation of the character's situation at particular points in the narrative.[3]

Leveraging the power of modern computational tools, my theory can allow a system to track when a character gazes back or ahead in time to reflect on experience, to contemplate roads not taken and roads that might be taken. My theory can also track the varying speeds at which time passes in a narrative, the modulation of which allows the reader to experience events at different levels of detail and to await long-expected outcomes with added suspense. It can also address the question of the span of time a story covers, given that novels said to be set on a single day often have references to times well before and after that. Pace and span together contribute to the reader's sense of how fast the narrative has flown.

Reading a story with pleasure involves a constructive activity by the reader; indeed, "expression creates being," as the French critic Gaston Bachelard (1964, xxiii) has observed. The experience of reading a narrative is similar, in some respects, to performing the music of a composer, except that reading involves an act of simulation. Time in narrative is especially interesting in this regard because the reader is carrying out her simulation in time, at her own pace, squeezing the reading into free moments. The reader can vicariously experience, as she travels about with other characters, entirely different experiences and thoughts in the past and the future, passing quickly over decades and even centuries; meanwhile, she also gratefully recognizes experiences and thoughts that echo her own. Most importantly, she can fast-forward or rewind — all of time is before her; she seems to be free at last of the weight of time. But at some point this freedom ends; the clock reminds one it's time to put away the book or the computer and to instead return to the day job, to run another errand or satisfy another master.

This contrast between real and imagined worlds becomes even more vivid when stories are digitized in various ways, from electronic texts to computer-mediated or computer-generated novels, allowing for nonlinear reading styles, and the co-opting of the reader in selecting or creating alternative futures. Overall, new modes of storytelling, along with the technologies of immersive game playing, have introduced rather novel ways of exploring time. These temporal aspects also have a variety of implications, some of them disturbing, for the way stories are and will be experienced. Chapter 9 ("Digital Storytelling") explores such issues.

Having spent several pages outlining this theory, I would like to briefly indicate what this theory is not about. The computational theory is not intended to model how humans understand narrative. A prerequisite for a theory of how humans understand narrative, given that my account is focused on language, would be an adequate explanation, backed by empirical evidence, of how humans understand language. Despite some very interesting proposals, linguistics is not quite there yet. Further, the computer programs that implement at least part of my computational theory rely on both induction, that is, having the system learn generalizations based on statistics collected from large bodies of linguistic examples, as well as rules. How rules and statistics interact in communication and language acquisition is far from clear.[4]

The computational approach also includes various modules that carry out arithmetic calculations related to calendars and that make logical deductions. It is extremely unlikely that the particular calculations, statistics, and logics involved in a model are actually those implemented in the circuits of the brain. Some of the evidence for specifics of time processing in the brain supports the idea of a system of circuits that oscillate periodically. My computational model, which does not even adopt the interesting biologically oriented perspective of cognitive linguistics, is far removed from any grounding in such biological mechanisms. This lack of grounding, while hardly uncontroversial, is nevertheless quite common in functionalist approaches to the philosophy of mind, where the mind is viewed as an abstract symbol-processing device; such a functionalism has been a strong influence in research in computational linguistics. The theories of cognitive linguistics, in turn, do not see much of a role for logic in representing meaning and, further, are somewhat sketchy when it comes to analyzing the details of how to represent time.

However, a weaker psychological claim can be made. Aspects of this computational model underlie some of the representations humans use in narrative understanding, as uncovered by psychological experiments. For example, psychologists have shown that in reading, humans carry out a simulation of the events in a story, modeling the characters, their events, and their passage in time, while experiencing feelings of empathy, repulsion, and so on at various points. Neuroscientists have provided further evidence for such simulation in experiments that reveal that the same areas of the brain are activated when reading about an action as would be activated when carrying out that action. These simulations have many points of correspondence with the computational model I propose. Studies of how children generate narrative show a progression from jumbled thoughts to simple timelines and eventually to plots and character models. This ordering supports my claim of timelines being more basic than plot and character. Further, it is simulation that contributes, in my theory, to the perceived tempo of events in narrative. Finally, my theory makes several predictions about narrative that can be tested experimentally. Even though much can be learned from human models, I do not believe it is essential for an artificial model to resemble the human one.

DEFENDING THE LINGUISTIC PERSPECTIVE

The focus in this book is on language rather than on extralinguistic factors such as the context of creation of a work, the time in which it was written, its relationship to writer and reader, its relation to prior literature, references to salient historical events or cultural allusions, and so forth. These extralinguistic factors, beginning with the reader, are of the utmost importance. Theorists beginning with Louise Rosenblatt in the 1930s have drawn attention to the importance of the cultural presuppositions that the reader brings to a text, allowing for a variety of meanings among readers. Postmodern critics such as Roland Barthes (1977) have taken this view to an extreme, minimizing the importance of the author and his or her biography to the understanding of a literary work, emphasizing exclusively the work as a linguistic object and the role of the reader in interpretation. Barthes buttresses his argument with an account of how writers like Mallarmé, Valery, and Proust went to great pains to blur the role of the writer, so much so that the narrator in Proust's magnum opus is a young man who has not yet written the book that is being read. The linguistic perspective Barthes advocates is in fact consistent with the view adopted in this book.

Barthes' argument is in keeping with the postmodern agenda of celebrating the subjectivity of interpretation. In principle two works created in different periods with exactly the same "text" might be viewed as quite different, a point made with effervescent wit by Borges in his story of Pierre Menard, the author who re-creates Don Quixote word for word: "He dedicated his conscience and nightly studies to the repetition of a pre-existing book in a foreign tongue. The number of rough drafts kept on increasing; he tenaciously made corrections and tore up thousands of manuscript pages" (1963, 54).

However, as mentioned earlier, I do require that interpretation be not entirely subjective to the point where anything goes; language does substantially constrain interpretation, in specific ways that are addressed in this book.

No matter what Barthes and other postmodernists might claim, situating a work in terms of the background of the writer is sometimes crucial. Reading *The Sound and the Fury* after perusing Faulkner's letters makes all the difference to its appreciation. Knowing the author's background is essential for understanding stories from cultures that the reader is utterly unfamiliar with. Of course, reading a book with hindsight makes a tremendous difference; imagine not knowing about the events of the 1930s and the Second World War when reading the repulsive *Mein Kampf* (first published in 1925).

Computer modeling capabilities today cannot satisfactorily address many of the extralinguistic contextual factors. However, the techniques of network analysis, in particular the computational analysis of various kinds of links (social or other) between individuals, can help build an emergent model of some of these factors. Such an analysis has been put to use in the tracking of academic citations (the counts of which are all too influential in measuring scholarly achievement and granting academic tenure); it is also used in the Page Rank algorithm of search engines like Google. With the growth of social networking sites on the Web, this area has also drawn the interests of governments. Given the history of such investments, and given the various U.S. and European government funding initiatives, new technologies relating to the contexts in which narratives (e-mails, calls to arms, and the like) are interpreted are likely to follow.

Turning away from the extralinguistic to the linguistic: narrative does essentially and inescapably involve language, and the ability to model textually provided linguistic aspects is clearly a necessary step. The modeling of narrative structure must address the popular languages of today as well as those endangered languages in which many of the stories that form our collective cultural patrimony reside. One disadvantage of focusing on language, however, is that linguistic constructions found in one particular version of a work may not be found in other versions, leading to inferences that may be invalid across versions.

Folktales are notorious in this respect. We find the animal stories from the Sanskrit *Panchatantra*, for example, traveling around the world, being altered as they go along; often there are multiple versions of the same tale with each rendering having a somewhat different treatment. The Greek myths, of course, have many different forms; the story of Demeter and Persephone, for example, has dozens of variants. *The Conference of Birds*, that great twelfth-century Persian poem by Farīd od-Dīn Attār, owes its framing narrative to the *Panchatantra* as well as *The Recital of the Bird*, by the tenth-century Persian physician and philosopher Avicenna (or Ibn Sīnā); a similar story is also seen in Chaucer's *Canterbury Tales*. The Indian epic the *Ramayana* has many different versions, in Epic Sanskrit (the original version), as well as other Indian languages such as Hindi, Tamil, Telegu, and Bengali, and, as it traveled east, in live performances in Thai, Malay, Javanese, Balinese, Burmese, Lao, Khmer, and so on.

In the world of printed books, writers often go on editing and rewriting their work, while printers and publishers try to keep pace, meanwhile hoping for a windfall from a yet another "new" or "critical" edition. Which version of *Hamlet* should we draw our inferences from—the second quarto, which Shakespeare may have seen, or the posthumous but official first folio? Does one prefer the first (1913) edition of Proust's *Du côté de chez Swann* or the more authoritative 1987 Pleiades edition? The problem of "critical" editions becomes much more an issue when one goes back to ancient texts, where manuscripts are often lost, damaged, or copied and reedited by unknown hands.

A similar problem is posed by oral narratives. The classic work of Milman Parry and Albert Lord, described in Lord's *Singer of Tales* (1960), illustrates vividly how certain varieties of epic poetry (from the songs of Serbo-Croatian bards to Homer) are transmitted through a process of creative improvisation by "illiterate" singers, so that stories change in each telling. Later research (most notably by Ruth Finnegan [1992]) has explored the varying degrees of improvisation in oral storytelling across cultures.

Discussions of world literature involve analyses of translations. This can weaken any inferences drawn from the language of a particular translation, since the devices found in a translation are just as likely to have been injected by the translator rather than by the author (as Borges quipped, "The original is unfaithful to the translation"). One way to address this latter problem is to consider multiple translations.

Fortunately, all these problems are faced by the reader as well, and many a reader experiences a much-loved work only through the prism of a particular edition and translation. Readers of English rather than Russian or Spanish should think of (and thank) Constance Garnett when reading *Crime and Punishment* (or Margarshack, or Pevear and Volokhonsky), and they should be eternally grateful to Gregory Rabassa for *One Hundred Years of Solitude*.

AGAINST THE INDETERMINACY OF INTERPRETATION

This emphasis on analyzing a particular version of a work raises the broader question of how different versions of a story relate to one another. Barbara Herrnstein-Smith (1980) has pointed out that the idea of a single version of a story, such as "Cinderella," is problematic when one tries to pin the story down in terms of a unique summary. She cites a folkloric compendium of 345 documented variants of the story of Cinderella! Although I certainly agree that there are likely to be many versions, I find this particular number suspicious. Folkloric classifications — such as the Aarne-Thompson classification — emphasize commonalities across collections of folktales at the expense of delineating differences; they are thus likely to be overinclusive. Also, the problem of a nonunique summary is entirely familiar to me from my work in automatic summarization, where getting humans to agree on a summary is hard. But agreement on summaries of, say, news stories is not random and is usually better than agreement across unrelated material.

The existence of multiple accounts or versions of a narrative (whether hundreds or thousands) does not imply a complete indeterminacy of interpretation, as Herrnstein-Smith appears to have mistakenly inferred.

Although there may not be necessary and sufficient conditions that define what it means for a story to be that of Cinderella, some versions of a story could still be more Cinderellaish than others. Some versions of Cinderella could (and in fact are likely to) agree on common properties much more than those versions compared, say, to versions of "Little Red Riding Hood." For example, if one clusters a set of stories by similarity, using features drawn from an enumeration of all properties contained in any of them, there are likely to be groupings that amount to the de facto Cinderella stories. Such clusters may have a centroid (a statistical average) that corresponds to a "typical" Cinderella story, or there may be a particular exemplar (or exemplars) chosen as a Cinderella "prototype" (prototypes).

Of course, version comparisons presuppose some way of comparing and enumerating properties (concepts). Once one settles on an account of what sorts of concepts one is considering, one can empirically determine the extent of human agreement across versions that will indicate what it means for a pair of stories to have similar sets of concepts. In other words the notion of whether two stories are versions of Cinderella is dependent on one's theory and classification of concepts (of plot, story, etc.) but is hardly indeterminate.

NARRATIVE SCIENCE

My perspective on computational modeling has been influenced by several decades of research in computational linguistics, a field that lies at the intersection of computer science, linguistics, and artificial intelligence (AI), a field richly influenced by developments in cognitive science and philosophy.[5] Another influence on my work comes from structuralist theories of narrative, developed mainly in France in the 1950s and 1960s and subsequently refined. The structuralist accounts (which in turn developed as an extension of earlier work by the Russian formalists in the 1920s) were descriptive, and like traditional models of say, the sound system in a language, provided elaborate classifications based on contrasting features of various kinds. In phonetics we have the *p* pronounced in "Paul" as a voiceless bilabial plosive, whereas the *b* pronounced in "ball" is a voiced bilabial plosive. Similarly, in structuralist narratology not only do we have a first-person versus a third-person narration but also mimesis (representation, or showing) versus diegesis (narration, or telling) — a distinction that originates from Plato — and a homodiegetic narrator (a narrator who is part of the story world, i.e., a narrator as a character) versus a heterodiegetic narrator (where the narrator isn't part of the story, roughly, a disembodied narrator). In some stories the narrator switches from one to the other, as in Nabokov's *Pnin*, where the heterodiegetic narrator suddenly becomes homodiegetic in the final chapter, along with a change from third person to first. Although these classifications were insightful, given the atmosphere in which they were conceived, they did not result in precise models with which one could compute. In this book we not only identify patterns in narrative but also describe programs that can identify those patterns.

Research in computational linguistics began with a Chomskyan perspective, based on rules for grammar that analyzed not only the forms of language, as structuralist linguistics had, but also tried to account for underlying similarities between different forms. Chomsky's earliest grammar formalism was developed in the mid-1950s, at a time when cybernetics and computing were revolutionizing the way scientists thought about systems and symbol processing systems like language. His approach was based on introspection about which linguistic forms were natural (grammatical) versus unnatural (ungrammatical). In parallel the research of the logician Richard Montague at UCLA developed a new view of language based on the idea of systematic correspondences between form and meaning, addressing many classic problems of reference that were a central concern in the philosophy of language and in the development of logic.

The theoretical paradigms developed by Chomsky and Montague were popular in computational linguistics since they were inherently computational and were stated algorithmically in precise and mathematically rigorous ways. They also were very expressive and allowed for the generation of an infinite variety of linguistic forms. Narratology, rooted in structuralist models, has not really made such a transition toward more expressive foundations.

Subsequently, in the early 1990s computational linguistics took a seriously empirical turn, moving away from introspection as a means of generating data to the use of large samples of real language, called corpora. In doing so researchers were taking advantage of the availability of inexpensive high-capacity computer storage and increasing access to vast universes of information. (As we shall see, corpora can be used to automatically induce linguistic structures by statistical methods.) The emphasis here was on forms that actually occurred in real data, as opposed to introspectively defined criteria for grammaticality, or to devoting attention mainly to rare phenomena that happened to illustrate interesting properties of language. The theories themselves were formally restricted in various ways, to allow for more efficient algorithms. Today both form and meaning are analyzed in terms of structure, but statistics as well as logic can be used in the analysis.

This striving for expressiveness as well as empirical validation, which will be explored in this book, is highly applicable to linguistic aspects of narrative. Just as we have come to rely on the ability to construct large-scale scientific models of all kinds of data—biological, meteorological, astronomical, and economic—we now have the computational tools to analyze vast universes of linguistic information, including the variety found on the Web.

The multiple disciplines that contribute to my account have convinced me that there is enough common ground to allow for a firm foundation for a scientific theory of narrative, at least as it impinges on temporal aspects, the focus of this book. Such a theory must develop precise, formalizable concepts (formality being merely a way of stating ideas precisely) and also be able to adequately test hypotheses and predictions against collections of example narratives in a replicable manner, rather than relying on informal, anecdotal observations (which nevertheless may provide a rich motivational background for a theory). Clearly, such a methodological requirement may be viewed variously as reductionist, foolhardy, and so forth, but it makes eminent sense from a computational standpoint.

To rebut one such accusation right away: such a scientific theory is not in any sense a reductionist one. There are many ineffable aspects of literary appreciation that will, by their very nature, defy any attempt at formal theorizing. Ultimately, the qualitative states that correspond to our feelings about a literary work could never be reproduced by a machine, for the simple reason that they are inherently subjective. In fact, it is hard to see how the quality of any mental state (as opposed to its occurrence, correlation, or cause) can be characterized by some particular physical state of a computer. As the philosopher Thomas Nagel pointed out more than thirty years ago in his famous essay "What Is It Like to Be a Bat?":

> We must consider whether any method will permit us to extrapolate to the inner life of the bat from our own case, and if not, what alternative methods there may be for understanding the notion. ... It will not help to try to imagine that one has webbing on one's arms, which enables one to fly around at dusk and dawn catching insects in one's mouth; that one has very poor vision, and perceives the surrounding world by a system of reflected high-frequency sound signals; and that one spends the day hanging upside down by one's feet in an attic. In so far as I can imagine this (which is not very far), it tells me only what it would be like for me to behave as a bat behaves.... Yet if I try to imagine this, I am restricted to the resources of my own mind, and those resources are inadequate to the task. (1974, 439)

The qualities of our mental states do seem sacrosanct, privileged in some respect; our minds have enshrined them with ineffability. It is doubtful if any of the programs described here or anywhere else, today or in the future, can savor the peculiar and particular thrills we experience in reading.

This does not mean, however, that we cannot model key aspects of our emotions and analyze features of a narrative that give rise to sadness rather than joy. It is possible to construct a biologically relevant computational theory of emotion that is entirely symbolic, one that makes specific predictions (in fact, AI researchers have done precisely that), without the computer program having a body and being able to experience any of the emotions we have of fear, anger, happiness, sadness, or disgust.

AI AND NARRATIVE

Since this book is all about artificial models of time in narrative, it is worthwhile reviewing the lessons learned from related AI work, and how my particular approach differs from it.

AI has had a long history of building narrative systems, that is, programs to understand and generate stories. Some of the inspiration for these approaches can be traced back to the 1930s, when the Cambridge psychologist Frederic Bartlett conducted experiments in which he asked subjects to repeat a given story over time. Bartlett found that the story was reconstructed in memory according to what he called "an active organization of past reactions, or of past experiences" (1932, 201), or a schema. The schema imposes a level of abstraction on the information in a story, favoring gists over details and biasing the assimilation of new information toward conformity with the schema, resulting in details irrelevant to the schema being left out.

The AI researcher Roger Schank and his colleagues gave these schemas a rich computational embodiment in terms of scripts, which are structures that represent a sequence of stereotypical activities, such as eating at a restaurant. As described in Schank and Abelson (1977), a restaurant script will involve characters typically found in a restaurant, such as waiters and patrons, and events such as arriving, perusing the menu (and perhaps other patrons), ordering, eating, paying a bill, and so forth, that may be arranged in a sequence. Characters have wants (such as food, i.e., they are hungry), and they know that they can carry out actions (such as paying for the food). These are some of the preconditions that a script requires in order to be applicable. When a script is "executed,"[6] postconditions also result, such as the person's hunger being satisfied. Every script will have to specify the characters, event sequence, preconditions, and postconditions.

The postulation of scripts as a means of organizing the experience of stories in memory is intuitively appealing.[7] However, for a computer program to use scripts, the programmer must be precise as to the set of scripts and the contents of each one. One of the basic challenges with scripts is determining which script applies in a given situation.[8] Even when a script can be identified for a given story, figuring out what the script should contain isn't easy. This is because of the large number of commonsense inferences that can be involved. If someone enters a restaurant, it sets up expectations that the person is going to eat there (unless the person is a waiter or an assassin). If the person pays up, one can infer that she has already eaten (unless she is in a place where one pays first). A person may eat with the intent of not paying (this results in an extremely uncomfortable outcome, as anyone who has been on the receiving end of this situation can attest). Of course, the presence of a waiter is only a default: fast-food places usually don't have waiters.

Research in the 1970s and 1980s tried to address the problems with scripts by reorganizing and simplifying them and designing them on an as-needed basis, driven by the particular domain of interest.[9] And scripts alone were soon recognized as insufficient for narrative understanding in AI. Researchers came to the conclusion that characters in a story needed to be modeled along with their goals and plans, schemes that are realized or foiled, with outcomes that matter to them.[10] The TALE-SPIN system of James R. Meehan (1977) instantiated this integrated vision, generating stories in the domain of Aesop's fables. The TALE-SPIN programmer provides the system with a cast of characters and a geographical setting and then gives each character a goal to solve. The goal spawns further "subgoals" involving specific actions, including cooperative or adversarial activities between characters; as the actions are carried out, the state of the world is updated. Despite these capabilities, the stories produced by TALE-SPIN are limited in scope: like bland running commentaries or documentaries, they are mainly a trace of the thoughts and actions of characters.[11] What is notably missing from this character-driven approach to narrative is any overall, global structure introduced by the author.

Later work on story generation has emphasized plot. The UNIVERSE system of M. Lebowitz (1985) is similar to TALE-SPIN but uses authorial goals rather than character-driven goals to structure narratives. UNIVERSE can be initialized with an authorial goal that calls for a couple to divorce, and then, like a meddling god, UNIVERSE will insert relationship obstacles into the narrative. In doing so it may use an existing plot fragment to achieve this goal. UNIVERSE is, however, overly author-driven; actions cannot occur unless they satisfy an authorial goal. Further research on story generation, including story "grammars" and temporal narrative, is discussed in chapter 9 ("Digital Storytelling").

Unfortunately, despite techniques for teaching systems to acquire new knowledge, AI narrative systems have relied on knowledge that is custom built (inserted by the programmer) for each story or type of story. The result is that story understanding (and generation) systems are brittle, unsuccessful in understanding (generating) stories on topics for which they weren't prepared. Also, given the large number of possibilities that can be inferred, the reasoning processes required to carry out commonsense inferences tend to face an explosion of possibilities that result in inefficient computation. Finally, these AI systems have been notorious for a complete lack of attention to issues of evaluation.

Some of the major challenges in story understanding (not time related, I believe) will continue to haunt the field, but I want to make it clear that this book isn't addressing the larger story-understanding problem. Instead, we are squarely focused on time, which can be addressed computationally (using methods from AI and computational linguistics) in a tractable manner.

THE STATE OF IMPLEMENTATION

This book develops a computational theory of time in narrative. The question that arises is how much of the theory has actually been implemented in a computer program.

Given the corpus-based approach to computational linguistics, the best practices followed today, based on numerous successes—discussed later in chapter 7 ("Tracking Narrative Progression")—involve collecting corpora and marking them up with the kinds of information and structures that the computer will be required to produce from that data. For example, a corpus of personal biographies might record the person, the author, the date of the narrative, as well as the chronology of events and the names of people mentioned in each biography. This sort of markup will be carried out in context, so that the computer can "observe" the surrounding text next to each mention of a person or an event. Once an annotation scheme for such markup has been developed, it needs to be tested so that humans can agree on how to mark up a given example. In other words the data on which the computer program will be trained must be of high quality. Usually an annotation editing tool is used to insert tags into each document, in a way that does not damage or alter the original document (otherwise, a sudden fit of sneezing might change "Arms and the man I sing" to "Arms around the man I fling"). The first phase, therefore, is one of data preparation.

Once a sufficiently large corpus has been marked up (a large quantity of data is crucial, especially for statistical approaches), then a variety of more or less off-the-shelf components are trained statistically to produce that markup for any text, along with any custom components that need to be built. The systems then have to be evaluated for accuracy.

The annotated data functions as a source of training material as well as a "gold-standard" data set for evaluation (the corpus is usually split up so that training and testing data are distinct). The problem of evaluating something as fine-grained and detailed as time in narrative becomes considerably simplified when a computer program is used to compare system-generated markup against the gold standard, allowing the time-lining program to be automatically scored for accuracy.

For many problems the challenge is more in the generation of sufficient quantities of high-quality annotated data (assuming that a gold standard can be defined) and less in the discovery of new algorithms.

A variety of annotated corpora and automatic tools now exist for generating timelines. However, given that fiction mining is not a high priority for funding agencies, timelining research worldwide (a highly active field) has focused on "real stuff" rather than corpora of fiction. Thus, we have sources such as newspaper articles, crime and accident reports, medical case histories, meeting discussions, e-mail, summaries of movies, and so forth, in a variety of languages, that have all been annotated with timelines, providing "gold-standard" data sets.

As a result, while there are lots of fiction sources online (Project Gutenberg being one major resource for such collections), no large-scale fiction corpora have been annotated with timelines. Therefore, the best one can do at the moment is to take timelining tools trained on nonfictional data sets and apply them to the rather different material found in fiction. This situation is far from ideal, since statistical systems tend not to thrive when tested on material that is as vastly different, in linguistic terms, as fiction is from news (even if there are storytelling elements common to both). There is, as a result, also no gold standard for fiction evaluation. This book suggests specific steps to address this situation, which of course will include efforts to annotate fiction corpora.

One reason we are not as far along in terms of processing fiction as we should be is, as mentioned earlier, the lack of a strong case being made to funding agencies. The situation was somewhat different in the 1970s, when story understanding and generation was a focus of more funded research. Such research, some of which was discussed earlier in this chapter, was mostly aimed at science for science's sake. Today, however, with the tremendous practical opportunities afforded by text mining, and the flow of dollars, euros, and yuans toward it, the idea of devoting time and energy to processing fiction seems almost quaint. Nevertheless, as we shall see, there is a somewhat livelier interest in the generation of interactive, multimedia stories, driven to some extent by the commercial and military interest in computer games.

THE FUTURE OF NARRATIVE COMPUTING

The fact that a computer could adequately model time in fiction shouldn't be taken to mean that computers might have substantially understood natural language. The focus here is on understanding time in narrative. That understanding is tested by asking the computer to answer questions about when and why events happen and how characters evolve. However, as any teacher knows, answering questions is not a sufficient condition for revealing understanding. The lively body of philosophical debate on the Turing Test, focused on whether a computer's answers to questions can be distinguished from a human's, leads to a similar conclusion.

One way of displaying understanding is, of course, to write an essay, to make a logical (or even, if one is inclined, an utterly Dada or antilogical) argument to tell a story. AI has had a distinguished history of story generation, with computers carrying out tasks such as the production of animal stories, fairy tales, murder mysteries, and Arthurian legends. By confining their output modalities just to text, these generation systems have not availed of the variety of multimedia content that can be synthesized with today's technology. They also do not involve the user.

A less ambitious role for AI in fiction is in machine-assisted authoring, where the system does not attempt to supplant the author's imagination. Already writers who aren't programmers are easily able to create Web content with a few clicks. Makers of home movies are today using digital video-editing tools to create professional-looking content. Just as people today make extensive use of such tools, it is only a matter of time before the average person will have AI-based story-authoring tools available. These authoring tools, which are already being created in laboratories, will allow authors to prepare conventional fiction as well as movies and multimedia stories, at first choosing from a palette of characters from preexisting video clips, and endowing them with sound bites, and eventually drawing from libraries of story lines and preprogrammed behavior elements that can be assembled together. Need a crooked cop? Or just some gumshoe-speak? How about an elegant and decadent aesthete? Such characters abound in fiction, are easily personified, and they all have only a certain number of ways of speaking.

Another important technological trend is the empowerment of the reader. In recent years systems for interactive fiction and interactive drama have started to gain prominence. As the technology of single-player and multi-player computer games starts to infiltrate fiction, authorial omniscience will give way to a view of fiction that is much more a collaboration between writer and reader. Today's interactive fiction and drama allow users not just to pause, rewind, or explore choice points, but also to completely change the story line and the perception of the characters. Clearly, there has to be some way of preserving authorial intent, while allowing for a high degree of interactivity and "player" autonomy.

These new trends face many challenges in terms of preserving the unity and authenticity of literary voice and vision. One way they can contribute to the creation of superior works of fiction is for topnotch "time management" tools to be used. Chapter 9 ("Digital Storytelling") discusses this issue further.

There are many aspects of narrative that we are still a long way from successfully modeling, such as the use of nonliteral language, which is a hallmark of narrative. Metaphor, humor, and irony have eluded computational solutions, even though research since the 1990s has explored small steps in this direction. The models of emotion that have been explored in computational work are still rather primitive, and the particular one I have used is extremely crude. Other researchers have explored richer artificial modes of emoting. Nevertheless, I see a time when computers might aim for higher aesthetic capabilities, such as analyzing the atmosphere of a scene, which is closely related to what some AI researchers call "situation awareness." Perhaps someday systems will even be able to appreciate the notions of "lightness" and "exactitude" that Italo Calvino (1988) identifies as among the enduring literary values.

This book sketches a platform for future research on time in narrative from both a theoretical and a practical perspective. For the interested scholar or budding scientist, I offer a list of topics that I believe are likely to yield considerable fruit in terms of near-term scientific investigation. For the reader who simply wants to enjoy fiction using computer aids, I recommend some tools that might be of use to her for semiautomated analyses of literary texts. All these resources are also available, along with live software demos, on the book's companion Web site. Unlike purely literary theories of narrative, this one comes with real embodiments.

TERMINOLOGY

A word on the often confusing topic of terminology. Since this book aims to be nontechnical, I have tried to keep definitions as simple as possible.

I consider a narrative to be any work of fiction or nonfiction in any medium that purports to tell a story, in the informal sense in which we use the term "story." For purposes of analysis, I focus on written texts, and I use the term "text" to stand for particular instances of these. I emphasize fiction, particularly novels and short stories, though other genres such as dramatic works and poetry, as well as cinema, are included on occasion. Plot is used in the Aristotelian sense, to express causal relations among events engaged in by characters with particular goals. A narrative, as embodied in a given written fictional text such as a particular edition of a novel, has a plot derived from that particular instance. Characters are particular agents in a narrative, whose behaviors can be tracked. Character, in the abstract sense, is the set of personal characteristics, virtues and vices, and dispositions that characters have; it can be something static, assumed, constructed initially, or developed through the narrative. These notions are further elaborated in the text; I commit to specific definitions, relating them to the narratological literature, in the glossary at the end of the book.

1 | Timelines

Time is central to narrative. In a few minutes or hours, a story can take us into the world of fascinating characters, where we experience their lives as lived in the moment or remembered and anticipated. A novel may advance the story forward, hastening toward a climax, or skip backward, filling in details of a deviant childhood; it may take time to set up the scene for a romantic evening, or it may flit quickly across decades of dullness and centuries of a culture languishing in desperation and squalor. The passage of time in narratives mirrors the key role time plays in our lives, in our sense of our own passage through life and who we have become. Yet we yearn for time to stand still; a human is, as Gaston Bachelard has observed, "a being who does not want to melt away and who, even in the past, when he sets out in search of things past, wants time to 'suspend' its flight" (1964, 6).

Given the importance of time, tracking its flow in a story is a nontrivial but fascinating task. This chapter explains how time can be modeled in a narrative, addressing the question of when events happen.

Constructing a timeline for a narrative is essentially a matter of ordering events in time. I will begin with a basic model of timelines, illustrating a timeline for a simple story by means of a diagram, of a kind generated by a computer program.

The timeline model has several important characteristics. It records events and times (including, of course, dates) mentioned in the narrative. This makes the model fairly fine grained, as the items recorded are within each sentence. The recorded times will be resolved (or "grounded") in terms of a calendar. Such a grounding must allow for times that are expressed, as humans are wont to do, in a form that is incomplete (e.g., "Let's meet at *three*") or vague ("I'm off to Santorini *this summer*," or "I'd love to have a drink with you *sometime*"). The times and events will be related by various relationships that will include their being ordered temporally.

I will then examine a series of more complex stories. Timelines will have to include events described as actual, or objective, though these events may be entirely fictional and given that 100 percent objectivity, despite what the pundits say, is never possible. Timelines will also include subjective events mulled over in a character's mind, where they might be remembered (in the case of actual events), anticipated (in the case of possible future events), believed, desired, imagined, and so forth. Also, a text can have many interpretations. I will emphasize what I call a "conservative" interpretation that makes the fewest commitments given the text.

One advantage of such a model is a practical one: the use of automated aids in the analysis and understanding of large volumes of online literary, historical, biographical, or other narrative texts. I hope to convince the reader, however, that there is also a theoretical advantage. When one is constructing a complex artifact, be it the Golden Gate Bridge, the Mars Rover, or the Taj Mahal, certain fundamental principles of both design and engineering come into play. These principles are well documented and form part of the best practices of institutions and organizations engaged in engineering, architecture, and related disciplines. For too long the details of principles by which literary narratives have been designed have been obscured by the lack of precise analytical tools. Timelines, as computed by our intelligent system, are just one such tool, and the logic behind them is well understood. The components in such a tool (events, times, and their relationships) use fairly simple representations for timelines and veer happily toward William of Ockham's dictum (or Razor) that entities should not be multiplied beyond necessity.

A BASIC MODEL

Let us begin with a simple story. Anyone with a grasp of English can piece together what has happened in the following story:

> Yesterday, Serena was running a marathon when she twisted her ankle. Her boyfriend, Francisco, had tripped her.

Although too simple to be of literary interest, the information that even a child can pick up from this story is quite remarkable. English gives us lots of clues to help situate the events of import along a timeline. The tense used in describing the despicable Francisco's action (the past perfect "had tripped") tells us that the tripping occurred before she twisted her ankle, explaining the poor girl's injury. The "when" and the past-tense progressive form "was running" indicate that the twisting of the ankle occurred during the marathon. "Yesterday" indicates that the marathon was held the day before the time of writing, which we'll call the "speech time." Obviously, the concept of a single speech time for a sentence or a passage involves a degree of abstraction, since speech (or writing) itself takes time.

The use of the progressive tense form "was running" means that Serena did run, even though she may not have run the marathon. In other words, even if she ran for only five minutes, for almost every time slice of those five minutes, she was still running. Of course there may have been parts of that run where she stopped to catch her breath, or parts where she lifted a leg or sneezed due to Francisco's overpowering aftershave, actions that in themselves hardly constitute running events. This allows us a little time before the twist.

Based on these deductions one can produce a little diagram for the narrative pertaining to Serena as follows (in the sample passage, events are shown underlined, and times are highlighted in gray):

Yesterday, Serena was running a marathon when she twisted her ankle. Her boyfriend, Francisco, had tripped her.

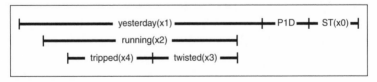

FIG. 1. Timeline for a simple story.

The diagram in figure 1 indicates that the tripping is during the running and before the twisting; the latter ends the running, all of which occurs during yesterday, which is one day before (P1D) the time of writing (the speech time, or ST). Here P1D stands for a period of one day. The narrative, like most others, is not told in chronological order.

Notice that the narration order is indicated with numbers, whereas the order of occurrence (the chronology) of the events is left to right. This is a crucial distinction, as it allows us to distinguish event order from narration order; for example, it means that flashbacks (sometimes called "analepses") will involve events with higher numbers occurring earlier (to the left) than those with lower numbers. Events or times under each other with the same horizontal extent take the same time. However, the box lengths do not reflect the lengths of the events; that is, the diagram isn't drawn to scale.

The participants involved in the running and the tripping are left out of the diagram, to conserve space; think of "running(x2)," for the time being, as shorthand for the (only) mention of the running event along with its participants. The timeline indicates both chronological and text order. The speech time (when the narrator said the passage) isn't explicitly mentioned, but we'll mark it as x0. It will represent a single time, namely, the time at which the passage is uttered. Of course instead of this abstraction, we could separately represent the speech time of various elements in the passage (e.g., sentence or word), but nothing is really gained from such a fine-grained distinction, unless the narrative specifically delineates different speech times. The latter situation, one can easily imagine, might occur in a genre such as a personal journal, where each passage is narrated at a different marked time. Speech times and event times (when the events are purported to happen) are aligned on the same axis, though of course they could be broken out on two axes at the cost of a more complex visualization.

This timeline was produced by an intelligent system that processed the narrative text, understanding English well enough to identify the events and times and link them with temporal relations (BEFORE, DUR-ING, ENDS, among others). The system then fed its output to a fairly trivial visualization program. We will discuss the details of the implemented system later, in chapter 3 ("Computing Timelines").

This model easily accommodates calendar times. Consider adding a dateline to the story:

[June 30, 2007] Yesterday Serena was running a marathon when she twisted her ankle. Her boyfriend, Francisco, had tripped her.

This dateline, a rough indication of the time of writing, allows us to anchor each of the boxes to a calendar date. In a nutshell, x0 is now June 30, 2007, and x1 is June 29, 2007.

In the following passage, while we know that John arrived at Mary's house after Mary left for dinner, we don't know which started earlier, John's hurrying or Mary's leaving.

John <u>hurried</u> to Mary's house after <u>work</u>. But Mary had already <u>left</u>.

The timeline is shown in figure 2. Instead of assuming multiple interpretations, we will represent an interpretation where the end of Mary leaving occurred before the end of John hurrying (more technically, the leaving OVERLAPS the hurrying), while leaving the temporal relation between John's working and Mary's leaving unspecified (indicated here with "?"). Most narratives involve such underspecified timelines. (More precisely the temporal relations in a narrative form what computer scientists call a "partial ordering," where the chronological ordering between a pair of elements may not be known.)

FIG. 2. Underspecified timeline.

TIME FROM TENSE

The clues for when events are happening are given by both explicit references to times, like "yesterday," as well as by tense, which expresses the distance in time of the event from the time of speech. But the influence of each can vary with the language in which the text is written.

In our story about Serena, we put the tense (the pluperfect "had tripped" and the progressive form "running") to good use in constructing a timeline. The event-flagging component of our system needs to understand tense, recognizing past-tense forms like "ate" or the future "will sleep." Actually English doesn't really distinguish the future tense from the present in terms of morphological marking, unlike the difference between present and past ("sleep" versus "slept").

Of course the present tense can easily be used for past events, as in (to quote something I overhead on the subway) "Like, then he smacks me" and also for future events as in (also heard on the same occasion) "I am slacking off in Provincetown this weekend"; there are also generic expressions that use the present tense, as in "Alice adores avocados." Note that "adores" is a mention of what linguists term an eventuality, a category that includes both things that can happen (e.g., "waltzing") or a circumstance that holds (e.g., "adoring," "being thrilled"). I will use the everyday term "event" to stand for eventuality (for more details, see the glossary).

While some languages mark a two-way tense distinction, for example, past versus nonpast in English, or future versus nonfuture in the Australian language Dyirbal, other languages make a three-way distinction; for instance, Catalan marks past versus present versus future. The Bantu language Chibemba deserves an entry in the *Guinness Book*. It marks four past tenses: remote past (before yesterday), removed past (yesterday), near past (earlier today), and immediate past (just happened), and likewise also four future tenses—immediate, near, removed, and remote. Chibemba speakers, most of whom live in Zambia, are blessed with a rich set of linguistic devices for expressing distance in time.

Many languages don't express tense as we do in English, by means of grammatical forms. Chinese, for example, doesn't have tense expressed by grammatical forms, like the past tense that results in forms like "ate," "eaten," "ran," and so on. It instead uses particles tacked on to words to indicate an event's "aspectual" properties: whether the event is ongoing, completed, terminated, or in a result state. Thus, while a system processing tense in English can use the tense markers to help figure out the event's relation to the speech time, a system processing Chinese has to rely on aspectual markers instead.

There is a further wrinkle. Tense and aspectual markers may be absent, and there may be no times mentioned at all in the sentence. In English we see tense markers absent when a teenager answers, surlily, "Watching TV," when we inquire tenderly about what he was, is, or will be doing yesterday, today, or tomorrow. We see a similar phenomenon in Chinese, where the aspectual markers may be absent.

我 看 电 视
wo kan dianshi
I watch / will watch / watched TV

As with speakers of English, Chinese speakers (who outnumber speakers of all other languages) are still able to understand one another from context. Thus an intelligent system that constructs timelines for Chinese stories (there are several such) must be able to make sense out of the context.

There are in fact a few languages that lack tense altogether. In Burmese, for example, events that are ongoing or that were observed in the past are expressed by sentence-final "realis" particles "-te," "-tha," "-ta," and "-hta." In other cases, that is, for unreal or hypothetical events (including future events, present events, and hypothetical past events), the sentence-final "irrealis" particles "-me," "-ma," and "-hma" are used. Of course this doesn't mean that the beleaguered citizenry of Myanmar (or Burma, as some continue to call it) aren't able to express, let alone conceive of, the tripartite distinction between past and present and future.[1]

Tense also has another important characteristic: it is tied to our subjectivity. For example, when a person exclaims (truthfully), "I cried the other day!" that day is experienced and remembered as being before the speech time, and thus the past tense is used. In a nutshell events are expressed as being before, at, or after the speaker's current time, that is, with respect to the "now" of the speaker. Likewise the hearer, or reader, of fiction also constructs a "now" that accompanies the reading, and so the event is ongoing, has passed, or looms ahead. (In the latter case the future is either known to the reader through a flash-forward or foreshadowing, or unknown but expected in the sense that an ending is expected.) The timeline, while representing a reader's interpretation, doesn't take such a subjective view of the reader moving through or experiencing time. Instead events are laid out for the passage in question for all the time involved in the passage, with the events related to one another by relations of precedence and inclusion. Because all the events are laid out in the timeline, one might imagine that a reader who visualizes the timeline after reading a passage (or a book) sees all the events more or less (subject to the time taken for a "visual" scan) in the "now."[2]

A CLAIM ABOUT TIMELINES

I will now go out on a limb and make a strong claim, to be elaborated in the rest of this chapter:

> The timelines that are needed for understanding the temporal aspects of all human narratives are the events and times in the narrative and their temporal and subordinating relations, as might be inferred from a conservative interpretation.

In the story about Serena, we had three events (running, twisting, and tripping) occurring in a specified order, one explicit time (yesterday), and one implicit time (the time of speech). We know that the three events took no more than a day, and very likely less than that; they also occurred one day before the speech time. These facts allow us to establish rough temporal distances among the events and between them and the speech time.

I will explain later what I mean by "subordinating relations," but first let us turn to "conservative interpretation."

CONSERVATIVE INTERPRETATION

There is much that a narrator will leave out, given that the human mind will usually fill in information.

The narrator doesn't tell us that the tripping occurred during the marathon. And the narrator doesn't tell us that Serena fell, though the most likely scenario, especially if the result was a twisted ankle, is that she did.

The narrator also doesn't tell us the exact temporal distance between the tripping and the twisting; we may assume the latter was "soon after" the former.

The narrator also doesn't tell us whether Serena kept running afterward. However, running with a twisted ankle is an unlikely occurrence, so her running of the marathon would most probably have ended once she twisted it.

Neither does the narrative tell us how long the marathon lasted.

Nor does the narrative tell us much about Francisco, other than telling us that he is her boyfriend and giving us grounds for disliking him intensely. Serena, by the way, is also stunningly beautiful.

To include these additional sorts of information may get in the way of efficient communication. Language gets by through leaving things implicit, relying on resonances induced in the reader. A skilled writer can provide a few hints, and the reader does the rest, constructing the scene in her mind. The opening lines of Hemingway's "Short Happy Life of Francis Macomber" take us into the scene very quickly.

> It was now lunch time and they were all sitting under the double green fly of the dining tent pretending that nothing had happened.
> "Will you have lime juice or lemon squash?" Macomber asked.
> "I'll have a gimlet," Robert Wilson told him.
> "I'll have a gimlet too. I need something," Macomber's wife said.
> (1954, 9)

Writers have often urged against including additional details. Chekhov, whose advice is well worth considering, even suggested (presciently, as it turns out) that the brain has a preference for simplicity in understanding narrative, as in this letter from him:

> Another piece of advice: when you proof read, cross out as many adjectives and adverbs as you can. You have so many modifiers that the reader has trouble understanding and gets worn out. It is comprehensible when I write: "The man sat on the grass," because it is clear and does not detain one's attention. On the other hand, it is difficult to figure out and hard on the brain if I write: "The tall, narrow-chested man of medium height and with a red beard sat down on the green grass that had already been trampled down by the pedestrians, sat down silently, looking around timidly and fearfully." The brain can't grasp all that at once, and art must be grasped at once, instantaneously. (1979)[3]

Now, what if the reader wanted to make things explicit, by elaborating the timeline further? Marathons don't last more than a day, so it seems safe to assume that the marathon ended the previous day, just like the running. The fastest marathon on record (at the time of writing—the record keeps improving!) is the great Ethiopian runner Haile Gebrselassie's time of two hours, three minutes, and fifty-nine seconds, achieved in a spectacular run in 2008 in Berlin.

So perhaps the marathon should have lasted at least an hour and a half? One can easily imagine all sorts of unusual circumstances, a sudden tornado, a runner endowed with extraordinary vitamin or other supplements, or even a truly bionic human of the future.

If the narrator wanted to tell us that the normal expectations we have about marathons were violated, for example, if it was a marathon run on the moon, he or she would have done so. Such a convention of informativeness, the philosopher Paul Grice has argued, underlies the use of human language as an efficient communication system. Grice's conversational Maxim of Quantity states: "Make your contribution as informative as is required (for the current purposes of the exchange). Do not make your contribution more informative than is required" (1975, 45). (We also assume, unless led to believe otherwise, that his Maxim of Quality is being followed: "Do not say what you believe to be false; Do not say that for which you lack adequate evidence" [46].)

Let us call an interpretation "conservative" if it is a minimal one consistent with the text. That is, it would not require committing to a specific length for a marathon or to events not mentioned in the text. It would not require an appeal to "unusual" circumstances not mentioned in the text. Nor would it require knowing about specific circumstances of the creation of the work or the circumstances associated with the reader or the audience for the work. These latter factors undoubtedly have an influence on interpretation. There are other factors as well: the prior reputation of the writer or publisher, the "marketing pitch" for a book, including the encomiums on the back cover, can all influence its interpretation. The goal of the conservative interpretation is to abstract away from such factors and arrive at a minimal interpretation. And a minimal interpretation may not necessarily be unique; there may be more than one such possible. In fact, just as people will react differently to a movie or a book, there may be multiple, even incompatible timelines that different readers might construct in certain "difficult" narratives. Nevertheless, as I have argued earlier, the existence of differences across readers doesn't amount to indeterminacy. Language must, and does, substantially constrain interpretation.

The conservative interpretation is carried out based on information from the text, the reader's knowledge of language, and her knowledge of the real world. In Serena's case a reader's knowledge of language and the name "Serena" will lead him to believe she is female. Further, since the text mentions tripping, not falling, the conservative interpretation will allow the reader to fill in an impression of someone losing her balance and stumbling, based on the reader's understanding of being "tripped" and his own experience. Thus, while the details of the tripping are not elaborated in the text (and constitute a "gap" of sorts), the reader can fill them in. The fall, however, is not committed to in the text and therefore should not be viewed as a gap and will not be filled in by a conservative interpretation.

A background assumption about interpretation here is Marie-Laure Ryan's (1991) Principle of Minimal Departure, which posits that readers fill in gaps in the text by assuming the similarity of the fictional world to their own experienced world. The conservative interpretation adds a further constraint to this principle: the only gaps filled in are those based on information mentioned in the text and the reader's knowledge of language and the world.

MODALITY

If humans thought only about the present, we would perhaps be a happier species. But we seem to be forever fretting about upsets in the past and are always wrapped up in plans for the future. Romantic fiction is full of such ruminations, as a snippet from Charlotte Brontë's *Jane Eyre* reveals: "Probably, if I had lately left a good home and kind parents, this would have been the hour when I should most keenly have regretted the separation; that wind would then have saddened my heart; this obscure chaos would have disturbed my peace!" (Brontë 1998).

Proust, a writer who apparently spent a great deal of time meandering through the labyrinthine passages of time and memory, was concerned with the interplay between moments of direct experience and moments recalled (perhaps we should say "reconstructed," for memories aren't faithful reproductions) and the anticipations of the future in those moments. Here is a well-known extract from Proust's abandoned first novel *Jean Santeuil*, which formed the model for his later *A la Recherche du Temps Perdu*. I chose this extract because it has been analyzed at length by the French structuralist scholar Gérard Genette (1980). Here Jean passes by the hotel where Marie Kossichef, whom he once loved, lives:

Sometimes passing in front of the hotel he remembered the rainy days when he used to bring his nursemaid that far, on a pilgrimage. But he remembered them without the melancholy that he then thought he would surely some day savor on feeling that he no longer loved her.[4]

As Genette points out, this pattern where the "future has become present but does not resemble the idea of it that one had in the past" (1980, 37) is a form that appears often in the *Recherche*. He notes that there are two times represented here, the time of the event of remembering, while Jean is passing in front of the hotel, and the time of the thoughts remembered, the rainy days; the narrative moves in a zigzag though highly deliberate manner, between these two poles of "now" and "once."

The rainy days are of course a set of days, uncounted, unanchored to the calendar, and therefore vague; further, these days exist in memory but also exist independent of it, as the "then" indicates.

The relations between a person and the objects of thought, such as things remembered, or regretted, believed, known, thought, predicted, and so on, are called modal relations. Modality, as developed in systems of modal logic, involves qualifications of various kinds on the truth of statements, qualifications expressed in English by verbal auxiliaries like "can," "may," "must," "will," "would," "should," and so forth. A statement such as "I believe OJ is a murderer" can be understood as meaning that in every (imagined) world of mine that is consistent with my beliefs, OJ is a murderer; thus the statement is true in the actual world if OJ is a murderer in each such imagined world. Likewise, if we say, "OJ ought to go to prison," this statement is true in the actual world if in all my "morally proper" worlds, OJ would go to prison.

There are some well-known philosophical problems with possible world semantics, not the least of which is the unresolved issue of the identity of individuals across worlds.[5] For example, is OJ in a belief world the very same OJ as in the real world or someone resembling him? If the latter, what sort of properties would OJ have? Would he have authored the book *If I Did It*? Although this issue of transworld identity is unresolved, this question is no different in principle from the question of identity across time, as in the case of a repeated event or a person at two different times. In the repeated event we know that it's not likely to be exactly the same, and in the case of a person two years earlier, we know that some personal characteristics have changed. As the Scottish philosopher David Hume observed:

> But this is still more remarkable, when we add a sympathy of parts to their common end, and suppose that they bear to each other, the reciprocal relation of cause and effect in all their actions and operations. This is the case with all animals and vegetables; where not only the several parts have a reference to some general purpose, but also a mutual dependence on, and connexion with each other. The effect of so strong a relation is, that tho' every one must allow, in a very few years both vegetables and animals endure a total change, yet we still attribute identity to them, while their form, size, and substance are entirely alter'd. . . . An oak, that grows from a small plant to a large tree, is still the same oak; though there be not one particle of matter, or figure of its parts the same. An infant becomes a man, and is sometimes fat, sometimes lean, without any change in his identity. (2003, vol. 1, bk. 1, pt. 4, sec. 6)

The problem of identity, as we shall see, extends to time itself. We shall have more to say about narrative and personal identity at the end of this chapter.

I will adopt the simple stance of assuming correspondences across worlds, so that the rainy days Jean remembered correspond to roughly the same days as the rainy days posited by the narrator, and thus the two can be viewed as co-temporal. Similarly, the hour in a world where Jane Eyre had recently left a good home and kind parents would be co-temporal with the hour that constitutes the current moment (or "Now") of the narrative; and the Jane Eyre who recently left a good home would correspond to Jane Eyre the narrator. Of course memories can be false, confabulated events that never occurred, or things might be foggy or distorted or falsely colored in memory; such subtleties will have to be acknowledged but passed over without any representational blurring.

Once we take modality into account in our model, we have the timeline shown in figure 3 for the *Jean Santeuil* passage, repeated here. In these and other directly quoted narratives, the underlining of events and highlighting of times are markup that has been added.

Sometimes passing in front of the hotel he remembered the rainy days when he used to bring his nursemaid that far, on a pilgrimage. But he remembered them without the melancholy that he then thought he would surely some day savor on feeling that he no longer loved her.

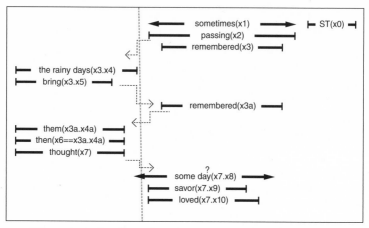

FIG. 3. Zigzagging in *Jean Santeuil*.

Several details of notation have been introduced into the diagram. These are simple enough once one gets used to them. The time frame of "x1" covers those occasions described by "sometimes," which are during the times of passing in front of the hotel, the time frame covered by "x2." The time frame of "x3" covers the times of remembering, which occur during the time frame of "x1." The fact that the rainy days are subordinated to the remembering x3 is indicated by "x3.x4," where "x4" is the mention of the rainy days. Now, "remembered them" is a subsequent reference to the earlier mention of remembering the rainy days; this so-called anaphoric reference is indicated with x3a instead of x3; this means that the second mention x3a ("remembered," where it is further qualified as lacking melancholy) is the same entity as the first mention "remembered" (x3). Accordingly "them" is indicated with (x3a.x4a).

Since the times and events indicated with periods (as in x3.x4 and x3a.x4a) are subordinated ones, they cannot directly be compared, as they aren't denizens of the same world. For diagramming convenience, rather than having to represent multiple dimensions, one for each world, we have laid these subordinated objects out in parallel with nonsubordinated ones on the timeline. To express correspondences across worlds, we have used a double equal sign (==). Thus "Then" (mention x6) refers to the rainy days that existed independent of memory, times during which Jean thought and so on, this corresponds to the rainy days he remembered (x3a.x4a, the mention of "them").

A final point of notation: "sometimes" and "someday" are vague times; these are indicated with arrows. Their temporal extents aren't precise, though we know that they occur after the rainy days. The relation between these two vague times is left underspecified.

Let's return to Proust. The mode of the passage is clearly retrospective. The imagining of the future from the past is used to compare where one is with respect to where one thought one might be. The passage reveals that Jean's thoughts of future melancholy, his feeling of no longer loving (x7.x10) during the pilgrimages were later remembered in front of the hotel, remembered (x3a) without the melancholy. The close reading of the timeline model clearly shows the zigzag effect Genette noted—this is observed from the ordering of the mentions. The two directions of subordination, one from the future into the past and the other from the past into the future, are also evident in the diagram, along with three clusters of events—beginning in the past, going far back into the past, and going back to the future from the past. This temporal pattern, involving parallelism, draws one's attention to something that makes one appreciate Proust's skill (or genius) even more: his ability to capture our capacity to sense an emotion from the outside (in this case from the future, where the emotion of melancholy doesn't exist) as well as from the inside (here from the past, where it is imagined for a future time when, Jean correctly predicts, he will no longer love Marie).[6]

Given the density of information in the timeline for two sentences of Proust, one might shudder to think what the timelines for entire novels would look like! Luckily the tools we have discussed for representing timelines can apply to entire stories or novels as well.

Proust, like other writers in Romance languages, makes good use of the "imperfect" tense, which can be used to indicate a habitual action. The *Jean Santeuil* passage above also reveals how sets of times ("sometimes," "the rainy days") are used to reinforce the idea of habitual actions. Habituality expresses a generalization, and literature captivates by way of particulars. Fortunately the two can happily coexist by means of exemplars. A particularly striking device is to express habituality in terms of a set of times and then to zoom in (i.e., drill down) to a particular scene as if it exemplified those times, though clearly the particulars of the scene are far too specific to be repeated. This is evidenced in the opening lines of Kafka's "Hunger Artist," where the narrative takes on a sinister tone:

During these last decades the interest in professional fasting has markedly diminished. It used to pay very well to stage such great performances under one's own management, but today that is quite impossible. We live in a different world now. At one time the whole town took a lively interest in the hunger artist; from day to day of his fast the excitement mounted; everybody wanted to see him at least once a day; there were people who bought season tickets for the last few days and sat from morning till night in front of his small barred cage; even in the night time there were visiting hours, when the whole effect was heightened by torch flares; on fine days the cage was set out in the open air, and then it was the children's special treat to see the hunger artist; for their elders he was often just a joke that happened to be in fashion, but the children stood open-mouthed, holding each other's hands for greater security, marveling at him as he sat there pallid in black tights, with his ribs sticking out so prominently, not even on a seat but down among straw on the ground, sometimes giving a courteous nod, answering questions with a constrained smile, or perhaps stretching an arm through the bars so that one might feel how thin it was, and then again withdrawing deep into himself, paying no attention to anyone or anything, not even to the all-important striking of the clock that was the only piece of furniture in his cage, but merely staring into vacancy with half-shut eyes, now and then taking a sip from a tiny glass of water to moisten his lips. (1975, 231)

Figure 4 shows the analysis.[7] For reasons of space, the diagram doesn't

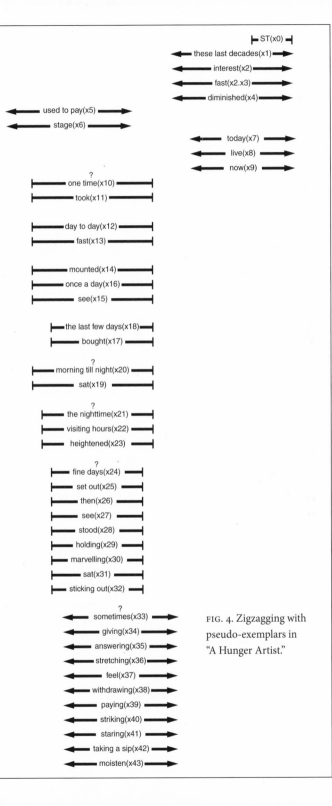

FIG. 4. Zigzagging with pseudo-exemplars in "A Hunger Artist."

directly indicate sets of times, which are, however, annotated with additional information. Thus "these last decades" will be marked as a set of decades ("PXDE"); more precise set expressions, such as "three days every month" (not from this passage), would be annotated as a set with a value of a period of one month ("P1M"), a quantifier of EVERY, and a frequency of a period of three days ("P3D").

As with Proust, we again see the zigzagging effect involving the first three clusters of times, with a zooming in, in the fourth cluster, that illustrates the pseudo-exemplars by means of eight subclusters of times. The parallelism here is a more elaborated one than with Proust, and the function it serves here is to highlight loss of freedom rather than loss of love. The passage culminates in an ironic account of brutality presented as entertainment, situated conveniently in the past.[8]

DELIBERATE VAGUENESS

Although writers can take advantage of expressions of habituality and pseudo-exemplification to situate events in particular cusps of time, there are occasions when a writer will choose to be deliberately vague about when things happen. In his brilliant novel *Austerlitz*, W. G. Sebald uses iterated events and ranges of time to create an impression of repeated journeys in search of something; the times and durations of these journeys are left intentionally vague. The following passage from Sebald is illustrative:

> In the second half of the 1960s I traveled repeatedly from England to Belgium, partly for study purposes, partly for other reasons which were never entirely clear to me, staying sometimes for just one or two days, sometimes for several weeks. (2001, 3)

This sort of vagueness is easy to capture in our model of timelines. There is no subordination, but there is iteration, with a set of traveling events, and varieties of times, a specified range of years (1966–69), sets of days (each 1–2 days long), and sets of periods of an indeterminate number of weeks.

The timeline is shown in figure 5.

Another sort of vagueness involves the deliberate sowing of confu-

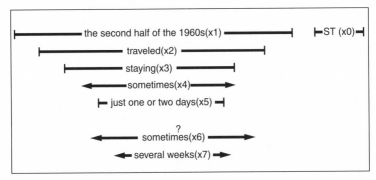

FIG. 5. Vague iteration in *Austerlitz*.

sion about time, as in the case of the Robert Hass (1990) poem "Misery and Splendor":

> Summoned by conscious recollection, she
> would be smiling, they might be in a kitchen talking,
> before or after dinner. But they are in this other room,
> The window has many small panes, and they are on a couch
> embracing. He holds her as tightly
> as he can, she buries herself in his body.
> Morning, maybe it is evening, light
> is flowing through the room. Outside,
> the day is slowly succeeded by night,
> succeeded by day. The process wobbles wildly
> and accelerates: weeks, months, years.

Here the poet captures the mood of an embrace as being "outside" time. The extent of subordination is left unclear: is their lovemaking "actual" or recollected? Disjunction is ubiquitous: the subordinated possibility of talking occurs either before or after dinner; the embrace is either in the morning or in the evening. The world outside is subordinated, one where time is allowed to pass swiftly in fast-forward mode, days turning into months, months into years. Meanwhile, there is a tantalizing vagueness as to the duration of the lovemaking. While such a high level of underspecification of temporal information is unusual, and more characteristic, perhaps, of lyric rather than narrative, a certain degree of underspecification, as we have seen, is part and parcel of most timelines, whether literary or not. Not all the events in a narrative will be ordered with respect to one another; some events will be anchored in time, and others may float.

There have been attempts to deliberately (some would say perversely) order events in reverse. *Time's Arrow*, by Martin Amis, is such a novel, where a character's life is explored in reverse, or "retrograde," order, to use a term from Gérard Genette. However, as Genette points out, "One can run a film backwards, image by image, but one cannot read a text backwards, letter by letter, or even word by word, or even sentence by sentence, without its ceasing to be a text" (1980, 34). The order is only reversed for particular text segments. Retrograde order is not all that rare; it is also common to segments of headline news, where the latest news is presented first.

Faulkner's *The Sound and the Fury* is a novel that appears to seriously scramble time in the narrative to the point of incoherence, at least in the case of the narratives by Benjy and Quentin. *The Sound and the Fury* is often referred to as a stream-of-consciousness novel in part because of the disjointed and possibly discombobulating style of these two subnarratives. What apparently confuses the reader are the breaks in segments (indicated in italics in certain published versions of the novel), with a lack of appropriate contextualization to indicate which thread in the narrative is being taken up after each break.

However, in reacting to this novel, certain literary critics have tripped up on their own words, confusing rather than clarifying matters. Cleanth Brooks, who describes the "idiot" Benjy's world rather memorably as "a kind of confused, blooming buzz" (1990, 326), goes on to maintain that Benjy "is locked almost completely into a timeless present. He has not much more sense of time than an animal has, and therefore he possesses not much more freedom than an animal does" (328). Yet a mere glance at the text and the verb tenses would reveal that entire segments of narrative in Benjy's account are told in straight chronological order.

Quentin's narrative includes numerous pontifications and asides on the nature of time by him and his father, for example, "Because Father said clocks slay time," and there is the overt use of props such as smashed watches. More generally, the young Quentin is concerned with loss of his southern heritage and of the ideal of innocence (tied to his obsessive love for his sister). These obvious features may have led Jean-Paul Sartre to hastily conclude that Faulkner's worldview was like that of "a man sitting in an open car and looking backwards" (1966, 89). But this focus on the present and the past rather than contemplation of the future is hardly unique to Faulkner.

Although multiple time frames are involved in Benjy's narrative, the essential treatment of time in it is not that complicated. Faulkner provided in a letter an eight-step chronology of this chapter, adding, "These are just a few I recall" (1994b, 220). The reader who is willing to take the pains to do so can map the chronology in Benjy's narrative. This has been done rather thoroughly, along with some fancy visualizations, by R. P. Stoicheff and his colleagues (2003), who reveal that Benjy's narrative is presented, as indicated here, in chronological order (once the flashbacks are taken out), and that the flashbacks themselves, when considered separately, are each presented in chronological order.

TIME AND PERSONAL IDENTITY

Let us reconsider the Proust passage. What Jean is doing through his excursion into the past is part of the construction of his identity through the narrative. The comparison of where one thought one would be with respect to where one finds oneself is part of the business of self-assessment. Writers make characters do this because they do it themselves, and because they recognize the level of resonance this can achieve for the reader. That is why such narratives make sense for us; they echo the paths through time we take in constructing our own identities.

Self-assessment through weighing of the past can expand our horizons, allowing us to take in the present from a broader perspective, taking it with a pinch or more of time's salt. Even more so it can help us rehearse and plan for the future. As we shall see in chapter 5 ("Time in Mind"), there is evidence that the brain uses similar subsystems to remember episodes from the past and imagine episodes in the future, suggesting the possibility that the reconstruction of the past, with all its rosy tints and false details, is an evolutionary strategy that allows humans to plan and survive in the future.

This chapter has introduced a basic model of a timeline for a narrative that can be computed by machines. The model adopts a conservative interpretation, namely, a minimal one consistent with the text. It includes a representation for times, a representation for events, and a means of temporally ordering them. Events and times can be relatively vague or precise. Subordinating relations among events, involving events that are believed, remembered, and so on, are taken into account.

Such fine-grained analyses can be applied in the large to literary texts. When we do so, patterns emerge. One pattern involves zigzagging back and forth in time. Another pattern involves introducing a repeated event and then zooming in to a particular scene as if it exemplified such an event. Yet another pattern involves iterated events and ranges of time, all of them deliberately vague. Another pattern involves simple interleaving of multiple chronological narratives. These patterns are devices that allow characters to travel back and forth in time and to make comparisons across these times that enable them to construct identities.

2   Stories within Stories

Narratives often have multiple narrators, with consonant or dissonant voices, resulting in the production of stories within stories, unfurling like scarves from a magician's hat.

When a character in a narrative imagines or remembers something, that something involves subordination. Quotation is also a form of subordination.[1] Thus the act of telling a story assumes a world, of narrator, the narrator's setting, the narrator's audience, what Genette (1980) calls the extradiegetic level. This world can be differentiated from the diegetic level, namely, the world of the events in the story. In this chapter I discuss subordination in relation to time, showing how it is addressed in the timeline model.

"The One Thousand and One Nights" is an oft-cited example where Scheherazade, while bedded down each night with a sultan who has lost all faith in women, tells a story, each one timed to stave off death at his depraved hands. Those stories contain characters who tell other stories, the stories being stacked one inside the other like a babushka doll. (These structures, called frame stories, are thought to derive in part from the much older Sanskrit *Panchatantra*.) Each of the narratives comes with a timeline, and these timelines can be related to one another by correspondences.

In addition to the narrator being a character in a superordinate story, a narrator can of course also be a character in her own story. There can be subnarratives that provide explanations: in the following text from Bonnie Webber (1988), the past perfect is used to shift focus to a prior time that serves as an explanation, which is elaborated for one more sentence, before the narrative is resumed. The corresponding timeline is shown in figure 6.

John <u>went</u> into the florist shop. He had <u>promised</u> Mary some flowers. She <u>said</u> she wouldn't <u>forgive</u> him if he <u>forgot</u>. So he <u>picked out</u> three red roses.

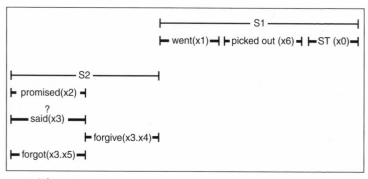

<small>FIG. 6. Subnarratives.</small>

In our model we will treat a subnarrative of talking to Mary (which includes his promise, and her threatening that she wouldn't forgive him—rather a short subnarrative!) like a giant event, called a macro-event. This giant event (s2) stands in a subnarrative relation to another macro-event, the supernarrative (S), of which the main narrative (the macro-event s1) is also a subnarrative. In our diagrams we can often leave out the supernarrative (S) when there is just one, as it is implicit in the presence of the outer box. Note also that the forgiving and forgetting is subordinated to the saying.

There will, inevitably, be cases where the subnarrative boundary will be unclear. For example, the last sentence in the following passage could describe an event that occurred before or after going to the hardware store.[2] The temporal relation between the two will be left underspecified.

Yesterday, Jack and Sue <u>went</u> to a hardware store as someone had <u>stolen</u> their lawnmower. She had <u>seen</u> a man <u>take</u> it and had <u>chased</u> him down the street, but he had <u>driven</u> away in a truck. Sue would later <u>see</u> the man <u>lunching</u> at McDonald's.

Polyphonic narration is another common device in narratives. A character in a story can be filled in with information from different narrators. In Cervantes's *Don Quixote*, as Charles Oriel (1990) shows, a character such as Cardenio emerges as a composite of the various glimpses of him in the subnarratives. In Virginia Woolf's *The Waves*, there are multiple narrators who aren't subordinated to one another, who may encounter (in their narrated worlds) similar or different events (with associated temporal relations) reported by other narrators.

The subnarratives may not always be consistent with one another or with the supernarrative. At the climax of Agatha Christie's *Murder of Roger Ackroyd*, the indefatigable Hercule Poirot reconstructs the sequence of events involving the murder, revealing that the narrator, Dr. Sheppard, is in fact the killer, at which point the supernarrative is explained as an attempt to tar Poirot, prior to Sheppard's committing suicide. Thus Poirot's narrative inside Sheppard's narrative undermines Sheppard's narrative. This sort of twist is hard to accept because it involves the violation of expectations about the reliability of the master narrator; in terms of our timeline representation, however, it presents no particular problem.

Kurosawa's *Rashomon* is a film in which two narrators, a woodcutter and a priest waiting out a storm, each tell a story pertaining to a samurai's murder, relaying their own accounts as well as the accounts of a bandit, the wife of the samurai, and the samurai himself (whose story is relayed through a medium). The stories are inconsistent, and to make matters worse, the woodcutter later revises his account. The existence of multiple narrators does cast a cold eye on the notion of objectivity, reminding us that it's all point of view. The point of *Rashomon*, in the eyes of some viewers and critics, at least, is that ego trumps truth; this is supported by research on Kurosawa's instructions to his actors. Emerging from these multiple stories is an underspecified narrative of what happened. I say "underspecified" because the events and their temporal relationships may involve a disjunction of various possibilities, some even inconsistent.

In his insightful book *Story Logic*, David Herman discusses certain cases of extreme temporal underspecification. He considers the story of Anna Seghers's "Der Ausflug der toten Mädchen" (translated as "The Excursion of the Dead Girls"), which, he argues, illustrates cases where the temporal ordering of events is "inexactly coded." He cites an example where "the narrator is troubled to discover in the young Fräulein Sichel a few gray hairs, not 'the snow-white [hair], that I had remembered her as having had at all times,' but rather just the trace (*Spur*) of her old age and of her later defilement for being Jewish" (2002, 226).

Herman argues that along with a reading of this passage as one where the past is being colored by the present, there is another interpretation where the narrator is claiming the existence of a trace of certain events that haven't yet occurred, due to his narrating from a speech time that is indeterminate (it spans a temporal continuum from the time of witnessing the young Fräulein Sichel to knowing about her old age).

Both these readings can be easily represented in my underspecified timeline, thanks to the key notion (missing in Herman's account) of subordination. The discovery (x1) is of a trace (x1.x5) of old age (x1. x5.x6) and of defilement (x1.x5.x7); we thus have a doubly embedded subordination:

> discover(x1) . . . not "the snow-white [hair], that I had remembered (x2) her as having had (x2.x3) at all times (x2.x4==x2.x3)," but rather just the trace (x1.x5) (*Spur*) of her old age (x1.x5.x6) and of her later defilement (x1.x5.x7) for being Jewish.

Thus, while the trace does "occur" earlier than the old age, its occurrence is subordinated to the discovery (much as "the rainy days" in figure 3 were subordinated to Jean's "remembering"), and that occurrence bears a further modal relation to the old age and defilement (much as Jean's "thought" relates to the melancholy he would one day "savor"). And the reading of the past being colored by the present is found in the hyperbolic description of remembering (x2) her having had snow white hair (x2.x3) at all times (x2.x4)—including childhood. In fact the two readings are not really alternatives, since the first arises from a different linguistic segment than the second—but they do create an opposition and tension between them.

VIRTUAL CYCLES

Yet another complex structure in narratives is the existence of a temporal subordination cycle. A cycle involves a chain of events that results in a circularity, for example, so that one event is before another one, which in turn shows up as being before the first. This is a particular form of inconsistency, one related to time.

One variety of cycle is a virtual one, occurring in the imagination, through an action that attempts to unwittingly execute an event long past. This virtual cycle is seen in the marvelous opening of *Swann's Way*, from Proust:

> For a long time I used to go to bed early. Sometimes, when I had put out my candle, my eyes would close so quickly that I had not even time to say "I'm going to sleep." And half an hour later the thought that it was time to go to sleep would awaken me; I would try to put away the book which, I imagined, was still in my hands, and to blow out the light. (1922, 1)

The timeline for this passage is shown in figure 7, where the attempted blowing out aims at executing the putting out of the candle, which has occurred before Marcel fell asleep. Since the diagram lacks adequate horizontal space, the boxed times beginning with put away (x15.x16), indicated with an arrow, are intended to be on the same line as and following try (x15).

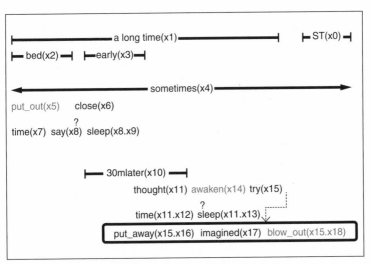

FIG. 7. Virtual cycle in *Swann's Way*.

In other words Marcel tries to blow out the candle after waking up (so that waking up is BEFORE blowing out), only to find that the blowing out occurred earlier, before falling asleep (i.e., blowing out BEFORE waking up). Thus the offending relation (waking up BEFORE blowing out) that causes the cycle is only in the character's imagination.

In this passage the virtual cycle records a character's error in assessing the temporal location of events. The thoughts of the subconscious imagination, articulated first during sleep, result in Marcel's disorientation with respect to the real world to which he wakes up. Sleep appears to involve, at first glance, an absence of awareness of the events and time that pass while one is asleep (though clearly one's biological clocks are still active). This absence can also introduce confused thoughts about the events in the period prior to falling asleep, perhaps due in this case to Marcel being sleepy at the time of registering the event, as well as at the time of recall.

Another type of virtual cycle involves repetition of the same incident at different points in the narrative. This device is seen in the Alain Robbe-Grillet (1965) novel *La Jalousie*, whose title was translated as *Jealousy* (though *jalousie* also means "window blind," the device through which some of the action is witnessed). The novel, set against the backdrop of life on a colonial African plantation (complete with patronizing and racist treatments of the native population), is told by an entirely invisible narrator. The novel obsessively scrutinizes the relationship between the narrator's wife A . . . and another planter Franck. The incident that we will focus on is the leitmotif of the violent squashing of a centipede during dinner. It is on a subsequent occasion, again during dinner, that we come across (on page 47) the first, retrospective mention of the squashing. The timeline is shown in figure 8.

The squashing ($x2$) is stated as occurring weeks or months before the moment ($x1$) during dinner.

Besides, she was no longer facing Franck at that moment. She had just moved her head back and was looking straight ahead of her down the table, toward the bare wall where a blackish spot marks the place where a centipede was squashed last week, at the beginning of the month, perhaps the month before, or later.

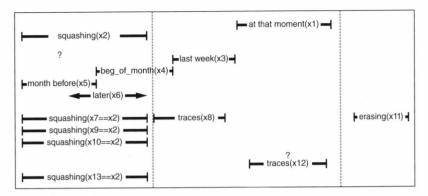

FIG. 8. Repetition in *Jealousy*.

This incident is then revisited on page 64, where the narration is now during the dinner where the squashing (x7) occurred. The focus here is on describing the centipede's body prior to the squashing, which is then quickly described.

On page 78 there is a passing reference to the result (x8) of the squashing, namely, the black stain on the white wall left by the squashed creature before it falls; on page 89, again set during the dinner where the squashing (x9) occurred, the focus is on the movements of the squasher, Franck, and the reaction of the other main character A . . . , whose hand is clenched around a table knife. On pages 96–97, the event of the squashing (x10) is described in the present tense, with the body of the centipede before and after the squashing (it is severely dismembered) delved into in considerable detail, followed by a description of the complete erasing (x11) of the stain with a typewriter eraser. On page 104, at dinner, the wall trace from the aftereffect (x12) of the squashing is revisited; and on pages 112–13, described in the present tense, the centipede's size is disclosed; it is now enormous, and its movement across the wall, the crackling and buzzing sounds it makes, and the squashing (x13) and subsequent fall are described quite vividly.

The Robbe-Grillet example is often taken for what Genette (1980) calls "achrony," where the order of event and speech times is left unclear. In the particular case of the squashing, there is just a single event, but the ordering of the narrations of this event is unclear. However, figure 8 shows that there is still a fairly well-fleshed-out timeline. There are really three main phases related to the squashing: the vaguely anchored squashing proper, all the descriptions of which refer to the same event (the co-temporality is indicated by a reuse of the double equal sign instead of x2a, x2b, etc., so as to reflect text order); the references to squashed traces, which are vaguely anchored; and the erasing, after which there are no more traces of the poor centipede.

The slow, repetitive description, most of it in the present tense, not only of events like the squashing (i.e., the cluster representing the first phase in figure 8) but also extensive descriptions of physical objects creates an effect of circularity. Along with this circling grows an atmosphere of lurking violence, as well as attraction and repulsion, emanating from the descriptions of objects and events rather than from accounts of mental states. The entire narrative, with its relentless camera-eye view of experience, is highly suggestive of cinema and the French New Wave.

Some narratives try to indicate circularity but don't quite carry it off. Gabriel Garcia Marquez's novel *One Hundred Years of Solitude* ends with Aureliano Babilonia, from the final generation of the Buendia family, deciphering ancient parchments written by the gypsy Melquiades (written in Sanskrit, Melquiades's native tongue, but encoded in an ancient cipher). The parchments foretell the entire history of the Buendias, in a manner reminiscent of *One Hundred Years of Solitude*, right up to the moment of reading, at which point everything comes to an end: Aureliano, the Buendia line, Macondo, and the book. This ending would represent a real cycle if the book he is reading is in fact *One Hundred Years of Solitude*; however, it can't be the same book, because the events in the old gypsy's manuscripts are narrated simultaneously rather than in the order in the book.

REAL CYCLES

Another type of cycle is a "real" one in which a subnarrative is also a supernarrative. This real cycle involves a real contradiction in the state of the world, in that events are ordered in a contradictory way.

In Julio Cortázar's short story "The Continuity of Parks" (2006), a reader of a novel is so absorbed in it that he witnesses the lead character, his dagger raised, about to exterminate him. One implication here could be that identity is being constructed by the reader, and that this construction involves a sort of destruction.

He had begun to read the novel a few days before. . . . That afternoon, . . . he returned to the book in the tranquility of his study which looked out upon the park with its oaks. Sprawled in his favorite armchair, with his back to the door, which would otherwise have bothered him as an irritating possibility for intrusions, he let his left hand caress once and again the green velvet upholstery and set to <u>reading</u> the final chapters. . . . Word by word, immersed in the sordid dilemma of the hero and heroine, letting himself go toward where the images came together and took on color and movement, he was <u>witness</u> to the final encounter in the mountain cabin. The woman arrived first, apprehensive; now the lover came in, his face cut by the backlash of a branch. . . .

The estate manager would not be there at this hour, and he was not. He <u>went up</u> the three porch steps and entered. . . . At the top, two doors. No one in the first bedroom, no one in the second. The door of the salon, and then the knife in his hand, the light from the great windows, the high back of an armchair covered in green velvet, the head of the man in the chair <u>reading</u> a novel.

This particular reader, we are told, is a witness to the events of the subnarrative, which involves the lover going up to the salon and, knife in hand, observing the reader. This is not presented as occurring in an imagined or remembered world, unlike the virtual cycle that opens *Swann's Way*. It can be seen that the subnarrative stretches to extend to the end of the main narrative, with the cycle closing at the reading event.

Thus, we have the thing read, for example, reading (x2), occurring after the reading, that is, reading (x1). In figure 9 we use elision (..) to hide some of the details.

"The Continuity of Parks" is an example cited by Genette illustrating metalepsis, which involves a transgressive change of narrative levels. Metalepsis in the form of real cycles seems to function to create a literary effect of closure, of the world folding into itself. It can be used to produce a destructive (though not necessarily violent) ending, where the writer proclaims his ability to wipe the slate clean. It is essentially a mannerist flourish, drawing attention to the writer's ability to confound logic and play with the reader's cooperativeness in suspending disbelief.

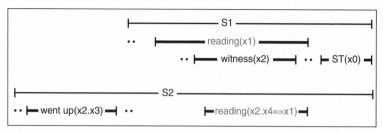

FIG. 9. Real cycle in "The Continuity of Parks."

The impossible is possible, the mannerist (or so-called magical realist) declares; the potential unreliability of the narrator comes only at the end, too late to cause any literary damage. In discussing this story Brian McHale (1987) notes that such violations of the ordering between narrating and narrated worlds are part of a more general trend in literature of foregrounding the ontological status of real and imaginary worlds, a characterizing feature, he argues, of "postmodernist" fiction. (In his view, while "modernist" fiction takes the world for granted, focusing on knowledge of it, that is, interpreting the world and man's [or woman's] relation to it, "postmodernist" fiction focuses, roughly speaking, on the existence and structure of such worlds, laying bare their construction within the artifact of the literary creation.)

It is worth pausing here to remark on the various units in our analyses. Elision allows one to mark the times of just a few pivotal or otherwise interesting events in the narrative. Further, we can temporally anchor chunks corresponding to entire stretches of text, not looking inside those chunks. Finally, in longer texts it is often helpful to analyze a summary of the text, where a single sentence of the metatext of the summary may correspond to variable-sized stretches of text, including one or more chapters. Such a summary need not be unique; nevertheless, we would expect a similar timeline across different summaries. Overall, the unit of analysis—entire text, pivotal events, chunks, or summary text elements—will be indicated where necessary.

This chapter has discussed how to capture stories within stories. Narrated stories within an overall narrative are represented by the same subordination mechanism used for representing events that are believed, imagined, and so on. Each embedded story is represented by an overarching event, called a macro-event. Narratives can result in cycles, in which a chain of events results in a circularity. One type of cycle is virtual, where the offending relation exists only in the character's imagination. One use of a virtual cycle is to express disorientation with respect to the real world. Another type is a real cycle, where there is a contradiction in terms of temporal ordering in the world; this can be used to create the impression of a world unfolding into itself. We shall have much more to say about cycles in chapter 4 ("Calendar Times").

3 | Computing Timelines

Thus far our model of timelines has been illustrated by means of diagrams. These diagrams may not seem to differ much in overall structure from the analyses of literary theorists.

The crucial difference, however, is that the timeline diagrams here are shorthand for representations that are computable. That is, these representations can be created automatically from texts in human languages; once created, they can be stored in a database to which questions can be posed. Further, these representations build on well-established mathematical and logical concepts. In what follows we will represent time expressions, mark events, and then introduce temporal relations among them. We first introduce a tagging scheme, in terms of which the timelines are represented for the computer. Then we describe how machines produce the tagging for any given text. All of these steps could be incredibly boring or absolutely fascinating to the reader, depending on how they are presented. (The computer, of course, doesn't mind either way; it just slavishly gets the job done.)

Let us briefly peek under the hood of an artificially intelligent system for timelining. There are three key components, nicely slotted into each other. The first component is one that recognizes mentions of events in a text, understanding some of their linguistic properties, and distinguishing between subjective and objective events. The next component understands the meaning of time expressions in the text. It turns out that across all human languages, time expressions fall into just a few classes that, even in cases of vagueness, can be represented precisely by computer programs. This component must be somewhat smart, for example, able to understand a reference like "one day" or "the next day," which may or may not be mappable to a particular date on a calendar.

The third component is more sophisticated, able to deduce whether one event is chronologically before, after, simultaneous with, or even a part of the other, no matter in what order the events are narrated. Thus, in the trivial mininarrative "Serena fell. She had slipped on a banana peel," we know the second event came before the first. In other words this component infers temporal relationships among events, linking them to one another and to times mentioned in the text. It also infers relationships involving subjective events. Working together these components can create very detailed timelines that can clearly be of aid to readers trying to keep things in order.

Assembling a timeline automatically can produce a database for one or more narrative texts, to which one can pose queries. One may ask when particular events happened according to the narrative or whether one event follows another, and how far apart in time they are. The answers, of course, will commit to no more than a conservative interpretation. The programs will be correct within a certain margin of error, discussed later. We will first examine the scheme for marking up linguistic information about time and then the actual computer programs that are trained to faithfully extract this information.

TIME AND EVENT TAGS

The simplest kinds of time expressions are absolute expressions (e.g., "June 2007," "summer 1968," "June–July 1970"). However, if we were forced to always express time in this fashion, communication would become extremely stilted and inefficient—think of never being able to say "yesterday" or "tomorrow!"

Accordingly languages provide relative expressions, which come in two flavors: deictic expressions, which depend on the speech time (st) (e.g., "yesterday," "next year," "the fall," "two weeks," all of whose meanings are dependent on when they are uttered), and anaphoric expressions, which depend on a reference time (rt) (e.g., "then," "a month later"), that is, on a time or event in the prior discourse. Speech time, as we have seen, expresses the time of the narration and accommodates any level of swapping or nesting of narrators; this is the time that moves inexorably on through the narration. The reference time represents the temporal point to which the narrative has progressed. It records where the narrative stands in time, as in this example of an extended flashback (from Kamp and Reyle 1993, 594), where the reference time is 6:30 a.m., even though the narrative is relayed from the temporal perspective of 10:00 a.m.:[1]

Fred arrived at 10. He had got up at 5; he had taken a long shower, had got dressed and had eaten a leisurely breakfast. He had left the house at 6:30.

Let us explore how the computer represents these time expressions, which is done by means of coded tags. An expression that maps to a date or time will be represented by a standard code, for example, 2001-09 for "September 2001" and "1968-SU" for "summer 1968." Here a small number of abbreviations are used to code fuzzy periods such as seasons and portions of the day like morning, afternoon, evening, and night. These periods are fuzzy because summer, for example, can mean different times to people living in Australia compared to those in the United States; and in some places the "break" for summer may last into the fall.

A period such as "two weeks" will be coded as P2W. A placeholder X is used to code unknown numeric information; for instance, "a Saturday afternoon" is coded as WXX-6TAF, meaning we don't know which week it is, though we know it's the sixth day of one, and the time of day is the afternoon. Recurring times are represented by indicating the frequency and any restriction on the set of times; for example, "three months every two years" would be coded as P2Y-EVERY-3M. Deictic and anaphoric expressions can be coded with arithmetic expressions; for example, "tomorrow" will be coded as ST+P1D, and "a month later" as RT+P1M. (In some cases ST and RT may be bound to particular calendar dates and times; in other cases they may be left as variables.[2]) There are various kinds of temporal modifiers, for instance, "early" in "early fall" or "at least" in "at least nine months," that are also coded.

An annotation editing tool called Callisto, which enables us to mark up time tags, is shown in figure 10.

The Callisto tool has been used for dozens of linguistic tasks.[3] It can work with most languages and certainly all the languages for which time annotation has been carried out, which include Arabic, Chinese, English, French, Hindi, Korean, Persian, Portuguese, Spanish, Swedish, and Thai.

The tags for times, it can be seen, are fairly straightforward. Let us

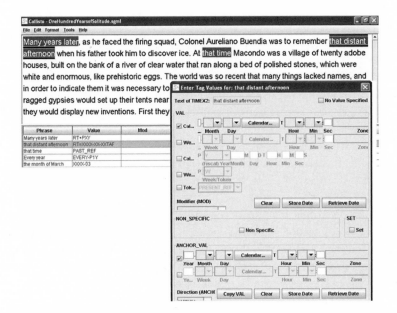

FIG. 10. Annotating time tags with Callisto.

turn to events. These are marked by flagging verbs, event nouns (like "war," "lovemaking," etc.), and certain other expressions, and marking them with tags. Consider the following famous opening sentence of *One Hundred Years of Solitude*:

Many years later, as he faced the firing squad, Colonel Aureliano Buendia was to remember that distant afternoon when his father took him to discover ice. (Garcia Marquez 1995, 5)

The time expression "Many years later" would be marked as RT+PXY. The event "faced" would be tagged as FACE[+PAST], "remember" as REME MBER[+INF+INTENSIONAL+STATIVE] meaning that it is untensed, that is, in infinitive form; it is an intensional verb, that is, what is remembered is in the mind; and it represents a state.[4] The time expression "that distant afternoon" is coded as "RT=XXXX-XX-TAF,"[5] "took" as (you guessed it!) TAKE[+PAST], "discover" as DISCOVER[+INF].

There are two main kinds of links among events and times: temporal links and subordinating links. Temporal links (TLINKs) are coded, for example, in terms of whether an event or time is simultaneous with another, is included in another, or precedes the other (for the cognoscenti, these are based on a system of logic called the interval calculus). Thus, where we placed an item to the left of another in the timeline diagram, the first was before the second; when it was under the item, it was either during the second or simultaneous with it, depending on the lengths of the item, unless of course it had a fuzzy extent or the relationship was marked with "?"

Subordinating links (SLINKs) are used for cases where an event stands in a modal relationship with another, as in the case of remembering or promising (or any of the other wonderful acts of our imagination); these are coded with features such as "factive," "modal," and so on.

To return to our Buendia sentence:

Many years later, as he faced the firing squad, Colonel Aureliano Buendia was to remember that distant afternoon when his father took him to discover ice.

We have the temporal links:

RT SIMULTANEOUS XXXX-XX-TAF
FACE DURING RT+PXY
RT+PXY BEFORE ST
FACE SIMULTANEOUS REMEMBER
TAKE DURING RT
DISCOVER BEFORE PXY

We also have the subordinating links:

REMEMBER SUBORDINATE XXXX-XX-TAF
TAKE SUBORDINATE DISCOVER.

These links can be automatically expanded further, for example, TAKE SUBORDINATE DISCOVER implies TAKE BEFORE DISCOVER, while

REMEMBER SUBORDINATE something implies that something BEFORE REMEMBER.

The resulting timeline diagram for the Buendia narrative is shown in figure 11.

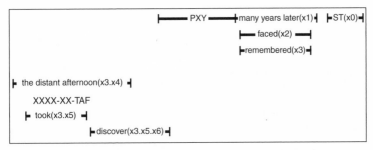

├─────── PXY ────────┤├many years later(x1)┤ ├ST(x0)┤
├── faced(x2) ──┤
├remembered(x3)┤

├ the distant afternoon(x3.x4) ┤
    XXXX-XX-TAF
├ took(x3.x5) ┤
    ├discover(x3.x5.x6)┤

FIG. 11. Timeline for opening sentence of *One Hundred Years of Solitude*.

The human markup is based on an extensive set of guidelines and a special editing tool that allows the human editor to draw links between events and times (which are in turn automatically translated into the tags). Both Callisto as well as another tool called TANGO can be used for the human annotation.

Given the vagueness and ambiguity in human language, annotators disagree about how to annotate particular examples, but with sufficient training on guidelines and adjudication of differences, a reliable human annotation is produced. A human might also unknowingly produce an inconsistent annotation, claiming, for example, that event A was BEFORE event B, which was BEFORE event C, which was DURING event A. These cycles may not be apparent to the human, especially in longer texts. Fortunately, a consistency-checking tool (called SputLink) is available during annotation by the human; its algorithm reveals the inconsistencies to the user, who is thus able to resolve them along the way. Of course in certain literary texts, cycles may be acceptable, in which case they may have to be retained.

The tagging scheme is part of an emerging international standard from the International Organization for Standardization (ISO) called TimeML and has been used for a variety of human languages.[6] The timeline model is represented internally by what computer scientists call a Temporal Constraint Satisfaction Problem (TCSP), in a restricted form that allows computer algorithms to efficiently query the model.[7] There is every reason to believe that the seven temporal relations represented (BEFORE, DURING, SIMULTANEOUS, IMMEDIATELY BEFORE, BEGINS, ENDS, and OVERLAPS) are adequate for human languages. The graphical representation of these temporal relations (from Allen 1983) is shown for any two events (or times) A and B in table 1:

TABLE 1. *Temporal relations in the interval calculus*

A before B	AAA BBB
A during B	AAA
	BBBBB
A simultaneous B	AAA
	BBB
A immediately before B	AAABBB
A begins B	AAA
	BBBBB
A ends B	AAA
	BBBBB
A overlaps B	AAAA
	BBBB

AUTOMATIC TIME TAGGING

So far we have seen how humans mark up linguistic phenomena connected with time and events in text. To peek under the hood further, let us first examine the internals of an automatic time tagger, shown in figure 12, based on one of the best of today's systems (from Ahn, Rantwijk, and de Rijke 2007).

The system breaks down the task into first flagging the time expressions, then resolving the times of fully specified time expressions. Next the system classifies time expressions into points (e.g., "3 PM"), durations (e.g., "3 minutes"), and so on. The tagger then tries to infer the direction of expressions like "last March" or "Tuesday," deciding whether it is a future, current, or past March or Tuesday; to do so it needs discourse tracking of the speech time and reference time. For resolving deictic expressions like "this year," some systems make the simplifying assumption that the speech time is the date of the document (e.g., as in the date of a news article), but such an assumption is inadequate for cases

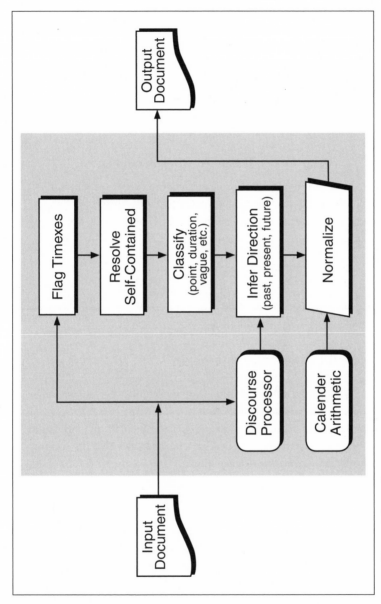

FIG. 12. Time-tagging engine.

of embedded speech like "In 1991, X said 'This year.'" For anaphoric expressions, such as "two months earlier," a system will have to consider time expressions mentioned earlier in the document, such as "In January 2005 . . ." to figure out, say, that November 2004 is being referred to. These inferences are carried out based on statistical training from examples. We will see shortly how this training occurs.

Finally, the tagger generates the official tags required, making use of a calendar in the process, and generates a document marked up with time expressions and their values.

AUTOMATIC TEMPORAL RELATION TAGGING

Let us now turn to temporal relations between events and times. First, it helps to explain why the problem is particularly difficult for computers. Events in narrative may be described in the order in which they occur, as in:

Serena fell. She lay on the grass.

However, this need not be the case. For example, we can have a past-tense sequence where the ordering is not chronological:

Serena fell. Francisco tripped her.

In the latter example Francisco's tripping Serena occurred before her falling; it is offered as an explanation.

In some cases, no doubt, linguistic cues will indicate the order, as in the following, where the past perfect tense indicates that the tripping occurred before the time of the falling:

Serena fell. Francisco had tripped her.

Even with linguistic cues inference can be difficult. In the following we infer that Francisco was brushing his teeth when Serena entered, and that he may have been brushing before she came in.

Serena stormed into the bathroom. Francisco was brushing his teeth.

Yet in a syntactically similar narrative, we infer that the room was dark only after the light was switched off.

Francisco switched off the light. The room was pitch dark.

These examples suggest that the inference of temporal ordering might require lots of knowledge on the part of the system, not only linguistic knowledge but knowledge about the consequences of actions, like tripping and switching off the light.[8] However, it may be difficult to find a knowledge base related to actions for use in computing timelines.

Instead of using a knowledge base, an important strategy is to have the human label thousands of such examples, indicating the temporal relation (e.g., BEFORE or AFTER) in each case, and then to have the computer analyze the data statistically to infer rules that cover the most frequent cases. If the statistical analysis is sufficiently general, it may be able to accurately predict the correct temporal relations without having to be injected with doses of world knowledge. The timelining system therefore uses a program called a statistical classifier trained on examples of narratives with their associated timelines.

Given a sufficiently large and broad collection of documents that humans have marked up with these timelines and coded in TimeML, the program automatically generates the markup for any given text document.

The program builds a statistical model based on frequency counts of how often particular types of time links co-occur with particular linguistic features of the sentences expressing them; the counts are computed in a large collection of documents that have been marked up with these links. In our Buendia example some of these linguistic features were shown in square brackets. The expectation is that these linguistic features will help predict the presence of particular types of links.

To train a statistical classifier, examples are grouped into classes, and the program tries to separate the classes by means of features, which are given weights based on statistics. For example, expressions such as "announce on Tuesday," "fainted on Friday," "broke up with my girlfriend over the weekend," and thousands of such examples occurring in real texts will all be marked up by the human as falling into a DURING class (meaning the event occurred during the time mentioned),

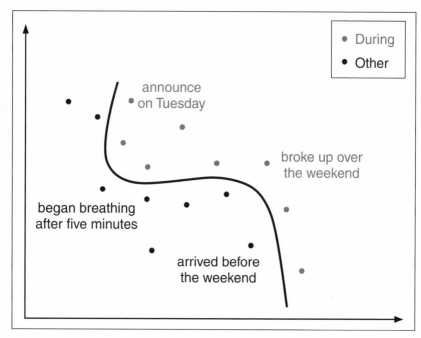

FIG. 13. Automatic classification of temporal relations.

whereas "arrived before the weekend," "began breathing again after five minutes," and such will be marked up as instantiating some other class (which could be BEFORE, AFTER, etc.). Linguistic features such as the type of verb, its tense, the type of time expression (day of week, period of months, etc.), and particular prepositions will receive weights corresponding to their frequencies in the marked-up corpus. Instead of a human rather arbitrarily stating rules for what the weights of features should be, a kind of democracy reigns; the feature counts in the data determine how they are weighted.

Of course, the program has to be given the features to begin with; these usually include the words in the text and sequences of words, along with other linguistic features, based on the researcher's hunches. Human intuition and ingenuity in selecting features are an indispensable ingredient in the mix.

A given training example will be placed, based on its feature weights, as a point in a geometric representation called a feature space. If we have

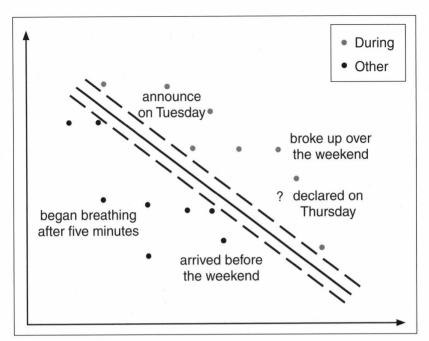

FIG. 14. Classification based on distance from margin.

three features, the space will be three-dimensional, but in general we will have many more features, making for a many-dimensional space.

This process is shown schematically in figure 13. Here we will use just two dimensions, corresponding therefore to two features, because it is hard to draw three dimensions on a two-dimensional sheet of paper and even harder to draw even more dimensions. Note that the two classes aren't separable by a line; this is a case (typical of temporal relations) where the classes are relatively hard to separate.

Fortunately, there are mathematical procedures that can transform the space into an even higher-dimensional one where a "line" in such a space can be used to separate the classes. (Actually, calling what we did a "line" would annoy a geometer—it is really a hyperplane, since we are dealing with many dimensions.) Typically the statistical classifier will try to thicken the "line" into a band, finding a band of maximum thickness that can separate the two classes. Finding the maximal band helps the learner generalize beyond the particular dataset (i.e., avoiding "overfitting" to the particular training data), as there may be more "marginal" separations that are overreliant on idiosyncrasies in the data sample.

When trained on a corpus of thousands of examples, the program tries to separate the DURING examples from the others. This is shown in figure 14.

Once trained, given a test example, say, "declared on Thursday" (let's assume this particular example hasn't been seen before), the program will place the test point, based on its feature weights, at some position in relation to the other points in the feature space. Depending on which side of the band it falls, the test example will be labeled by the program as DURING or some other class. Since "declared on Thursday" is similar to the DURING examples, it will be closer to those than the others and will likely fall on the same side of the band margin and so will be labeled as DURING.

Even though statistical classifiers work well, they still need to be supplemented by rules from human intuitions, since the statistical features will not pick up patterns that are relatively rare in the training data.[9]

The architecture for a temporal relation tagger is shown in figure 15, derived from a system called TARSQI (described in Mani et al. 2006). The classifier module is the statistical classifier described earlier. It is supplemented with three other modular components that use linguistic rules developed by a human.

The module called s2T takes a subordinating link (SLINK) and infers a temporal relation, so that remembering rainy days means that the rainy days preceded the remembering. Likewise, forgetting that one wrote the letter means the letter was written before the forgetting, whereas forgetting to write the letter means the letter was not written.

The next module, Gtag, uses nearly two hundred hand-developed rules to infer temporal ordering, such as recognizing a past-tense event verb joined by a conjunction to another past-tense event verb as being BEFORE the latter, for example, (Hemingway's) "lifted her mosquito bar and crawled cosily into bed" (as it happens, this particular rule was accurate nearly nine times out of ten). Of course such a rule (like most "rules") will have exceptions.

Another module, A2T, infers temporal ordering from aspectual verbs, such as "begin," "end," "continue," and so on; for example, if I started

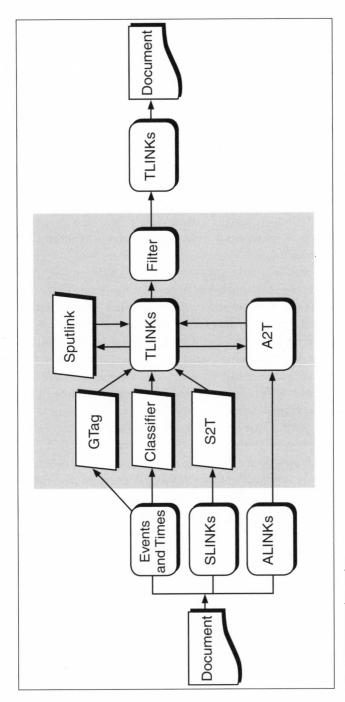

FIG. 15. TLINK tagging engine.

walking to campus after the movie, this implies I walked to campus after the movie.

All these components are integrated with SputLink, which expands the links and resolves inconsistent links that might be introduced within and across modules. The result can include both contradictory links, such as an event being both BEFORE and AFTER another, but also cases where the temporal relation is underspecified (i.e., there may be more than one possible relation). Such links may be thrown out or preserved, depending on user preferences—as we saw earlier, narrative can include temporal cycles, which should be preserved. SputLink uses nearly 750 rules, most of them automatically generated from templates. For example, one rule is

> If event A is BEFORE event B and event C is DURING event B, then A is BEFORE C.

These rules may seem to be breathtakingly obvious, but they allow the computer to weave the warp and woof of the timeline, filling in links in the timeline and detecting inconsistencies.

The output from all these systems is passed to a module that makes a final decision, based on the evidence it has, regarding what the temporal relation is. It can be seen that the system uses linguistic knowledge as well as temporal reasoning, combining logic as well as statistics from training data, to arrive at a timeline for a text.

To revisit the beginning of the Buendia narrative:

> Many years later, as he faced the firing squad, Colonel Aureliano Buendia was to remember that distant afternoon when his father took him to discover ice. At that time Macondo was a village of twenty adobe houses, built on the bank of a river of clear water that ran along a bed of polished stones, which were white and enormous, like prehistoric eggs. The world was so recent that many things lacked names, and in order to indicate them it was necessary to point.

Figure 16 shows an automatically generated visualization of a human-annotated timeline for this paragraph.[10] Here arrows represent BEFORE, circles DURING, and squares SIMULTANEOUS relations.

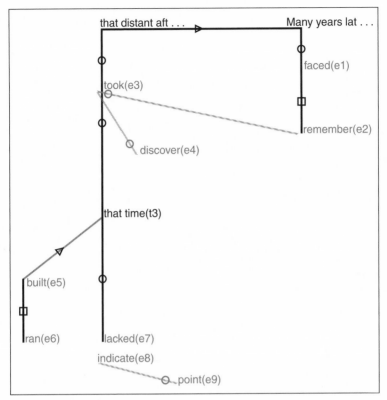

FIG. 16. Timeline for *One Hundred Years of Solitude*. (This figure is based on an actual screen image from a system but redrawn to make the contrasts clearer in gray scale.)

The dark links in figure 16 are TLINKs, and the light ones are SLINKs. In comparison, figure 17 shows the additional links inferred by SputLink as a result of temporal reasoning.

As "that distant afternoon" is earlier in time than the "many years later," SputLink has dutifully inferred that his father's taking him to discover ice (event e3) is before his facing of the firing squad (event e1). It has also inferred that the building of Macondo (e5) precedes the remembering (e2). Loyal and robotic, SputLink has filled in all the links that can be inferred from figure 16 without considering whether any of these links are particularly significant. Nevertheless, the linking is useful,

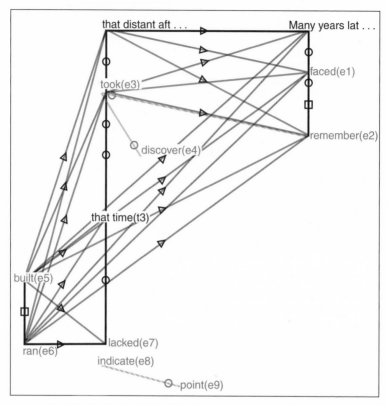

FIG. 17. *One Hundred Years of Solitude* with Sputlink expansions. (This figure is based on an actual screen image from a system but redrawn to make the contrasts clearer in gray scale.)

as it allows the system to answer questions about the temporal orderings of the events, even orderings not mentioned in the text.

ASSESSMENT

It is time to ascend from Vulcan's forge, away from all the grimy machinery and the sound of drills and the threat of flying bits. Let us now assess how well these tools work.

Figure 18 shows a run of the TARSQI system on the opening sentence of the Garcia Marquez novel. It can be seen that the temporal relations are ordered correctly except for the event "faced," which is left unrelated to the others.

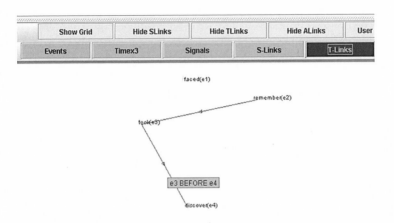

FIG. 18. Opening sentence of *One Hundred Years of Solitude* as seen by TARSQI.

As is obvious from our exposure to the innards of the system, computers have indeed come a long way from the kinds of techniques that made them well known in the area of authorship identification. Computer systems today are digging much deeper into the way we talk about and understand and reason about events and times, in a way that makes it possible to map timelines for complex narratives, shedding light on that complexity.

A collection of 250 English news documents annotated in TimeML with events, times, and temporal relations has been released by the Linguistic Data Consortium for use in research. The TARSQI system scores around 75 percent on timelines of English news stories from this collection when compared to humans. This means that the program is good enough to run on large bodies of news stories, but the output will require some correction by humans. Specialized editing tools have been developed to facilitate such correction.

The accuracy of such programs in recognizing and resolving time expressions in different languages in international timelining competitions is around 90 percent, and comparable with the accuracies of humans when the latter are matched against them. (In 2004–5, the best-performing systems for English included those from the Language Computer Corporation in Dallas and the Center for Scientific and Technological Research in Trento; the best one for Chinese came from the Hong Kong Polytechnic.) Programs that do this task therefore require very little, if any, correction by humans, provided the programs have been fed sufficient training examples.

Systems designed to recognize TimeML events in news text (such as that described in Sauri et al. 2005) score about 80 percent. This result can be contrasted with the 60 percent accuracy ceiling that has been observed in research on extracting more abstract events, such as the Message Understanding Conference competition (MUC) described by R. Grishman and B. Sundheim (1996), where one must recognize a given news story (e.g., a failed hijacking attempt) as an instance, for example, of a terrorist event, and identify in addition the location, the participants, and so on. (Other tasks have included recognizing instances of corporate takeovers, money laundering, etc.) The reason for the higher accuracy for TimeML events is that these events are at the "surface" of the text, expressed by particular morphological and syntactic patterns within a sentence for the most part (e.g., finite verbs, event nouns), whereas the MUC events require a large number of inferences involving semantic and pragmatic reasoning over the entire document.

Subordination relations, as in the case of Jean remembering the rainy days or of Aureliano Buendia being taken to discover ice, are annotated as part of TimeML. Accuracies for subordination relations over nearly seven hundred events are in the 70 percent range, based on published results from the TARSQI system. Performance is expected to improve with additional quantities and variety of training data.

Research has also begun on annotating subnarratives, based on aspects of an annotation scheme for macro-events, which are not yet part of TimeML, based on a corpus of more than a thousand articles, from materials used to assess reading comprehension in schools, as well as current-event stories from the Canadian Broadcasting Corporation aimed at schoolchildren.

All these developments bode well for the timeline analysis of literary texts by computer. Existing programs that have been trained in news and other genres can be used without retraining, but when used in this way they are likely to be less accurate with literary text corpora, because different genres can have very different linguistic and literary characteristics. Although they might seem to work reasonably well on particular fragments of the sort we have discussed here, for a more precise understanding of their accuracy, a corpus of literary examples will have to be marked up in TimeML to train such programs.

Timelining systems such as TARSQI have so far been applied in eminently practical settings, mainly to corpora consisting of newspaper articles, crime and accident reports, medical narratives, discussions about schedules, e-mail, summaries of silent films, and other such sources. Commercial products have also been developed to answer "when" questions from news documents. My prior research has focused on some of these genres. However, this book represents the first time these computational models have been extended to fiction and poetics.[11]

In the future, assuming corpora of literary classics marked up with TimeML were made available to train computer programs, these methods could be applied to thousands of literary narratives, changing the way literary scholars conduct research. Generalizations about the use of time in different literary subgenres should then be easier to make. Particular patterns of timelines, including those we have investigated in this book but no doubt many more, will start to emerge across varieties of narrative texts.

One can envisage all the online narrative texts from Project Gutenberg (or other such resource) having timelines generated for them. These timelines can then be adjusted, if necessary, by humans and used as a resource for students and scholars alike. Since humans don't really have the time to construct timelines for every story, having a computer do it, if it can do so accurately, is a sensible option. The resource could be stored in a database, which can then be queried to determine when particular events happened, which events follow one another in a story, which are included, and which ones are simultaneous. This can of course result in queries about relationships that aren't mentioned in the text, from the trivial fact of telling us that Serena was tripped yesterday, to the subtle relationships of correspondence across times in Proustian or Borgesian narratives. Further, the timelines could be constructed for entire novels or fragments of them; they could be restricted to events involving particular characters, so that we would have timelines just for events involving Molly Bloom or Mrs. Dalloway.

Such a database of timelines for the world's literature can help launch (or revive) an empirical discipline of literary studies of time, one based on observation of the frequency and distribution of particular patterns of temporal narrative. Such a discipline could determine whether particular schools or authors have characteristic styles in the way they represent and express time. They could determine the time spans of different genres of narrative, measure the pace and rhythm of each, characterize patterns of recurrence. They might, in the best of worlds, also make us better readers and writers.

There are undoubtedly many subversively creative activities, many of them of little consequence but still wildly interesting, that can be practiced by lovers of fiction. For example, for recurring characters we might construct timelines across stories or across novels. Research has already been done on matching structures similar to our timelines, to compare different versions of the same story; such research leverages thesauri (to help match paraphrases) and allows for a degree of sloppiness in matching. These timelines might be connected by common events or times or characters. For example, one might connect parallel stories of the Spanish Civil War or the Battle of the Bulge. In P. G. Wodehouse's works the Woosters are shown to be late risers, but timelines can reveal other habits, such as the times of the day when Bertie sallies forth into the world; perhaps there are particular times when he is more likely to meet up with an aunt or the dreaded Sir Roderick Glossop, and, finally, it would not hurt to get a better handle on the schedule of that most orderly of valets, Jeeves.

I suspect that at least some of these projects will be of interest to literary scholars. However, it is hard to envisage carrying out any of them, even for a single work of art, without the benefit of computers.

This chapter has introduced a tagging scheme for timelines, called TimeML. The scheme includes a markup for time expressions, events, and the temporal relations between them. The markup is part of an international standard. Tools to automatically generate this markup are available and have begun to make their presence felt in commercial systems. These tools thrive on the availability of collections of texts marked up with timelines. These collections, or corpora, are then mined by standard, off-the-shelf statistical classifiers, which can automatically generate the markup. To enhance the accuracy of these tools, rules developed by humans can be integrated into these statistical frameworks.

Although these tools have been applied to a variety of different types of narrative, this book represents the first attempt to apply them to literary narratives, in particular, fictional ones. Once corpora of literary texts are created and marked up with timelines, using specialized editing tools, the statistical classifiers can be applied to them to automatically create timelines. The computer can do this for thousands of literary narratives, allowing for empirical studies of time in narrative to get off the ground, based on observation of the frequency and distribution of particular forms of temporal narrative. This capability can help uncover patterns, test hypotheses about authors, genres, and so on, and in general establish a science of narrative analysis. It can also, one hopes, enhance the reading experience.

4 | Calendar Times

Proust, who suffered from insomnia, drew attention in the opening paragraphs of *Swann's Way* to the disorientation that can result when one wakes up confused about time:[1]

> When a man is asleep, he has in a circle round him the chain of the hours, the sequence of the years, the order of the heavenly host. Instinctively, when he awakes, he looks to these, and in an instant reads off his own position on the earth's surface and the amount of time that has elapsed during his slumbers; but this ordered procession is apt to grow confused, and to break its ranks. Suppose that, towards morning, after a night of insomnia, sleep descends upon him while he is reading, in quite a different position from that in which he normally goes to sleep, he has only to lift his arm to arrest the sun and turn it back in its course, and, at the moment of waking, he will have no idea of the time, but will conclude that he has just gone to bed.

Not to know when one is can be extremely disorienting. One of the first things a person does on waking up on a weekday morning is to look at the time. There is a sense of relief and satisfaction in knowing that one is "on time," and that things are starting off on a good foot; one can become quite panic stricken on finding that one has overslept. It is helpful to be able to check one's bearings in this way, to know where one is on the map of time.

The disruptions that occur when our biological clock gets out of phase with the rhythms of day and night, as in the case of jet lag, can be most uncomfortable and disorienting.[2] These disruptions have often been the subject of literary narratives. In his novel *Pattern Recognition*,

William Gibson has an engaging description of waking up at an unseemly hour as a result of jet lag: "Five hours' New York jet lag and Cayce Pollard wakes in Camden Town to the dire and ever-circling wolves of disrupted circadian rhythm. It is that flat and spectral non-hour, awash in limbic tides, brainstem stirring fitfully, flashing inappropriate reptilian demands for sex, food, sedation, all of the above, and none really an option now" (2003, 1).

As in Proust's case, when our clock is out of synch, we may have no idea where we are in time. Our technology of clocks and calendars is thus vital in keeping us tethered to our schedules of work, rest, and pleasure.[3] Clocks and calendars help reorient us to the official schedules of both the heavens and the earth. Calendars in particular are used to distinguish occasions for festivals and times for prayer and planting.[4] They provide a means of recording births and deaths, and the succession of empires, the launching of wars and proclamations, as well as apparently mundane quotidian events, often of even more significance to people than the doings of empires. These include birthdays, wedding anniversaries, the day of one's initiation into sexual or religious activity, and so forth.

Due to these associations, it is not surprising to find a variety of uses of calendar times in narrative. They can be used evocatively, to evoke particular events associated with those times. Calendar times can also provide a way of organizing events along a timeline, into what we will call chronicles. Narratives may also begin and end, and repeat themselves, in cycles that make explicit reference to heavenly cycles. We will explore each of these in turn.

CALENDAR TIMES USED EVOCATIVELY

Consider the Hemingway short story "In Another Country," which begins with a reference to a season:

In the fall the war was always there, but we did not go to it any more. (1954, 243)

Astronomical principles inform us that fall runs from equinox to solstice (September 23 to December 21 in the Northern Hemisphere, and March 21 to June 21 in the Southern Hemisphere). But these dates are only approximate. The TimeML annotations scheme we introduced would conveniently sidestep this issue by representing the fall as XXXX-FA. Hemingway's use of "always there" implies that the war was an event that persisted throughout the fall, that is, the "fall" lasted for part of the "war." Our TimeML annotation would represent this relationship as the fall being DURING the war.

However, we also happen to know that fall is a season when leaves descend to earth; it is the season that transitions from blossom to frost. "Know'st thou not at the fall of the leaf / How the heart feels a languid grief" goes a verse from Dante Gabriel Rossetti (2006). TimeML is unaware of all these connotations.

By the end of "In Another Country," we have become aware that fall is experienced as a season of dislocation and distress, of soldiers sequestered in a hospital while their comrades fight on—soldiers wounded by war in body and spirit. In other words this particular fall has a special gravity to it.

"The Short Happy Life of Francis Macomber," as we saw earlier, opens with the characters about to have lunch:

It was now lunch time and they were all sitting under the double green fly of the dining tent pretending that nothing had happened.

When is "lunch time"? It becomes clear soon enough, as Margaret openly flirts with Robert Wilson during the meal, that the time is really noon. It is clear, however, that "lunch time" isn't really about the time on the clock. Lunch time is the time for a prescribed ritual in which social and interpersonal relations among the white colonials are reaffirmed or unraveled. The time that is used to situate the story is clearly distinguishable because it corresponds to a ritual event. In our annotation scheme the two times, "now" and "lunch time," will be linked as being SIMULTANEOUS.

The use of time words and phrases to denote ritual events is in fact built into our calendar terminologies. There are times of the day marked out for prayer, as in the (Latin) "matins," "lauds," "primes," "terces," "sexts," "nones," "vespers," and "complines" in monastic Catholicism, and the (Arabic) *fajr, dhuhr, asr, maghrib*, and *isha* in Islam. We have days of the week, such as the Sabbath, when special observances are called for, and particular months, such as Ramadan, the month when the Koran was apparently revealed, a time for fasting, feasting, and reflection. These times, which are marked as time expressions in TimeML, are charged with historical and mythic associations and claims about the human's role and responsibilities in relation to a higher moral order (all of those connotations are of course absent from TimeML). Historical events, or mythical ones, mark out times in the calendar with a special glow.

One function of named times (days of the week, months, holidays, religious days, etc.) in narrative is thus to evoke particular events as part of the setting; such times, in other words, are a convenient shorthand for those events. These events need not always be the mythic ones that are of significance to an entire culture. For Proust's character Marcel, Sundays were highly significant in relation to the Easter holidays the family would spend in Combray, the occasion for Marcel's extensive, retrospective riffs on personal history and experience. And for Marcel, Saturdays too, as Genette (1980) shows, were of special significance, for that was the day that lunch in Combray (itself a ritual occasion, associated with particular conversational peculiarities and social attitudes) would be had an hour early so that Françoise could go off to the market.

In short any calendar time can have a ritual significance, connoting a significant event or set of events typically associated with that time; the significance can be known to entire cultures, to smaller units such as families, or just to individuals.

CALENDAR TIMES IN CHRONICLES

One might imagine that the simplest timeline is one where calendar time is explicitly used as an organizing principle for a narrative, as in the case of a journal or history, where events are described according to a fixed chronology. Travelogues, diaries, histories, ship logs, and such are all forms of what I call a chronicle.[5] Calendar times are used primarily to organize events in a chronicle.

The earliest stories orient the opening events of a narrative in terms of a mythical creation story that constitutes a critical part of the culture's historical memory. This type of precalendrical chronicle is seen in an ancient Sumerian legend from about 2100 BC, about Gilgamesh, the hero-king and fifth ruler of Uruk, in modern-day Iraq (here from Black et al. 1998):

When dawn was breaking, when the horizon became bright, when the little birds, at the break of dawn, began to clamour, when Utu had left his bedchamber, his sister holy Inana said to the warrior Gilgamec: "My brother, in those days when destiny was determined, when abundance overflowed in the Land, when An had taken the heavens for himself, when Enlil had taken the earth for himself, when the nether world had been given to Ereckigala as a gift; when he set sail, when he set sail, when the father set sail for the nether world, when Enki set sail for the nether world—against the lord a storm of small hailstones arose, against Enki a storm of large hailstones arose. The small ones were light hammers, the large ones were like stones from catapults (?). The keel of Enki's little boat was trembling as if it were being butted by turtles, the waves at the bow of the boat rose to devour the lord like wolves and the waves at the stern of the boat were attacking Enki like a lion. At that time, there was a single tree, a single halub tree, a single tree (?), growing on the bank of the pure Euphrates, being watered by the Euphrates. The force of the south wind uprooted it and stripped its branches, and the Euphrates picked it up and carried it away. I, a woman, respectful of An's words, was walking along; I, a woman, respectful of Enlil's words, was walking along, and took the tree and brought it into Unug, into Inana's luxuriant garden."

The speech time of Inana's narration is given as a time of day, whereas the events of her story (the carrying away of a tree after a storm) are positioned after a sequence of mythical creation events.[6] No calendar is used to situate these mythical events.

By the time of the ancient Greeks, historical memory is tied to a calendar filled with specific historical events. We are now in a world that seems almost modern by comparison with that of the Sumerians. Consider the opening of Thucydides' history of the Peloponnesian War (431–404 BC; the war was a twenty-seven-year, protracted event that would end up destroying Athenian civilization). Thucydides goes to some length to pinpoint its beginning. He anchors most time expressions to the historical calendar determined by the period of a priestess or magistrate holding office and to specific battles, as in this extract:

The thirty years' truce which was entered into after the conquest of Euboea lasted fourteen years. In the fifteenth, in the forty-eighth year of the priestess-ship of Chrysis at Argos, in the ephorate of Aenesias at Sparta, in the last month but two of the archonship of Pythodorus at Athens, and six months after the battle of Potidaea, just at the beginning of spring, a Theban force a little over three hundred strong, under the command of their Boeotarchs, Pythangelus, son of Phyleides, and Diemporus, son of Onetorides, about the first watch of the night, made an armed entry into Plataea, a town of Boeotia in alliance with Athens. (Thucydides 1903, bk. 2, chap. 6)

Novels concerned with historical events, such as *War and Peace*, include elements of chronicles, organizing the narrative into calendar years, months, and so on. The title of the first chapter of *War and Peace* is "Book One: 1805," and each of the subsequent sixteen chapters has a title indicating a particular year or period of years. For a voluminous work like *War and Peace*, organizing the chapters by years along a timeline is eminently sensible, especially since the story is concerned with historical events, fictionalized to varying extents, associated with military campaigns. However, this date-based scaffolding is only an exoskeleton; within each chapter we see a full variety of timelines of great intricacy.

Another type of chronicle that organizes events in terms of chronology is the journal. Samuel Pepys, a charming and addictive diarist, provides engrossing and judiciously selected observations on life in seventeenth-century London in his posthumously published *Diary*. Here is an extract from September 1660 that includes a sample of fairly gruesome historical events, though the narration is still unfailingly amusing in parts:

SEPTEMBER 25TH

To the office, where Sir W. Batten, Colonel Slingsby, and I sat awhile, . . . And afterwards I did send for a cup of tee (a China drink) of which I never had drank before, and went away.

OCTOBER 13TH

To my Lord's this morning, where I met with Captain Cuttance. But my Lord not being up, I went out to Charing Cross to see Major-general Harrison <u>hanged</u>, <u>drawn</u>; and <u>quartered</u>; which was <u>done</u> there, he <u>looking</u> as cheerful as any man could <u>do</u> in that condition. He was presently <u>cut down</u>, and his head and his heart <u>shown</u> to the people, at which there was great <u>shouts</u> of joy. . . . Thus it was my chance to <u>see</u> the King <u>beheaded</u> at White Hall, and to <u>see</u> the first blood <u>shed</u> in revenge for the blood of the King at Charing Cross.

OCTOBER 20TH

This morning one <u>came</u> to me to <u>advise</u> with me where to <u>make</u> me a window into my cellar in lieu of one that Sir W. Batten had <u>stopped</u> up, and <u>going down</u> into my cellar to <u>look</u> I <u>put</u> my foot into a great heap of turds, by which I <u>find</u> that Mr. Turner's house of office is full and <u>comes</u> into my cellar, which do <u>trouble</u> me. . . .

. . . This afternoon, <u>going</u> through London and <u>calling</u> at Crowes the upholsterer's, in Saint Bartholomew's, I <u>saw</u> the limbs of some of our new traitors set upon Aldersgate, which was a sad <u>sight</u> to <u>see</u>; and a bloody week this and the last have been, there being ten <u>hanged</u>, <u>drawn</u>, and <u>quartered</u>. (Pepys 1893)

Journals as a whole tend to be fairly "flat" in timeline structure. Although they have an exoskeletal timeline capturing a series of speech times, along with subsidiary timelines for each journal entry, the latter tend to be simple, since journal entries are typically short and involve events for particular times of the day. The diary fragment here presents no problem for the computational model, the only wrinkle being the situating in time of the expression "it was my chance to see the King beheaded at Whitehall" in the entry of October 13th; the fact that the king's beheading isn't described means that it must have occurred earlier, before the speech time of the text.[7]

With the growth of publishing on the Web, journaling has become widespread. Travel blogs, in particular, are ubiquitous. Consider the first two paragraphs of a travel blog from Ride for Climate:[8]

MARCH 7, 2006

<u>Leaving</u> San Cristobal de las Casas, I <u>biked</u> with Gregg and Brooks for one more day. We <u>climbed</u> over the mountains, and then <u>de-</u>

scended to the east, where a thick green rainforest grew up around the road. We arrived in the town of Ocosingo and we were advised the road ahead was unsafe in the afternoon or night. I did not ask if there was a fire station and went straight to a cheap hotel that I split with Gregg and Brooks.

The following morning, as I was planning to ride farther that day, I left at dawn while Gregg and Brooks were still asleep. I biked 30 miles to the town of Agua Azul where I played for 4 hours in waterfalls and clean cool pools.

Such blogs incorporate route descriptions embellished with significant anecdotes, while confining themselves to a fairly flat exoskeleton. We shall see in chapter 6 ("Characters in Time") that the relatively simple timeline as well as the salience of the route in such blogs make for a rich spatiotemporal visualization.

Not all chronicles are uniform in the way they represent time in the exoskeleton; even in a short chronicle, relatively lengthy events may be sprinkled with mentions of more instantaneous ones. Further, events may be iterated and interpolated between times marked on the calendar and used to bound other events that can be single or repeated, to convey habituality.

In the following excerpt from a historical blog by the writer Amitav Ghosh (2005), the first sentence covers two decades and the remaining sentences one year:

In the course of the two decades he spent in Kabul, Babur led four expeditions into India. His fifth and final campaign was launched in October 1525: it had a characteristically light-hearted beginning: "We mostly drank and had morning draughts on drinking days." Between marches Babur and his nobles wrote poetry, collected obscene jokes, and gave chase to the occasional rhinoceros. Despite internal dissensions the Lodis managed to field an army of 100,000 men and 1,000 elephants against Babur's paltry force of 12,000. The armies met on April 20, 1526, at the historic battlefield of Panipat a few miles north of Delhi.

In this narrative, the emperor Babur's times set aside for leisure are marked out by a habitual event (drinking), and the gaps in an another event (marching toward a battle) are used to bound the repeated events of writing poetry, collecting obscene jokes, and chasing the occasional rhinoceros.

The timeline is shown in figure 19.

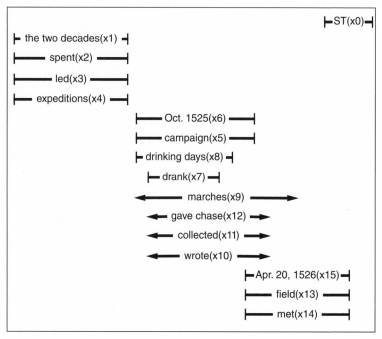

FIG. 19. Timeline with gapped intervals and zooming.

Notice that the marches are a fuzzy interval, which in this case involves gaps. The giving chase, collecting, and writing are also gapped but roughly overlap during the marches. In this chronicle the times in the exoskeleton involve zooming down to a specific day, which results in a culmination of the narrative.

Virginia Woolf's *Mrs. Dalloway* is a novel that mixes elements of chronicling with the use of evoked times, both melded into a complex, stream-of-consciousness narrative. The story, set on a perfect summer's day in London in the middle of June 1923, seamlessly marks time by clocks, most notably Big Ben. The timeline's bound is indicated at the beginning; we know the day is expected to end with Clarissa's party, which seems to be her main concern, a valiant attempt to keep up appearances. While Big Ben's movements serve a journaling function to track the progress of the day toward this anticipated culmination, they also coincide with particular events, of considerable significance to the characters, most of which have to do with the past catching up with them in different ways.

The philosopher Paul Ricoeur has argued, in an analysis of the temporal structure of this novel, that Big Ben marks what he calls "monumental time": "Clock time, the time of monumental history, the time of authority-figures—the same time!" (Ricoeur's words in Ricoeur 1990, 106). Big Ben's striking, in his view, is a symbol not just of the merciless passage of time but also of imperial power, in a London that continues to rule over the colonies (most notably, India, from where Clarissa's old flame Peter has just returned), and where the establishment doctors Holmes and Bradshaw are utterly unsympathetic to the mental condition of Septimus, the shell-shocked suicidal-depressive war veteran and aesthete, described, in Woolf's words, as "aged about thirty, pale-faced, beak-nosed, wearing brown shoes and a shabby overcoat, with hazel eyes which had that look of apprehension in them which makes complete strangers apprehensive too. The world has raised its whip; where will it descend?" (Woolf 1996, 11).

The same strikings of the clock are heard by different characters as they move about London, characters whose lives are linked at different degrees of proximity to Clarissa Dalloway's. The characters also experience other events in common, a plane flying overhead, the Prince of Wales' car passing, and so forth. A highly schematic timeline, using summary elements as the units of analysis, is shown in figure 20.

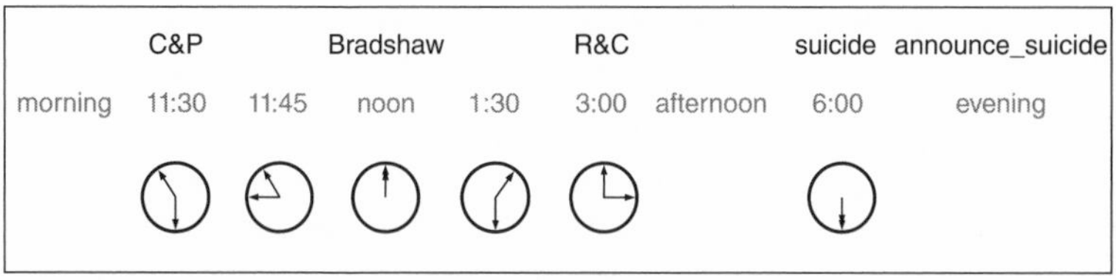

	C&P		Bradshaw		R&C		suicide	announce_suicide
morning	11:30	11:45	noon	1:30	3:00	afternoon	6:00	evening

FIG. 20. Timeline of *Mrs. Dalloway*.

As Ricoeur notes, the first time Big Ben is heard, it is morning. As Woolf's narrator says: "First a warning, musical; then the hour irrevocable" (1996, 4). The clock strikes as the emotionally fragile Clarissa, an upper-class woman in her fifties, is out walking through an elegant part of London on her way to the florist's, remembering her days with Peter, unaware that the latter is in fact back in London.

When the clock is heard again, events have advanced; Clarissa has returned home from the florist's, mulling over her youthful passion for a girl called Sally, while Peter, the one-time socialist who had been sent down from Oxford and had gone off to find his fortune in India, where he hasn't quite succeeded (the book has quite a few disparaging remarks about coolies and the like), has arrived at Clarissa's, where he gives way to tears. Clarissa kisses him, at which point Peter seeks to confront her, seizing her by the shoulders to ask her if she's happy with her husband, Richard, just as Clarissa's daughter Elizabeth comes in; he leaves just then, the question is left dangling, as the clock strikes 11:30.

There are other instances of clocks striking, one especially at noon, the time when Septimus and his wife, Lucrezia (Rezia), have their ominous appointment with Dr. Bradshaw, where "it was merely a question of rest, said Sir William; of rest, rest, rest; a long rest in bed" (Woolf 1996, 71).

At six in the evening, Holmes comes to fetch Septimus, giving rise to the dramatic moment when Septimus, hearing Holmes advancing up the stairs, reasons, "Holmes would get him. But no; not Holmes; not Bradshaw. . . . There remained only the window, the large Bloomsbury lodging-house window, the tiresome, the troublesome, and rather melodramatic business of opening the window and throwing himself out" (Woolf 1996, 108).

Later that evening, when the suicide is brought to the attention of the upper-class party guests, Clarissa identifies with Septimus: "She felt somehow very like him—the young man who had killed himself. She felt glad that he had done it; thrown it away. The clock was striking. The leaden circles dissolved in the air. He made her feel the beauty; made her feel the fun" (Woolf 1996, 135).

The main point of Ricoeur's analysis is to establish that this is in fact a story mainly about the experience of time. He goes on to argue that each character's experience of time is essentially solitary, but that each solitary experience resonates in the solitary experience of another character, forming a network of time experiences that exists in a state of conflict with monumental time. The conflicts themselves seem not, to my mind, to be primarily about time, though the clock times do evoke connotations of power and authority, in addition to the intimations of the relentless march of time toward death, which is experienced in different ways for different characters.

In summary the way calendar times function in narratives is quite varied. Times may be used to evoke events of significance to the individual, group, or culture. In the case of chronicles, a fairly simple calendar-based exoskeleton is fleshed out with events of different lengths and possibly complex timelines for each element. The calendar times in chronicles may not all be of the same granularity, and zooming may occur within the exoskeleton. Narratives can use the exoskeleton for symbolic purposes, in such a case fusing the evocative and organizational functions of calendar times.

CALENDAR CYCLES AND NARRATIVE STRUCTURE

Yet another role of calendar times in narrative is to re-create the cycles expressed by calendars. There are actually two very different kinds of concepts of cycles in time: the predictable recurrence of certain types of events—such as sunrise, sunset, spring, sleep, and supper—and the rather shocking case of recurrence of all events.

All-event cycles, involving the recurrence of all events, posit an extreme situation of the past being repeated exactly, perhaps eternally, as in Nietzsche's myth of the eternal return. The negative consequences of a world of this sort have been explored in various literary works. In the Milan Kundera novel *The Unbearable Lightness of Being*, the narrator points out that "in the world of Eternal Return the weight of unbearable responsibility lies heavy on every move we make" (1991, 5). In the Alan Lightman (1994) novel *Einstein's Dreams*, a few unhappy people caught up in such a fictive world are tragically aware that all the mistakes of their previous lives will be repeated.

Cycles of the former kind, event-type cycles, are uncontroversial but nevertheless quite fascinating. Different cultures have come up with a variety of narratives that explain these cycles. In Greek mythology Persephone, the daughter of the fertility goddess Demeter, is abducted by Hades into the underworld. Her mother, distraught, neglects the earth, allowing it to become barren. Zeus tries to ameliorate matters by prevailing upon Hades, who agrees to let her go. But first he gives Persephone a pomegranate seed to eat; as a result of having partaken of the fruit of the underworld, Persephone is condemned to spend four months of each year underground, ascending to earth just as the seeds blossom and restore the earth to abundance.

Event-type cycles do not always stretch back forever. Time usually begins in the calendars of these cultures with an event of the founding or initiation of a civilization or religion, which occurs in a time lost in the fog of myth and collective memory. The heavens and the earth are usually created around this time. As the imagination of a culture that has preserved its historical memory stretches back toward the time of origin, it populates the time of creation with all kinds of fanciful events. In this respect the calendar is rather like an axis mundi. While the latter tethers the world spatially to the heavens, the calendar tethers the world to its origin in time.

Narrative, too, can stretch far back in time; thus, to pick a few well-known examples, we have the creation story of Macondo in *One Hundred Years of Solitude* and the elf myth of the creation of Arda in Tolkien's *Silmarillion*. The Mayan epic, the *Popul Vuh*, provides a mythology for the Quiché-speaking Maya of Guatemala, starting from the creation of the universe by three meditating feathered serpents to the founding of the Quiché nation. The serpents' first two attempts to make humans, out of mud and then out of wood, failed, so the first humans were made from corn. The *Popul Vuh* explains the origin of the moon as well as the sun, or *kin*, meaning "day," from the god Hunahpu (literally, Blow-pipe User, or Hunter), whose name is given to the twentieth day of the *tzolkin* calendar; Hunahpu is the child of Hun-Hunahpu, the sun of the winter solstice. The mythology of the *Popul Vuh* has been woven into two remarkable twentieth-century novels, Miguel Angel Asturias's *Men of Maize* and Rosario Castellanos's *Book of Lamentations*.

The event-type recurrences in specific calendars can influence the underlying structure of stories told in the corresponding culture. The event-type cycle governed by the sun's daily trajectory has of course been a standard resource for poets of all times and stripes. The anthropologist Andrew Hofling has studied narratives among the speakers of the dying Itzaj Mayan language, spoken (as of 1993) by fewer than three dozen people in northern Guatemala. He has found their narratives, whether personal or mythic, to be highly formulaic. These Mayan narratives, according to Hofling, usually involve a subnarrative of a dangerous journey, beginning and ending in the home. The length of the journey is often indicated, and the journey ends at a time of day; the narrator then relates that time to the speech time of the narration. The journey, marked in days (*kin*), mirrors the journey of the sun (*kin*) across the heavens. Here is an ending of an oral personal narrative, which also shows the use of repetition as a formulaic element:

Then I began to <u>walk</u>
and <u>walk</u>
until I <u>arrived</u> here at my home.
When I <u>arrived</u> here, at my home,
it was already dawn.
And from that day until now,
I haven't <u>returned</u> again
to that milpa,
I'm still afraid of it. (Hofling 1993, 170–71)

The timeline is shown in figure 21.

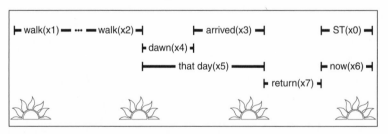

FIG. 21. Symbolic cycles in Mayan narrative.

Narrative here emerges as an exploration of the cycles experienced in life. A journey in time comes to an end, and a new one begins, on and on, mirroring the journeys of cosmic bodies across the heavens. The narrative ends in a coda with a movement back to the speech time, bringing the hearer back to the outside world.

The formulaic nature of narratives in the form of epic poems has been well established ever since Milman Parry and Albert Lord analyzed the epics sung by the living bards of Bosnia. They found that formulaic phrases were used to fill out each line of hexameter, and that the bards made use of stock episodes (journeys, weddings, etc.); these devices simplify the demands on memory. Lord also drew attention to the formulaic use of time expressions with "Homeric overtones," such as "When dawn put forth its wings," or "When the sun had warmed the earth" (Lord 1960, 35). The point here is that for these Mayan narratives, their formulaic nature involves event-type cycles.

THE LONG VIEW OF TIME

It is worth remembering that many a culture has viewed time in terms of an infinite set of event-type cycles. Such views have been incorporated into the calendars of these cultures. Let us examine the most fecund calendarists in this vein: the ancient Mayans, who reached their zenith from 250 to 900 AD. They used a 365-day solar civil calendar called the *haab*, consisting of eighteen 20-day months followed by a 5-day unlucky period called *uayeb*. The Mayans also had a sacred calendar called *tzolkin*; it was embodied in a wheel embedded within another wheel, the inner one consisting of numbers one to thirteen rotated successively within a larger one of 20 named days, the entire sequence covering a sacred year of 260 days. The Mayans, incidentally, believed that each calendar day or larger period was ruled by one or more different gods, who needed to be propitiated with various rituals, including human sacrifice.[9]

But the Mayans didn't stop there. They also had a lunar calendar (the lunar month is roughly 29.5 days), involving a half-year cycle, and a 584-day Venus cycle, which tracked the appearance of Venus as the morning and evening stars. The most famous Mayan calendar, however, is the Long Count, a solar calendar in which each 360-day year was called a *tun*. The Long Count counted days from the beginning to the end of the world, and then beginning again, in a never-ending event-type cycle; each cycle lasted almost 3 million days (approximately 7,885 of our years). To accommodate its vast temporal horizons, the Long Count used time units that ranged from *kin*, a day, to *alautun*, which is more than 60 million years (63,081,377 years, to be precise). The earth, based on today's best science, is just 4.54 billion years, or 72.12 *alautuns*, old. And the universe, at roughly 13.7 billion years, clocks in at 217.63 *alautuns*.

Fortunately, a narrative passage that references *alautuns* and so forth can be represented in our timeline. The TimeML annotation scheme we have been using has a calendar attribute (called "CAL") that indicates which calendar is being used. The specifications currently cover the Gregorian calendar as well as the traditional Chinese solar and lunisolar calendars, the Islamic calendar, and the various Persian calendars.[10] Other calendars could certainly be added if desired, including extinct ones. Modern technology provides software to convert between dates across various calendars, including the Mayan ones, and it is available off the shelf.[11]

Do those cultures that take the long view of time, namely, those that measure time out in very long cycles, like the Mayans and the Hindus, produce narratives that, on average, have longer narrative arcs?[12] Do such long-view cultures allow for longer time spans in narratives compared to cultures that measure time out in teaspoons? The answer seems to be in the affirmative, if we consider certain mythological narratives, in particular, creation myths. To pick an arbitrary example of ordinary mortals, in the Indian narrative of the "Birth of Ganga" (the Ganges), a king lives for 30,000 years, whereas the record in the Old Testament is 969 years, held by Methuselah.

I also wonder if the long-view cultures allow for more "sediment" in their narratives, namely, a kind of weight that accrues across time, as opposes to lighter, minimal narratives that reflect our sense, in cosmopolitan Western culture, of life and time being circumscribed and punctuated by much shorter horizons. Narratives involving longer temporal cycles, for example, involving annual rituals such as the Japanese tradition of viewing cherry blossoms (which plays a significant role in Japanese novels, such as Tanizaki's *Makioka Sisters*) or even the American one of family reunions at Thanksgiving, can convey a more measured sense of the trajectory of life, compared to those that focus on events associated with diurnal cycles, such as the rituals involving the packed schedules of commuters, soccer moms, and other sub- and exurbanites. We will explore time spans further in chapter 8 ("Time Management").

The idea of narrative as a theatrical performance is something that lives on in cultures that practice oral recitation of traditional stories. With each such performance the performer and audience are linked together in each moment in an imagined world of creation. In some cultures the experience of being at a live performance can involve re-creating and reliving in imagination an ancient myth; a notable instance of this can be found in dances associated with the *Ramayana* performed throughout India and Southeast Asia.

In many tribal communities, time and space are very closely linked together in mythology, creating a landscape imbued with myth, one that takes on sacred overtones. The Australian concept of the Dreamtime, or Dreaming (called *alcheringa* in the Arrernte language), represents both the time period of creation of the earth and the spatial realm of heroes and ancestral spirits of humans and animals who leave their imprints in sacred places. The tracks left on the earth by these spirits are called songlines, and they carve out a sort of atlas of the continent. Each song tells of the adventures of ancestral spirits along a particular track through the land; the content and melody of the song may remain the same as the track crosses through different tribal territories with their distinct languages. The Dreaming is thus a highly multifaceted narrative realm, pulsating with stories of the origins of the Australian native peoples.

Time is one way, of course, of viewing space. The properties of places can change, often for the worse, over time. A hallowed land, filled with places touched by myth, the caves where ancestral creatures made their home, or the valleys where native peoples buried their elders—these are places where the bulldozers now roam freely, trampling on ancient memories. As we move up and down the twisted lanes of life, our paths cross, at particular places and times; likewise characters in narrative come together, fall apart; battles are fought and won or, more usually, lost. Places thus become imbued with all sorts of properties, the most significant ones lasting through time.

Although I do not discuss spatial representation at length in this book, my colleagues and I have been active in integrating timelines with information extracted from spatial descriptions in the text (using a markup language called SpatialML). Suffice it to say that we can add an additional dimension or two (or even, if desired, three) to represent space. All events on the timeline that have a common spatial location (including those occurring at different times) can be anchored to a common location in the spatial plane. In some cases latitude and longitude can be inferred from a textual description, such as a place name or an object said to be at some distance away from a named place. Using such a scheme a constant spatial location can be the locus of a history of narrated events. We will return to this issue in chapter 7 ("Tracking Narrative Progression"), examining spatiotemporal trajectories of characters in a narrative.

In summary, calendar times are rich in meaning, going well beyond simply pointing to a particular clock position or cell in a calendar. They are tied to events of significance to an individual, group, or culture, and they express recurrences of particular types of events. References to calendar times in a narrative function in many different ways: to evoke significant events, to organize narratives into chronicles, and to mimic, in the narrative arc, different types of cycles of recurrence. These different facets, as well as the calendars involved, can be represented in our timeline model. Certain cultures, in their calendars, take a very long view of time, and this may well influence their narrative perspective. While time spells change, space appears to persist, allowing stories to extend across time via spatial regions that harbor, so to speak, temporal memories.

5 | Time in Mind

So far we have not addressed how humans actually understand time in stories. One would expect human processing of time in narratives to rely on more-general cognitive abilities, especially a capacity to reason about time. Such reasoning would involve the human brain's ability to cleverly position events in time. But with respect to what time?

The time in terms of which we mentally position events is not tied to any official calendar; rather it is tied to our subjective sense of time, the tensed view of time that we explored in chapter 1 ("Timelines"). We think of events looming ahead or receding into the past, and of ourselves as traveling into the future, and of events as having lasted for a particular time. And yet the only time in which things happen to us is the present. It is from the vantage point of the present that we look back into the past and reach out into the future.

Augustine was one of the early philosophers to point out that in our subjective experience of time, it is the present that we seem to "live" in. Here is his account (from Augustine 1974, bk. 11): "What now is clear and plain is, that neither things to come nor past are. Nor is it properly said, 'there be three times, past, present, and to come': yet perchance it might be properly said, 'there be three times; a present of things past, a present of things present, and a present of things future.' For these three do exist in some sort, in the soul, but [elsewhere] do I not see them; present of things past, memory; present of things present, sight; present of things future, expectation."

He went on to imply that the present is instantaneous (here when the text says "space," we should infer "extent"): "In other words, it [time] is coming out of what does not yet exist, passing through what has no duration, and moving into what no longer exists. But time present how do we measure, seeing it hath no space?"

He answers the question of how long the present lasts by pointing out that since things flit by in the present moment, our sense of duration involves a computation in memory: "It is in thee, my mind, that I measure times. Interrupt me not, that is, interrupt not thyself with the tumults of thy impressions. In thee I measure times; the impression, which things as they pass by cause in thee, remains even when they are gone; this it is which still present I measure, not the things which pass by to make this impression."

The subject-centered view of time, with its lived present, elapsed past, and anticipated future, is different in many ways from the objective, mathematical abstraction of time as an arrow of successive moments, or instants. In the tensed view something that was described as being in the future at one speech time can be in the past at a later speech time. The subjective view also involves the notion of events, which reflect changes in the world. As George Lakoff and Mark Johnson (1980) indicate, languages have metaphors that express the notion of time as moving, as when we say, "Christmas comes before New Year's Day," where time moves from future to past. As Gentner (2001) has noted, many of these metaphors for time are spatially derived; we speak of moving the party forward by a day, of having a long holiday and then falling behind in one's work. In contrast, the mathematical view has no notion of change per se: time is just a sequence of instants, and the sequence itself is static. Correspondingly, languages also have "ego-moving" metaphors, where time is viewed as standing still, as when we say, in another example from Gentner (2001), "The holiday season is before us," in which case the observer is what is moving through time and toward the future.[1]

Note that any instant, treated as a mathematical point, is duration-less; there are an infinite number of them. A time structure made up of instants is what mathematicians call "dense": between any two instants there would be a third, a never-ending apparition of instants. In contrast to Augustine's notion of the subjective present being instantaneous, human language does not wholeheartedly embrace the notion of instants. Languages happen to treat events as having a certain duration. Although we have words in human languages for short events like "blink," "emit," and so on that can be short-lived, we don't have verbs or aspectual markers in any language that describe truly instantaneous events. We do have calendar-time words for short intervals such as the nanosecond and the picosecond, and also the even stranger one called the yoktosecond (10^{-24} seconds, or one septillionth of a second), but no units for the far, far shorter instant. An interval may of course be viewed abstractly as a "point" as when we think of Tuesday as a point in time, but even in such a view an interval is not an instant. Intervals take up time and likewise the events that occupy them. (Of course this is not to say that we cannot talk about instants, which we have just done.)

Another crucial difference between subjective experiences of time and the mathematical view involves the fact that the mathematical view of time is acyclical, that is, there are no circles in time—or, as Heraclitus was supposed to have said, "One can never step into the same river twice." However, we have seen many examples of narratives that have a cyclical structure.

Finally, there is also a disconnect between the perceived, subjective duration of an event and its actual clock time that is measured by the mathematical view. Depending on one's attentional state, thirty minutes' wait in a doctor's office may seem to take forever, whereas the same time spent beachcombing may seem to pass far too swiftly. Likewise, a narrator can devote more or less length to recounting an event, so that the wait in the doctor's office might be dealt with at length, while the beachcombing may be passed over in a quick phrase. This can result in readers experiencing different durations of the two thirty-minute events.

In our timeline model both events and times are represented as intervals.[2] The temporal ordering of events and times using TLINKs in TimeML of course comes from the mathematical view. We also, as we have seen, allow for cycles, in keeping with the subjective view. We do not, however, represent instants explicitly, which differs from the mathematical view.[3] However, if desired, instants can be derived from events, by viewing instants as cuts in time.[4] As for subjective durations of events, we will see in chapter 8 ("Time Management") that these will correspond to the durations that readers estimate for narrative events.

In the remainder of this chapter, I will examine a little more closely the experience of time and events in human (adult and child) minds and how it affects our processing (i.e., interpretation and production) of narratives. It is important to first examine the brain's underlying abilities to perceive time and events, creating temporal structure out of the flux of sense impressions. I will focus on the time windows during which such perceptions occur and their possible influence on narrative. Next, it is worth reviewing empirical research that studies how humans interpret time in narrative, including memory effects, the way readers' brains react when reading stories, their understanding of timelines, and the evolution of children's narrative capabilities. Finally, I will reiterate the points of connection between these empirical results and the computational model used in this book.

THE BRAIN'S TIME WINDOWS

Earlier, when describing Serena running, I mentioned that for almost every time slice of those five minutes, she was running. Within such a time slice, however, there will be a subslice that is not a running event per se but an event of her lifting one leg, or of bending her knee, and so forth. We can keep slicing these events into smaller and smaller events, down to the most primitive movements. However, at some point our brain can no longer detect an integral event, because the slice is too small, that is, its temporal extent is too short.

Let us now descend from the Parnassian heights of concepts in the mind to actual hardware, namely, to what goes on when the brain tries to detect an event in time.

Detecting an event, even at a preconscious level, requires that different qualities in the sensory input be linked together. When perceiving a familiar person calling out one's name, the auditory wave that corresponds to the continuous speech signal needs to be sampled at a particular rate and then segmented into phonemes before words can be recognized. The brain is sampling from a set of features that have continuous values, and it has to segment them into discrete objects and events. When watching the friend's face, many features must be sampled to recognize the movement of the lips and classify it as a smile (something even babies can do rather well). It takes time for the brain to receive and integrate this information via neuronal connections.

According to the neuroscientist Ernst Pöppel (1994, 1997), an event must last at least thirty to forty milliseconds (that is, three to four hundredths of a second) for it to be distinguished from another event. This observation is borne out by a wide variety of studies and experimental paradigms. For example, in an experiment by Magdalena Kanabus and her colleagues (Kanabus, Szelag, and Pöppel 2002), pairs of auditory stimuli (low and high tones) and, separately, visual stimuli (green and red lights) were presented to subjects, with the interstimulus interval being varied. Subjects had to judge the order of the stimuli by pressing two buttons in the same order as the presentation of the stimuli. If a low (or high) tone was heard, the subjects had to press the lower (higher) button, and likewise for a green (or red) light. They could also press a third button if they instead perceived the stimuli as being simultaneous. The results showed that for stimuli to be viewed as successive, that is, that one was BEFORE the other, they had to be separated by at least forty milliseconds. This was true for both auditory and visual stimuli.

The interval of thirty to forty milliseconds is called the threshold for event identification. This time is certainly very small on the human scale of the times we normally worry about and points to the inherent sensitivity of our event-detection capabilities, which have been finely honed for survival.

So much for detecting individual events. To continue to perceive and act, the brain must keep the information it is perceiving and hold the percept it has formed in memory, while querying the outside world as to what has changed. This holding can only last for up to three seconds, after which the brain updates the information. For example, consider an experiment in which subjects are presented with a Necker cube (figure 22).

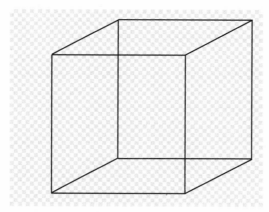

FIG. 22. The Necker cube.

TIME IN MIND

The Necker cube is an ambiguous picture where the lack of depth cues results in it being interpreted in one of two possible ways. As indicated in the literature review by Pöppel (1994), when a subject looks at the Necker cube for some time, the perspective changes to the other interpretation; this change (or reversal) takes place after roughly three seconds. Similarly, when subjects are made to hear computer-generated sequences of syllables such as "cu" and "ba" (or "so" and "ma"), they perceive either "cuba" or "bacu" (or "soma" or "maso"), switching to the alternative interpretation after roughly three seconds.

How do these time windows imposed by the brain influence the structure of narrative? Frederick Turner and Ernst Pöppel (1980) have speculated that the present lasts at most three seconds, and that this limit corresponds to the average duration of what they call a "line" of verse across cultures and languages. For example, the "line" "Shall I compare thee to a summer's day?" (the opening line of Shakespeare's "Sonnet 18") lasts a little over three seconds when recited at "normal" speed. As for the thirty-to-forty-millisecond threshold for event detection, I suspect that it influences the minimal durations for phonetic segments, constraining how short lines can be.

MEMORY AND NARRATIVE STRUCTURE

Let us ascend even higher up in cognitive terms, to look at the mind's representation not of individual events but of narratives as a whole. In order to understand how people represent narratives in their minds, we have to come to terms with the peculiarities of human memory. The classic experiment of Bartlett showed that when people were asked to repeat a given story over time, the story was reconstructed in memory according to "an active organization of past reactions, or of past experiences" (Bartlett 1995, 201) or "schema." (The story in question was "The War of the Ghosts," a folktale that the anthropologist Franz Boas had collected from the Kathlamet Chinook tribe of Oregon.) The existing schema in people's minds biases the assimilation of new information toward conformity with the schema, resulting in details irrelevant to the schema being left out. In retelling "The War of the Ghosts," a considerable amount of detail was omitted, and subjects invented quite a bit of material that was more in keeping with the (Western) subjects' cultural stereotypes. Among the transformations they carried out was changing the order of events. Although the outline or gist of the story for a given subject remained more or less the same over subsequent recalls, subjects differed considerably in their versions.

Bartlett's findings point to two important considerations: first, that schemas guide understanding, and second, that long-term memory involves confabulation. The first idea has guided much work in psychology, AI, and computational linguistics, especially research on story understanding and generation. We will revisit schemas later in relation to the stages of children's narrative development. The second consideration, which underlines the fact that memory is constructive, that is, an active process of imaginative reconstruction, has been borne out by a considerable body of recent research. Let us briefly explore this latter point further.

The idea that only the gist of a story is remembered makes excellent sense in evolutionary terms, as it allows the brain to store experiences and perceive in an efficient fashion. Otherwise we might suffer the fate of Funes in Borges's witty short story "Funes the Memorius":

> We, in a glance, perceive three wine glasses on the table; Funes saw all the shoots, clusters, and grapes of the vine. He remembered the shapes of the clouds in the south at dawn on the 30th of April of 1882, and he could compare them in his recollection with the marbled grain in the design of a leather-bound book which he had seen only once, and with the lines in the spray which an oar raised in the Rio Negro on the eve of the battle of the Quebracho. These recollections were not simple; each visual image was linked to muscular sensations, thermal sensations, etc. He could reconstruct all his dreams, all his fancies. Two or three times he had reconstructed an entire day. He told me: I have more memories in myself alone than all men have had since the world was a world. And again: My dreams are like your vigils. And again, toward dawn: My memory, sir, is like a garbage disposal. (1963, 112)

Studies of the neuroscience of constructive memory, reviewed by Daniel Schacter and Donna Addis (2007), reveal that common regions of the brain (the parahippocampal gyrus in the medial temporal lobe and areas of the lateral cortex) are activated when we remember details of the personal past and imagine details of the future. Such findings (with healthy subjects), further supported by a substantial experimental literature dealing with less fortunate souls subject to amnesia and dementia, have lent credence to the intriguing hypothesis that one biological function of memory is to help humans to prepare for the future. As Schacter and Addis put it, in order to simulate future events, humans need to "draw on the past in a manner that flexibly extracts and recombines elements of previous experiences—a constructive rather than reproductive system" (2007, 774). Constructive memory, in a nutshell, allows one to reassemble the past so as to prepare for the future.

What else can we conclude from this evidence of confabulation? Some of our notions of self-identity, to the extent that they are based on long-term memory, are apparently built on quicksand. Thus we perceive, from the vantage point of the present, a past of events that actually transpired, of good times and lost opportunities, as relayed by that often treacherous companion, memory. The precise events are colored by memory, reconstructed with each retrieval; while there is a "real" past that constitutes a history, there are many pasts born of reverie where one might invent oneself in different ways. Autobiography is one genre that thrives on such invention, though of course deliberate lying is not looked upon favorably by the reader who, having sobbed her way through scenes of deprivation and despair that constitute the childhood of the young unfortunate, is now told that all her tears were for nothing, and that the author is now laughing all the way to the bank.

The lack of authenticity in our memory of the past doesn't mean that the grasp of self-identity through the past is an utter chimera.[5] Nevertheless, who is to say that the single path actually taken by a person should define him or her compared to the large, perhaps even infinite, set of possibilities he or she might have taken? We are determined as much by the paths we did not take, by errors avoided as well as risks and opportunities foregone, with such nonevents providing a rich sediment to support our fretting and rumination about the past. And with a branching past, only one of which is the actual, comes a branching future, a set of many possibilities, of which exactly one, unknown to all except perhaps soothsayers and foretellers of election outcomes, will come true. Yet when all is said and done, a person must be characterized by her imagination and dreams as well as by her actions. We define ourselves as much by fears and hopes, by the possibilities of the future as by those of the past. As Stephen Albert tells his assassin Hsi P'eng in Borges's story "The Garden of Forking Paths": "This web of time—the strands of which approach one another, bifurcate, intersect or ignore each other through the centuries—embraces every possibility. We do not exist in most of them. In some you exist and not I, while in others I do, and you do not, and in yet others both of us exist. . . . Time is forever dividing itself toward innumerable futures and in one of them I am your enemy" (1963, 100).

NARRATIVE TIMELINE COMPREHENSION

It is time to return to matters at hand. Narratives can be complex temporal artifacts. A narrative such as a novel may attempt to capture, in an allotted time span, the trajectories of lives lived and moments experienced in one or more times. This can involve skipping forward, hopping backward, taking time to set a scene or portray a fight, or racing through decades of a life, as in the narrative of Solomon Grundy, who was born on Monday and buried on Sunday. As creators of narrative, writers seem to prefer inventiveness, but with regard to readers, one may wonder whether human brains have a preference for simplicity. Does the reader's mind prefer certain kinds of timelines?

Experiments by Rolf Zwaan (1996) have shown that in reading narrative passages, readers expect that successive sentences will describe chronologically successive and contiguous (i.e., temporally adjacent) events. Deviations from this narrative format (as we have in the preceding example passages) will result in delays in processing information. For example, Zwaan (1996) discovered that sentences with a time shift between events (expressed, for example, by "an hour later") take longer to read and result in subjects taking a longer time to answer questions about whether a particular word occurred in the story, compared to when there isn't such a shift. These experiments ensured that when (the single sentence in) each story was varied to introduce different time shifts, there was a control for the effect of sentence length (each sentence variant was of the same length). Events separated by a time shift were less strongly connected in long-term memory than those that were not separated by a narrative time shift. The body of experimental research supports the hypothesis that readers build cognitive models in their minds of the situation described by the narrative, including representations of whether events are before or after each other and how far apart they are in time.[6] In other words readers do construct timelines, with a strong preference for simple ones.

There is also evidence that when reading a story, readers carry out a simulation (at least partly subconscious) of the events in the story, almost as if they were making a movie in their heads. As part of that simulation they represent how far apart events are in time. As shown by Zwaan (1996), when processing a narrative sequence of immediately successive events without a time shift, readers took longer to access events that, although mentioned recently, were temporally somewhat remote from the current narrative "now." This temporal distance effect was absent when the text had a time shift.

As in the case of "The War of the Ghosts," dealing with unfamiliar cultural situations can result in a loss of understanding. The thought-experiment of a novel *Einstein's Dreams*, by Alan Lightman, explores situations where normal assumptions about time do not hold. In one chapter time is circular, where "for the most part, people do not know they will live their lives over" (1994, 8). In another, time can occasionally branch back to the past; in such a world the transportees from the future are fearful that any change they make in the past will have dire consequences for the future. In one effects can precede causes; in another time stands still; in one there is no time; and in yet another, people know when the world will end. In experiments conducted by Arthur Graesser and his colleagues (Graesser et al. 1998; Graesser, Olde, and Klettke 2003), subjects predictably found it hard to imagine the abnormal situations in *Einstein's Dreams* and fared relatively poorly in making inferences based on such situations.[7]

EMPATHY IN NARRATIVE UNDERSTANDING

The idea that people subconsciously reenact actions they read about or perceive is borne out by experiments that peer directly into the brain. The accidental discovery of mirror neurons—where neurons that fired when a monkey did something also fired when it observed that action—has led to speculation about the role of the mirror neuron system in learning and evolution. Researchers doing fMRI brain scans, which measure changes in the flow of oxygen-rich blood in an area of the brain (a sign of increased mental activity in that area), have found that when people read phrases describing actions involving particular parts of the body (e.g., a hand), the same sections of the frontal cortex are activated as when observing a person carrying out actions with those body parts. These results (from Aziz-Zadeh et al. 2006) further suggest that narrative understanding might involve reuse of the mechanisms that underlie inferences about others' actions and intentions.

In his cross-cultural examination of narrative and emotion, Patrick Hogan (1993) has argued that prototypical narratives allow the reader to empathize with particular characters through priming of their own emotions. This heightened emotional response is how we put ourselves in other's shoes, able to nod sadly and wipe away tears as Oedipus blinds himself.

STAGES IN NARRATIVE PRODUCTION

Let us now turn to how children progress in their narrative skills. Research by Arthur Applebee (1978) has shown that they acquire the ability to produce narrative in stages, beginning with very rough capabilities at the age of two and with mature capabilities as early as nine. These capabilities have been viewed in terms of the development of what have been variously called story schema or macrostructures. The stories produced by the youngest children are in the form of unorganized "heaps," namely, sets of characters, objects, and events, which aren't linked together in any way, as in the case of the characters in this three-and-a-half-year-old's beginning:

A girl and a boy, and a mother and maybe a daddy. And then a piggy. And then a horse . . . (Applebee 1978, 53)

There is clearly no timeline to be derived from a heap. Next, the child passes through a stage of "sequences," focusing on a series of events all linked to a single character, without any explicit causal connection between the events.

Little boy played. He cried. He's all right. He went home. (Applebee 1978, 65)

Here the timeline has emerged. But there is no sense of narrative progression. In a subsequent stage, of "focused chains," the child, by around five years of age, is able to track the events associated with a principal character and express their causal connections. These are the kinds of stories that preschoolers in kindergarten are able to express.

> Davy Crockett he was walking in the woods, then he swimmed in the water to get to the other side. Then there was a boat that picked him up . . . (Applebee 1978, 65)

It can be seen that goals and outcomes are important in giving the narrative a sense of direction. In the final stage the child can express the plot of the story, paying attention to both principal and subsidiary characters. Here is an example of a more plot-oriented story from a child at this stage:

> There was a boy named Johny Hong Kong and finally he grew up and went to school and after that all he ever did was sit all day and think. He hardly even went to the bathroom . . . (Applebee 1978, 66)

This progression shows that timelines, at least simple ones, precede causal explanations in terms of goals and outcomes.[8] However, as indicated by Maya Hickmann (2003), it appears that while children do have an overall schema for a story at the age of three or so, their narrative powers are not developed enough to express causal connections. An ability to produce descriptions of an agent's mental states and construct subnarratives also comes later. Hickmann (2003) carried out experiments in which English-, French-, German-, and Chinese-speaking children narrated a story from a series of drawings. Her results show that children start out ordering events sequentially (with a heavy use of "then," "and then," and "after that"). With age these give way to relations that express inclusion and overlap (using "while," "just as," etc.), with Chinese-speaking children using them the most frequently.

Hickmann also found an increasing use of tense shifts with age (except for children speaking Chinese, which lacks grammatical tense). These were used to indicate a temporal overlap with a previously mentioned situation. For example, in her translation of this seven-year-old's German narrative, there is a shift to past tense (see the underlined words below) to indicate that when the dog looks up, the cat is already almost on the tree.

A bird <u>has gotten</u> children and the bird flies away and the cat wants to eat a bird and there the cat runs up and there the dog looks and then the cat <u>was</u> almost on the tree and the dog pulls it down with the tail and then a bird comes with a caterpillar. (2003, 307)

These results indicate that the narrative skills of children depend on an interaction between the stage of linguistic development and the type of temporal relation they are able to describe. This in turn influences the structure of the narrative timeline they are able to create.[9]

THE INFORMED COMPUTATIONAL MODEL

What is the relation between these psychological results and our computational model? Let us turn first to the elements in our representation. The subjective view of time, as we have noted, takes events as a basic element for individuating changes in the world. We have found some empirical limits for how short events can be and how long the present seems to be. These provide clear grounds for treating events as primitive elements in our computational model. Further, the fact that events are noninstantaneous and require at least thirty milliseconds to be individuated provides support for our claim that instantaneous events are not part of our experience, and thus instants are not represented directly in the timeline model. Timelines were also found to be basic to narrative strategies used by children, preceding causal explanations; this result helps motivate the representation of timelines as a separate component in narrative.

When reading a story, subjects prefer simpler timelines and require more processing time to deal with complex timelines. Since our timelines provide an explicit (though underspecified) representation of event chronology and narrated order, different types of anachronies and their complexity can be measured (in terms of number of order reversals, TLINKed elements and temporal relation types, etc.), so that psychological experiments can be based on them.

We also found evidence that readers carry out a simulation (at least partly subconscious) of the events in the story, and that in that simulation they represent how far apart events are in time. Simulation also forms a basis for the perceived tempo of a narrative, namely, whether it is seen as fast or slow paced at particular stretches. In chapter 8 ("Time Management"), I will argue that such a simulation by the reader allows her to estimate how long events have lasted (when not otherwise specified) in the narrative. These durations, when compared with the length of the text used to render the events, can provide empirical measurements for narrative tempo.

It also appears, from neurological studies, that subjects subconsciously reenact actions they read about, providing a basis for an emotional response to the text. In chapter 6 ("Characters in Time"), I will show how such responses can be attached to events on the timeline.

It is now time to recapitulate. I have argued that in the world of our experience, events are primary. Research shows that to parse events out of the flux of experience, they have to last at least thirty to forty milliseconds. Further, the sensation of being in the present lasts for up to three seconds, after which the brain refreshes its impressions of the world. Psychology has also established that memory is a process involving imaginative reconstruction, and that this process holds for remembering narratives. The timeline of a story can be altered over time in the reader's mind, which has not evolved for dealing efficiently with complex timelines. There is evidence that readers carry out a simulation (at least partly subconscious) of the events in the story and their distance in time. They reenact actions they read about, providing a basis for an emotional response to the text. Finally, psychologists who have studied children's ability to tell stories have found that timelines, at least simple ones, precede causal explanations.

I have argued that these various psychological results can be brought to bear on the computational model of time in narrative. In turn the model can help provide a rich structure for psychological experiments. However, there is clearly much more that neuroscientists and psychologists can do to improve our understanding of temporal aspects of narrative. Here are some possibilities for future investigation.

One might expect that, in estimating the durations of events, people would be able to distinguish between things that take three minutes long versus ten minutes long, but not between two versus three minutes. There is likely to be considerable individual variation; we all know and are usually either amused or irritated by people who are habitually late for appointments, seemingly incapable of realistic time estimates for various events that they have so boldly scheduled for the day. The extent to which distances in time are scaled and aggregated is also an important question. Addressing this question can help us understand what sorts of durations people construct for events occurring in a novel. We shall return to this point in chapter 8 ("Time Management"), where we explore both human annotation and machine computation of event durations.

There are undoubtedly a large number of simplifications related to temporal aspects of the story that are carried out when we understand and remember stories. Psychological experiments can guide us to the specific collapsing operations involved. One question here is the variety of temporal relations involved: Are temporal inclusion and precedence between time intervals sufficient? Are more fine-grained models of precedence used, for example, to distinguish between events where there is no "perceived" gap between them? Consider ordering "try on" with respect to "realize" in the following:

Shapiro said he tried on the gloves and realized they would never fit Simpson's larger hands.

My research with Barry Schiffman (2007) has shown that human annotators find it hard to decide whether the trying on dovetails in time into realizing, or whether there is a pause between the two actions.

Another set of questions concerns subnarratives. How well are subnarratives understood? One would predict that more-complex subnarratives would require more time to integrate into memory, with more likelihood of errors in inference.

Does instructing the reader as to the timeline improve appreciation of other aspects of a work? The timelines we examined certainly suggest that this is true; it would be nice to have supporting experimental evidence. If available, it would allow us to measure how important timelines are to the pleasure-inducing aspects of narrative.

6   Characters in Time

Consider the *Epic of Gilgamesh*, one of the world's most ancient poems. Gilgamesh starts out as a tyrant, hardly a character the reader identifies with. Enkidu, when introduced at the beginning of the epic, is immensely strong but almost entirely animalistic, a barbarian until Gilgamesh has him tamed by the love of the temple harlot Shamhat. Enkidu then becomes Gilgamesh's shadow, his friend and advisor; when Enkidu dies, Gilgamesh is inconsolable, and the experience launches him on a quest for the secret of immortality. Here is an excerpt from Tablet 8 (found in the library of Ashurbanipal in Nineveh, ca. 700 BC, and now in the British Museum), where Gilgamesh laments the death of Enkidu:

Weep. Let the roads we walked together flood themselves
with tears.
Let the beasts we hunted cry out for this:
the lion and the leopard, the tiger and the panther.
Let their strength be put into their tears.
Let the cloud-like mountain where you killed
the guardian of woodland treasures
place grief upon its sky-blue top.
Let the river which soothed our feet overflow its banks
as tears do that swell and rush across my dusty cheeks.
Let the clouds and stars race swiftly with you into death.
Let the rain that makes us dream
tell the story of your life tonight.[1]

By the time we've finished reading this passage, we are not only more enamored of Enkidu but are also entirely in tune with the great Gilgamesh; his suffering is ours as well. Each of these characters has, over the course of the narrative thus far, undergone a transition in our assessment.

The view of character as a mental construct formed by a reader, including the ascription of properties across different time frames in the character's existence, has been discussed previously in narratological studies. Uri Margolin (2007) describes the construction of character models by the reader as a process involving the assignment of properties to characters based on text-provided data (in the form of character behaviors and character descriptions by the narrator, the character, or others). He characterizes this process as involving both data-driven as well as expectation-driven inference. Once a certain number of properties of an agent have accumulated in the reader's mind, the reader constructs a character model that identifies the character as being of a certain type. The reader then proceeds top down, filling in more information, coming up with expectations, and explaining facts that have been learned by relating the agent's actions to the goals and dispositions of that particular type of character. Here, too, comparisons are made of the behavior of the agent across time frames, resulting in judgments about the agent's inconsistency or vacillation.

Other narratologists have also viewed readers as carrying out inferences. Seymour Chatman (1980), for example, sees these inferences as involving the labeling of a character in a narrative in terms of traits drawn from the psychologist's inventory of personality traits. (In psychology such traits are identified based on empirical evidence and are given different weights. A personality may be complex and have conflicting traits.) Chatman views inferences about fictional characters as empirical in nature, assembled from text and background knowledge and experience. This process is similarly haphazard and as multifaceted as the inferences we make about real-world characters. Although I agree with Chatman's view, it seems a bit of a stretch to commit to a reduction of fictional (or real) characters to a fixed set of personality traits proposed by psychologists. (Perhaps my view reflects the historical fact that in the twenty-first century, personality theory is rather passé.) Further, I believe that the appeal to traits, which are in themselves morality free, obscures the moral underpinnings of our notions of character.

In the rest of this chapter, I will elaborate my notions of character, proposing a model of how the reader evaluates, as the narrative evolves, the characters of particular agents in the narrative. I will first explain who the reader I have in mind is, namely, the "actual reader." Next, I will describe how character evaluations are marked on the timeline. This leads to a discussion of what sorts of cues are used by readers to build character models, and a definition of the notion of character. I then take up the issue of modeling changes in character evaluations over the timeline, which gives rise to certain varieties of narrative progression. As the timeline unfolds, agents in a narrative may also move; I supplement my notion of narrative progression with an account of the spatial trajectory taken by the agent over time.

THE ACTUAL READER

Let us now focus on the identity of the reader. Although a reader's reactions can certainly be subjective and variable, the emphasis here is on the case that the text makes for specific characters, with certain background assumptions made by the author about morality and related matters. Literary critics have long acknowledged the role of morality in a reader's interpretations; as Rabinowitz has argued, "there can be little doubt that the process of moral evaluation plays a central role in the reading of narrative fiction" (1988, 85). The moral assumptions can of course vary given the reader's background; however, one cannot allow (and no society allows) that all morality is up for grabs.[2]

Put another way, the author can boost or cast aspersions on a character or remain neutral; we have to consider the "actual" reader who responds to these signals, ignoring readers who are hung over or otherwise ill-disposed toward the work (as editors and reviewers sometimes are). The actual reader is a member of Rabinowitz's "actual audience," that is, a flesh-and-blood reader. Note that what is being evaluated here is the outcome of an action for a particular character for the reader, rather than the outcome for that character. Thus an outcome that is perceived as negative by a character may be perceived as positive by the reader and vice versa (we are still confining ourselves to a Boolean model of emotion).

Literary judgments are often said to be fundamentally "subjective" and prone to variability, given that people themselves differ in so many ways, and this difference can of course affect how they interpret a work. Some might view the mere suspicion of variability as casting doubt on the whole idea of an "actual" reader as a valid generalization across samples of readers. To dispel such doubts I would like to argue that the nature of literary judgments is in fact an empirical question. The empirical methodology I have advocated throughout this book involves developing a linguistic annotation scheme that is then statistically tested for reliability across subjects, so that the corpora marked up with the annotation scheme are of high quality. Annotating reader evaluations is thus a task that is no different in principle from other linguistic tasks such as annotating time expressions, a task we have discussed in some detail. However, since annotating reader evaluations hasn't as yet been carried out on a corpus, it is premature to commit to any particular evaluation by an actual reader. The judgments I provide in this chapter are thus mine alone and may differ from those of other readers.

Once the task of annotating reader evaluations has been carried out, and high reliability has been proven by actual measurements, the judgments resulting from the annotation can be viewed as those of the actual reader. To make this more precise, we will view reader evaluations in an experimental setting, where a story, say, Chekhov's "Lady with the Pet Dog," is selected, and an appropriate sample of readers is chosen. The story's timeline will include a sequence of events in narrated order; this sequence will be provided to the reader. Each reader will rate each successive event outcome in the sequence with exactly one of three categories: positive, negative, or neutral. A statistical measure can be used to compare agreement among readers while correcting for chance agreement.[3]

I am not going so far as to hypothesize that a random sample of readers will in fact agree 100 percent of the time; I leave it as an empirical question to determine what sorts of levels of agreement hold among readers. However, I do believe that the agreement should be significantly more than that which would be obtained by the readers simply guessing at random. The annotation of evaluations for events where the readers disagree can be arrived at by picking a single reader's evaluations throughout, or by choosing the majority opinion, or else by (the more expensive process of) having the disagreements discussed among readers and a consensus decision arrived at for each case. Even if agreement turns out to be poor, the empirical approach will allow one to pinpoint specific situations where there tends to be higher or lower agreement. In other words the nature of subjectivity can be winnowed down further.

This treatment of the "actual" reader as if she were some sort of statistical abstraction may be startling to some lovers of literature. However, we experience such dichotomies all the time, for example, in medicine, where we are familiar with the notion of a patient as a statistical everyman, with an expected range of normal behavior (with a range of acceptable values for various parameters like blood pressure, mood, pain level, blood counts, etc.). This notion is a similar (and necessary) abstraction that coexists with the unique characteristics of each suffering and experiencing patient.

My idea that the hearer of a narrative responds emotionally to characters' situations is hardly new, dating back to Aristotle. In his *Poetics*, Aristotle suggests that tragedy works upon the viewer by arousing emotions, specifically pity (sympathy) and fear (antipathy), on the part of the viewer: "For the plot ought to be so constructed that, even without the aid of the eye, he who hears the tale told will thrill with horror and melt to pity at what takes place" (1932, chap. 14). The idea of emotion being an evaluation or appraisal of events is rooted in Aristotle's theory of emotion in his *Rhetoric*.[4] The notion has been developed substantially not only in narratology but also in cognitive psychology (see Oatley, Keltner, and Jenkins 2006), as well as, to a lesser extent, in recent film studies.[5]

Now, character evaluations are often already present in stories. They may be expressed by the author, by the narrator, or by a character in a story. Such evaluations need not be shared by the reader. Nevertheless, the reader's attitudes can be manipulated by the author's use of particular narrative devices. James Phelan (1989) discusses some of the devices involved in narrative progression that can cause the reader to adopt a particular set of attitudes. For example, consider the closing scene of Orwell's *1984* discussed by Phelan:

> He gazed up at the enormous face. Forty years it had taken him to learn what kind of smile was hidden beneath the dark mustache. O cruel, needless misunderstanding! O stubborn, self-willed exile from the loving breast! . . . But it was all right, everything was all right, the struggle was finished. He had won the victory over himself. He loved Big Brother. (from Orwell 1982, 197)

The scene ends with Winston's eventual defeat through indoctrination. Instead of being repelled by Winston's behavior, we are moved to pity. This is especially so because the principal character plays the role of an individual attempting to rebel against the totalitarian state. As Phelan explains (1989, 42), until that point the events in the narrative had been presented from Winston's point of view, with the authorial audience expected to share Winston's evaluative comments. At this point, however, the reader's evaluations depart from Winston's, and the reader sees him as pathetic rather than triumphant, with the reader's reactions reinforcing a sense of opposition to the totalitarian state.

MARKING CHARACTER EVALUATIONS

Consider the following Serena story, adapted from Wendy Lehnert ([1981] 1999):

[1 Francisco <u>felt thrilled</u>]

[2 when Serena <u>agreed</u> to his <u>proposal</u> of <u>marriage</u>.]

[3 But when Franciso <u>found out</u> about her father's illegal dogfighting ring, he was <u>torn</u> between his <u>love</u> for Serena and his responsibility as a police officer.]

[4 When Francisco finally <u>arrested</u> her father]

[5 Serena <u>canceled</u> their <u>engagement</u>.]

When Serena's father is punished, let us assume that the negative outcome for Serena is evaluated by the actual reader as positive. As a result Serena's retaliation is evaluated by that reader as negative. And that leads the reader to sympathize with Francisco. These assumed emotional reactions are shown in figure 23.

A positive evaluation (marked ^{++}C) means that the reader expresses sympathy with the outcome for the character C (irrespective of whether it is positive or negative for C), and a negative one (marked -C), we could say, means that she expresses antipathy toward C. Character evaluations are marked on the mentions of events, indicating that they are evaluations of the particular character based on the outcomes of such events (these events in turn have been highlighted in the passage of interest). This markup scheme is crude but provides a useful starting point for computational analysis.[6]

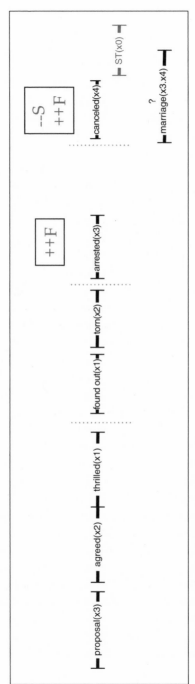

FIG. 23. Character evaluations for Serena and Francisco.

It can be seen in figure 23 that by unit 4 the markup indicates that the actual reader appreciates Francisco (F) for his action, and by the end of the passage (unit 5), the reader sympathizes with him for his loss. This is not the only evaluation possible. It may be that the actual reader instead sympathizes with Francisco for the problem he faces when he discovers her father's role, rather than agreeing with the solution he adopts.

It is worth remembering that this particular example is mainly for illustration of the nature of the markup—the three-sentence story is too short and factual to allow the reader's emotions to be engaged and thus for character evaluations to be developed properly. Now that the framework has been introduced, we will return shortly to more-literary stories that will allow for proper evaluations.

DEFINING CHARACTER

We still need to explain how we arrive at our character evaluations as readers and, eventually, to model that using computers. The accounts of Margolin and Chatman lay the ground for an empirical approach, based on evidence from data in the text, expectations based on reader's experience in the real world, and so on.

In *Oliver Twist* we (or at least Victorian readers) applaud when the criminals Fagin and Bill Sykes end up hanged and cheer wildly, perhaps wiping away a tear or two, when Oliver is rescued by a rich man. I would like to argue further that our impressions about the motives and actions of a character are made in relation to some set of moral principles that the reader has adopted (or has been made to adopt).

For the sake of argument let us discuss what might lie behind the approval of Francisco's action of arresting Serena's father. Clearly, some notion of poetic justice is involved; her father is an evildoer ("bad guy" in contemporary American parlance) and must be punished. We might summarize the morality here as "comeuppance." There could be other, even more enjoyable stories that have an entirely different morality, for example, "crime pays" or "liars win." Underlying these moral principles are attributions of morality to characters, that is, Serena's father is a criminal. In this particular case the fact that he had a role in illegal activities was indicated explicitly.

The Francisco example might suggest that mention of an agent's occupation or role is enough to establish a default model of character;

thus policemen have a disposition to heroically uphold the law, they often arrest people for real or imagined violations of the law, and they tend to be brave and handy with firearms. People who are criminals are unacceptable until they repent and atone for their crimes. Such a notion is built into classical thinking about character. Horace, in his *Ars Poetica* (2004), recommends that the essence of an occupation or role be represented in a character: "He who has learned what he owes to his country, and what to his friends; with what affection a parent, a brother, and a stranger, are to be loved; what is the duty of a senator, what of a judge; what the duties of a general sent out to war; he, [I say,] certainly knows how to give suitable attributes to every character."

This sort of argument might appear to be further reinforced when we change Francisco from cop to crook:

> Francisco <u>felt thrilled</u> when Serena <u>agreed</u> to his <u>proposal</u> of <u>marriage</u>. But when Francisco <u>discovered</u> that her father was a stool pigeon, he was <u>torn</u> between his <u>love</u> for Serena and his <u>job</u> as an enforcer for the Genovese crime family. When Francisco finally <u>arranged</u> for her father to be <u>taken out</u>, Serena <u>refused</u> to <u>speak</u> to him ever again.

Here Francisco's role as a hired killer should make him repugnant to the reader; however, we are reading a Mafia story, and given that the reader today lives in a culture immersed in innumerable pulp fiction and celluloid works that celebrate the trials and tribulations of crime families (from *The Godfather* to *The Sopranos*), not to mention satires on such topics, the stereotypical enforcer is not really all that intolerable. Further, since Serena, too, comes from a crime family, her father being taken out at some point is not entirely unexpected. Clearly, one cannot assign the default virtues of the heroic policeman to Francisco in our main story—it is far too liberal an interpretation. In short, it isn't clear that particular moral characteristics can be necessarily associated with an occupation or role. Nor can particular personality traits be inferred; in an ideal world salespeople shouldn't be introverted, nor should test pilots be neurotic, but the world, as many a commentator has astutely pointed out, is far from ideal, and human flaws make for interesting copy.

Today, although we still thrill to a well-told tale of good triumphing over evil, literary characters can nonetheless lack traditional virtues and still be appealing or interesting. Dostoyevsky's Raskolnikov is one of the great characters of fiction and invites sympathy, even though he has murdered two innocent women and has wild mood swings most of the time; his seeking redemption earns our sympathy. In *Lolita* Nabokov creates an engaging character in the pedophile Humbert Humbert, not just because of the satirical tone of the novel but also because of the narrative's exhilarating style and vivid wordplay. And let us not even mention the enjoyment readers and literary critics have derived from the pages of Sade's *Justine* or from scenes of the movie *Pulp Fiction*. As for the much-loved characters of Shakespeare, we must not forget the hot-blooded killer Hamlet.

Still, for a given occupation or role, certain types of behavior are extremely probable; policemen, after all, do detain and arrest, pedophiles do what they do, and baristas, for that matter, do prepare coffee (sometimes very well). In a nutshell, mention of a policeman or a pedophile or a barista cues particular default expectations about behavior, which may of course be violated.

So what is moral Character? Let us simply say, at the risk of sounding banal:

Character is the set of personal characteristics, virtues and vices, and dispositions that agents have at any given time in a narrative.

This is a very loose definition; obviously, much more can be said on the topic. However, I think it is sufficient for our purposes. Sometimes the narrative will tell us of a character's virtues and vices, dispositions and personal characteristics; sometimes it will, more indirectly, reveal them to us through a scene or action. And sometimes we will not know. As for personal characteristics, those that an author gives to an agent are often arbitrary, little details and images that a writer adds to make a character become fixed in the imagination of the reader. These are often not without symbolic value; as Keith Oatley (2006) has pointed out, Long John Silver's wooden leg is an emblem of strength and fortitude, for Long John is warm, intelligent, and stoical despite his disability.

It is worth pausing for a moment to compare my notion of Character with the influential existentialist account of Paul Ricoeur. For Ricoeur, Character is "the set of distinctive marks which permit the reidentification of a human being as the same" (1995, 119). Character is thus tied to the notion of personal identity. Character exemplifies what he calls "idem" identity, or "selfhood as supported by sameness," which he differentiates from the notion of a self that evolves, where "the narrative constructs the identity of a character" (147). The dynamic self maintains its individuality and integrity through narrative actions that express commitments over time: "Self-constancy is for each person that manner of conducting himself or herself so that others can count on that person" (166).

Ricoeur examines aspects of time in narrative based on refinements to the concept of mimesis. These refinements include the integration of the structures that emerge at the level of plot with the reader's own experience, specifically, as Ricoeur states, "the intersection of the world of the text and the world of the reader" (1984, 71). This process results in the reader evaluating his or her own life.

The differences between my notions and Ricoeur's can now be stated. I view character as a set of properties ascribed by the reader to an individual, indexed at a particular time. Thus the set of characteristics that constitute Ricoeur's idem identity are a proper subset of the characteristics found in my definition. Ricoeur's notion of dynamic identity and self-constancy is not represented in my scheme; however, mine is dynamic to the extent that as the agent participates in events with different outcomes, some of the agent's properties will change. Finally, the aspect of the intersection of text and reader that I focus on is the reader's evaluation of agents at crucial stages of the narrative.

Another insightful analysis of character is offered by Phelan (1989). He views character as composed of mimetic, thematic, and synthetic elements. The mimetic element arises from agents in narrative representing possible people. The thematic element reflects the use of character to assert generalizations about human nature, for example, "power corrupts." The synthetic element is based on recognizing the fact that character is a construct and thus artificial. Thus a character might have attributes that are mimetic (he is short), thematic (he has a lust for power), and synthetic (he lives in Oceania). Phelan also distinguishes between a character's dimensions and his or her functions in the narrative: "A dimension is any attribute a character may be said to possess when that character is considered in isolation from the work in which he or she appears. A function is a particular application of that attribute made by the text through its developing structure" (9). A character may have many mimetic and thematic dimensions, for example, but they may or may not contribute to the development of thematic assertions, that is, thematic functions, as the work progresses. Finally, Phelan also differentiates two varieties of unstable relations that characterize narrative progression: instabilities "between characters, created by situations, and complicated and resolved through actions," and tensions, that is, "instabilities—of value, belief, opinion, knowledge, expectation—between authors and/or narrators, on the one hand, and the authorial audience on the other" (15).

Let me now assess aspects of Phelan's framework that are relevant to the concerns of this chapter. Phelan's notions of character are more fine-grained than mine. His analysis sheds light on the means by which an author, over the course of a narrative, can manipulate the reader's (or narrative audience's) sympathy for a character. His accounts of the way these devices work to influence reader evaluations are convincingly argued across a variety of literary examples (including *1984* as outlined earlier). His work is concerned mainly with narrative progression, and he analyzes changes in character evaluations in terms of the framework introduced here. However, he does not address the nature of character evaluations, in terms of say, Boolean judgments. As a theory, however, his approach can be seen as complementary to mine. His approach differs from mine in its lack of any analysis of time per se; in my view it is helpful to have a timeline in terms of which to analyze narrative progression along with its concomitant character evaluations.

It is now time to return to my definition of Character and apply it to Francisco (as policeman) and Serena. At the beginning of the story, we are told Francisco's name; given that Serena is a first name, Francisco is probably a first name, rather than a last, therefore indicating a level of familiarity on the part of the narrator. In the terminology of Genette (1980), this third person narrator is "heterodiegetic," that is, not a character in the world of the story, and involves "external focalization," that is, revealing a character's mind from an external perspective, as opposed to entering into the character's mind. Francisco is a male name, with a Latinate etymology. If probing into Francisco's religion or denomination on behalf of, say, the Homeland Security department, we might even guess "Catholic," though of course he could very well be an agnostic or an atheist. We are also told that he is thrilled to have his marriage proposal accepted, which suggests he is excitable and innocent. These elements constitute his character at that point. No personal characteristics, twitches, limps, and such are provided. Then Francisco is identified as a policeman. This introduces his disposition to uphold the law, to arrest violators, and so forth. These inferences are based, one might say, on social conventions that Rabinowitz calls "Rules of Signification" (1988, 76).

All these bits of information are integrated into our model of Francisco's character. Francisco is torn when facing a dilemma, reinforcing the innocence. He roots for good over evil, and in doing so sacrifices "love for justice."[7] His sacrifice, that is, his loss, is something the actual reader might applaud, largely because the author has built a case for him.

With Serena, the name is female, also of Latin etymology. She is clearly not as central as Francisco, since less space is devoted to her. Thus, when it comes to how the action is focalized, her acceptance of the proposal is presented factually, without any information about her feelings. When she retaliates, any dilemma she has faced isn't described. Her character is opaque. The narrator has not exposed enough of her to make us sympathize. In reading of her retaliation (an appropriate tabloid headline might be FAMILY TRUMPS LOVERBOY), an actual reader may express antipathy rather than sympathy, and having supported Francisco, the reader is pulled toward him and away from her. The narrator has not chosen to make her actions worthy of sympathy.[8]

There are many other aspects of this story that narratologists of the structuralist school would find typical, namely, the impediment that her father represents to Francisco's goal, the power represented by Francisco's office, the asymmetry between the two genders, and so forth. These are interesting in themselves and also add more dimensions to the conflicts experienced by the characters. There are also psychoanalytic aspects—the father versus lover conflict, and perhaps even (for creative psychoanalysis can be quite fanciful) the symbolic castration of the father, but in my view these don't contribute anything useful for purposes of modeling, though they might certainly stimulate further discussion.

We have made much of a constructed, artificial story, short as it was, to introduce ideas. Let us turn now to more-literary texts. Consider Hemingway's short story "The Short Happy Life of Francis Macomber." Rather than drawing a full timeline, we use sentences as mnemonics for entire timeline diagrams constructed from the source. My character evaluations (applied to the mnemonics but derived from reading the source) are shown alongside.

[1 Francis flees from the lion that morning.]
[2 Margaret humiliates Francis over lunch in front of Robert and slips into Robert's bed that night.] ⁻⁻M
[3 Hunting the next morning, Margaret shoots at a buffalo charging at Francis and kills him instead.] ⁺⁺F, ⁺⁺M
[4 Robert browbeats Margaret.]

It can be seen that I do not appreciate Margaret's retaliation, positive as it may feel to her, for cuckolding a man in revenge for his physical cowardice is not desirable behavior in my book. I also sympathize with Francis's moment of crisis when faced by the buffalo, but after Margaret's bungled action (she can't shoot straight!), her feeling positive gives way to horror, and I sympathize with her. Another reader may have entirely different judgments, of course; one would prefer to measure agreement across a sample of readers before committing to these evaluations as those of the actual reader. Hopefully, such an experiment on interannotator reliability in character evaluations will soon be carried out.

One might wonder at this point whether the timing of character-related information is critical to the reader's assessment of characters of agents. In this regard Chatman observes that some of the inferences about character may arise from states whose temporal location is not specific. He uses such an example to argue that traits are not tied to the chronology of a narrative but are "parametric" to the event chain. For example, he discusses the following constructed story:

Peter fell ill. He died. He had no friends or relatives. Only one person came to his funeral. (1980, 43)

Chatman argues that the temporal location of not having friends or relatives (significant as a trait) is not specified and cannot be ordered in relation to the events of falling ill, dying, and being at a funeral. He assumes, therefore, that such states are not part of any narrative timeline. I would beg to differ. Since we have been dealing with partial orderings in our timelines (rather than just chains or sequences of events), and since we accommodate fuzzy extents (as shown in many of the literary examples in this book), it is perfectly acceptable to have a state with an indeterminate temporal location as part of the timeline representation. In any case, as Chatman points out, the position of such a state in the discourse may be relevant (e.g., as a personal characteristic that appears later in the story and that is elaborated with some event data in the next sentence). Since his example is easily accommodated within a timeline-driven model of the acquisition of agent characters from narrative, I do not see any reason to postulate "trait-related" states as somehow distinct and not foregrounded temporally compared to events.

Let me turn away from tales of revenge and consider a story of which Nabokov opined, "All the traditional rules of story telling have been broken in this wonderful short story. And it is one of the greatest stories ever written." Let us analyze character evaluations for Chekhov's "Lady with the Pet Dog" (from Chekhov 1988). Rather than drawing a full timeline, we again use sentences as mnemonics for entire timeline diagrams constructed from the source.

[1 Gurov, a married womanizer on vacation alone in Yalta, seduces Anna, a married woman visiting Yalta with a pet dog for company.]
[2 Anna is ashamed and feels spiritually debased.] $^{--}$G
[3 When Gurov returns to Moscow, the memory of their time together haunts him.]
[4 He confronts Anna at a theater in her hometown S——, where he kisses her, begging her to understand his love.] $^{++}$G
[5 She confesses how much she has suffered, longing for him.] $^{++}$A
[6 They meet regularly in secret in a hotel room in Moscow, where they contemplate the great difficulties that lie ahead.] $^{++}$G, $^{++}$A

In this story I do not appreciate Gurov's womanizing, successful as it seems to Gurov. Coercion is viewed negatively by this reader. Nevertheless, Gurov's seduction of Anna is presented against a backdrop of scenes so skillfully constructed that his actions are presented nonjudgmentally and in a way that seems entirely natural and in keeping with his character. Anna's remorse and shame at her adultery arouses my sympathy; subsequently, Gurov too gets into my good books with his falling in love, where he is no longer a conqueror but a victim, stricken and haunted by love. The initiative he shows in seeking her out at the theater and her positive response result in my enhanced appreciation for each.

The ending, where they carry out their furtive affair in full face of the troubles that lie ahead, expresses a tension between following one's heart and experiencing the many negative consequences that will follow upon their choice. None of these consequences are spelled out, as we are at the end of the story. The story ends sadly, with them looking into a future that is unknown yet likely to be filled with trouble.

NARRATIVE PROGRESSION THROUGH TRANSITIONS

Characters can be static and unchanging, as in the case of the stereotypical valet Jeeves, or they might evolve (or implode) over the course of a narrative. The traditional dictum (from Forster 1963) that characters should be "rounded," capable of change and surprise, rather than "flat" and one-dimensional often appears in reviews of books and movies. As Mieke Bal (1997) points out, this excludes entire genres of fiction, including fairy tales and detective fiction, and also the works of Proust, where the characters are deliberately "flat" so as to convey the challenges in trying to address that most elusive of goals, the sense of personal identity (not only who one is but the impression of who others are).

As we readers peruse a narrative, tracking the path of a particular character and her experiences, including interactions with other characters, we react, evaluating the outcomes of events for a character. As we have seen, these reactions can be modeled, somewhat crudely, using a Boolean system. In many narratives, as the narrative evolves there will be outcomes that give rise to further evaluations. This is by no means required of all narratives. In some the author may provide no clue as to how to evaluate the character. Thus in our Serena story we had no evaluations of her until she retaliates; until that point, one could argue, the author has simply not bothered to make her worthy of sympathy or antipathy.

I would like to make another simple claim:

> Character development can be assessed by the changes in character evaluations over stages of the narrative.

We can classify character development in terms of transitions in reader evaluations for a character over the course of the narrative. A character can reiterate, increase, or decrease readers' evaluations, or there may be no (i.e., a neutral) evaluation. An increase from negative to positive is expressed as switch_to(+), since the polarity of the evaluation has switched; likewise a decrease from positive to negative will be termed switch_to(-). These polar changes will be distinguished from ordinary increases, incr(+), or decreases, incr(-), from neutral. We will distinguish reiteration of a previously positive evaluation (i.e., with the last evaluation being positive) with repeat(+) and of a previously negative one as repeat(-). Over the course of a narrative, a character's evaluation can be plotted as a function. A character's evaluation over a narrative will be described as monotonically increasing if it increases at least once and never decreases. Likewise, a character's evaluation will be described as monotonically decreasing if it decreases at least once and never increases.

To pick a familiar example, consider Gregor Samsa's sister, Grete, in Kafka's *Metamorphosis*. We start out sympathizing with her, but later our antipathy grows, as she joins her parents in their callous attitude toward poor Gregor, while our sympathy for Gregor keeps mounting throughout the piece, as he becomes more and more dehumanized. Grete's evaluation is nonmonotonic, whereas Gregor's is monotonically increasing. The ending, when one considers Gregor and any other character, is divergent. Gregor is the only light on the otherwise bleak horizon.

In saying that transitions in character evaluations occur over the course of the narrative, I mean that they occur as the narrative unfolds. Transitions are thus defined over events as they appear in narration order, rather than the underlying chronological order. As an example, in the first two chapters ("Bela" and "Maxim Maximych") of Lermontov's *Hero of Our Time*, the mature Pechorin is shown to be brave and energetic but also extremely dissipated, cynical, and manipulative. In the remaining three chapters (from "Pechorin's Journal"), which chronologically precede the other two, he is shown to possess considerable insight into his own character, justifying his cynicism as a reaction to his frustration with the mediocrity of his fellow men. Thus the actual reader may end up showing a little more sympathy for Pechorin as she learns more about him, even if that additional knowledge is derived from events that transpired earlier in time.

To return to our stock example, if we plot the character of Francisco (see the numbered list on page 116 in the section titled "Marking Character Evaluations"), we see that by the end the poor man has paid the price in the reader's eyes for taking a stand on the side of justice. This ennobles him, relative to the neutral position he was in at the end of the first sentence. The reader has sympathized with the outcome in step 4 incr(+); this sympathy is reiterated in segment 5 repeat(+). His character evaluation is clearly monotonically increasing. Serena is an elusive character; she arouses the reader's antipathy incr(-) in segment 5. Serena's character evaluation is clearly monotonically decreasing. This results in an ending that involves divergence (a difference of polarity) between the evaluations of these two characters.

The character of Margaret, on the other hand, evolves from an oppressor to a woman in mourning. She starts off arousing our antipathy, incr(-), in segment 2, but this turns to a polar increase, of sympathy for the outcome in segment 3, switch_to(+), as we sympathize with Francis, incr(+). Her character evaluation is nonmonotonic, whereas Francis's is monotonically increasing. The ending is convergent.

As for Gurov, he too evolves from what this actual reader judges to be a negative figure, of a womanizer, into a sympathetic victim of love armed with the courage of his conviction. Anna evolves from a woman who feels she has transgressed into someone who is determined to stay the course of her passion. Here lust, unromanticized and calculating when initiated by Gurov, and impulsively engaged in by Anna, gives rise to a courage that suggests a grim resilience as the lovers jointly face up to the future onslaughts of fate. Gurov's evaluation is not monotonic, but Anna's is monotonically increasing. The narrative progression involves not a resolution but a heading forward, almost a vector that points, with a particular gravity, beyond the timeline of the story. All this is of course expressed in just a few pages of Chekhov's highly distilled writing style.

In the case of Gurov, at segment 4 there is a polar increase, followed by reiteration in segment 6. Anna's evaluation follows in lockstep; in segment 5 there is an increase, followed by reiteration in segment 6. It ends with convergence, with both having positive evaluations, but a key difference is how they got there: Gurov's increase is polar, that is, he has moved from a situation of being despised to one where we are in sympathy with the outcome. There is a special appreciation for such upward progress; analogously, a student who evolves from a sluggard and incompetent at the beginning of the semester to a whiz kid by the end is often the student who is most appreciated.

To actually measure the progression, we can lay it out on a timeline, shown in figure 24, which is defined over summary elements as the units of analysis.

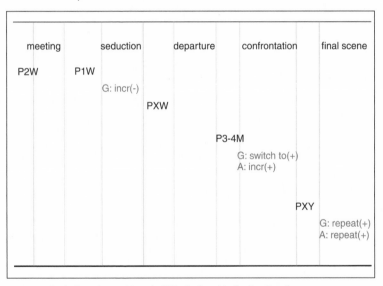

FIG. 24. Scale-based transitions in "The Lady with the Pet Dog."

Gurov, on a summer vacation in Yalta, is there for at least two weeks before meeting Anna; after that, seduction (incr(-) reader evaluation for Gurov) is swift (by nineteenth-century standards). They spend several weeks together, before she is summoned back home to S——. As he sees her off at the station, autumn is arriving, an appropriate season for setting off.

> Here at the station there was already a scent of autumn in the air; it was a chilly evening.
> "It is time for me to go north too," thought Gurov as he left the platform. "High time!" (Chekhov 1988, 151)

Anna starts to grow on him over the fall, back in Moscow, and in December he confronts her at the theater in S——, switch_to(+), and her positive response, incr(+), results in our enhanced appreciation for each of them. The ending scene in the Slavyansky Bazaar Hotel in Moscow, marked by a grim and heroic resilience, repeat(+) for each, is situated a few years later.

We can see clearly that the three groups of transitions occur on three time scales, respectively: weeks, months, and years. It seems appropriate to have the movement toward seduction be swift. The path to moral action by Gurov (confrontation) takes three to four months, which is the interval between the first hint of fall and December. And the final scene of a long-drawn-out affair with no end or resolution in sight comes after the evidence of at least a few years of stasis. Passions have a swift onset, but their consequences last, in many cases, entire lifetimes.

In some narratives nothing much happens that changes our evaluations of the characters. And yet the stories are still enjoyable. These are stories that we value mainly for the way they are told, for their writers' sleight of hand, the vivid imagery, the surprising juxtapositions of philosophical ideas and unpredictable events. Some of these stories, in fact, do fascinating things with time and space that interact with our sense of narrative progression. I am thinking particularly of some of Julio Cortázar's short stories, such as "The Island at Noon."

In "The Island at Noon," the Mediterranean island in question, named Xiros, is seen by Marini from a plane on the Rome-to-Tehran flight thrice a week around noon. Marini serves as a flight attendant on this route, and when he's not romancing the stewardesses, he's obsessing about the island, with the events in between the noontime sightings being severely compressed in time. (These sorts of variations in tempo are of considerable interest; however, their analysis is deferred until a

CHARACTERS IN TIME

fuller discussion of tempo in chapter 8 ["Time Management"].) Marini escapes to Xiros eventually. He goes for a swim, after which he climbs up a hill, where he reclines, gazing up into the sky, wondering whether he will be able to successfully forget his past and kill his former self. It is noon, and the plane is flying overhead, at which point things end badly for the plane, and Marini is unable to save anyone.

The mystery of Marini grows, our sympathy increases monotonically, but there isn't any tension with any other characters, either by way of convergence or divergence. Here it is the recurrences of noonday events that come to an end, as the spatial perspective is now inverted (instead of an island spotted from a plane window, the plane is seen from the island). The final transition is therefore related to an ending of a temporal recurrence; the island will still be there, but it won't be "seen" anymore at noon.

As I mentioned earlier, some of my research has involved integrating spatial representations with timelines; this allows a system to anchor all the noon "plane" events to Xiros. Alas, Xiros doesn't have any real geo-coordinates nor are fictive ones provided.

One would expect narratives to gather more transitions toward the end, or at least to have some transitions at the end. But sometimes the sympathy has already been built up or down, and there is not much going on with respect to evaluations at the end. And perhaps in some cases the author is too weary as she nears the end of the book to bother. The writing of a book, enervating as it can be, is a constant reminder of how elusive perfection really is; by the end there is a sense of resignation.

SPATIOTEMPORAL TRAJECTORIES

We have seen that characters experience events at different times, undergoing various transitions in the reader's estimation. Characters are also always evolving, however slightly, just as we are, experiencing events, and changing their properties. But certain points in their evolution, namely, the points of transition, are more significant for the narrative.

These transitions occur, of course, in particular places. As we noted earlier, time is one way of viewing space. Although the coordinates of a place stay more or less constant (except for geological changes), its properties can change over time. Anna's hotel room in Yalta during seduction is a rather different place than Yalta with a hint of autumn in the air. And the Slavyansky Bazaar Hotel in Moscow, where Gurov and Anna meet, is of course a very different setting from Gurov's house there. We can view the paths a character takes in space and time as a trajectory of motion. From the standpoint of narrative, the interesting points in a trajectory are the crossings, where one character's trajectory intersects another's.

For example, in figure 25, we see Anna's trajectory away from Yalta, followed by Gurov's a little afterward, and then we have Gurov confronting Anna in S——. (Here we have assumed an arbitrary hypothetical location for S——.) We can see that Yalta and S—— form two places where these intersections occur.

FIG. 25. Trajectories in "The Lady with the Pet Dog."

For reasons of space the events at the Slavyansky Bazaar Hotel aren't shown. Since this image is a snapshot from a demonstration, the trajectories can naturally be shown in their temporal order, as a multimedia tour.

With trajectories at hand, we have choices in terms of how we want to deal with the temporal properties of space.[9] For the lover's trajectory in Moscow, why not pop up a picture of the Slavyansky Bazaar or even the hotel? As background why not indicate more-detailed province and city information on the map? We have a choice of such interpretive elements in today's setting, or else we can try to be more authentic and collect archival maps and pictures from Chekhov's day. In the former case the reader is visualizing space as it is organized today, in a contemporary reader-response setting; in the latter case she will be taking a stab at emulating the atmosphere of Chekhov's day.

Trajectories inherit whatever subordinations are present on the timelines. Thus, in Gogol's short story "The Terrible Vengeance," when Katherine tells Danilo the crucial information that she has just had a nightmare of her father telling her that he (her father) will make her a fine husband, the events in the dream are subordinated to Katherine's act of telling, which occurs by the Dnieper river in Ukraine. This means that trajectories are inherently branching, just as timelines are.

In order to compute trajectories, as we shall see, we will need a capability to understand spatial language. Fortunately, there are many parallels between the language of time and the language of space. For example, times and places may be given in absolute terms ("June 16, 1904, Dublin"), as well as in relative terms ("after dinner, some miles from Combray"). Events can be situated in time analogous to the way objects are located spatially ("lunch on Saturday" or "he was crossing the threshold"). The frame of reference in both space and time can be absolute (based on a calendar or a coordinate system) or deictic (based on the speaker's speech time or location).

However, the spatial frames of reference we use in everyday language include political and administrative distinctions, which are by their nature prone to change much more so than calendars. It is commonplace to refer to a country that no longer exists, like Czechoslovakia or Prussia (not to mention entirely fictional countries like Atlantis or Ruritania, or worlds where real and imaginary places are intermingled). In other words space is inherently temporal.

These issues cause practical problems in locating entities in space, since different places may have the same name, an old place may have a new name, a place (such as a town) may be distinguished both geographically and administratively, and which country a place is in may be disputed. These issues will be addressed in chapter 7 ("Tracking Narrative Progression"), in the section "Computing Trajectories."

Trajectories themselves are a basic foundation for the much richer literary notion of the chronotope. The chronotope, a concept introduced by Mikhail Bakhtin, is "the intrinsic connectedness of temporal and spatial relationships that are artistically expressed in literature" (1994, 84). In a chronotope certain spatiotemporal properties of the real world are organized together and used as a metaphor in a work of fiction. The chronotope of the road, which expresses a course through space and time, is the best known. The road is a locus for significant encounters between people of all social classes, nationalities, and characters, and is a motif found not only in travelogues but also in novels from Apuleius through Cervantes, from Banerji to Kerouac, as well as slogans and ads of all sorts (e.g., "Life's a journey—take the scenic route!"). Other examples cited by Bakhtin include the chronotope of the castle in Gothic fantasies, and that of the salon in the novels of Balzac and Stendahl. Clearly, the concept today must be extended to chronotopes involving places that are virtual not due to their fictive status but because of their existence only in cyberspace.

In this chapter we have analyzed character simply as the set of personal characteristics, virtues and vices, and dispositions that agents have at any given time in a narrative. A text, it is argued, makes a moral case for a given character by means of outcomes of events in which the character is involved. This has the effect, in the reader's mind, of boosting approval of or casting aspersions on a character, or her evaluation of the character remaining neutral. We imagine an "actual" reader who responds to these signals with appropriate emotions by means of character evaluations, which are viewed as expressing sympathy or antipathy to the outcomes of certain events for a character. Annotations to that effect are attached after particular points (events) in the narrative. Annotating reader evaluations is a task that is no different in principle from annotating time expressions; once high reliability in this task has been proven by actual measurements, the judgments resulting from the annotation can be viewed as those of the actual reader.

These evaluations, when integrated with timelines, give rise to different varieties of narrative progression. We can model the upward and downward transitions in evaluations over the course of a narrative and compare the evaluations of characters at the end to identify convergent and divergent endings. Time is patterned in interesting ways in relation to these transitions. As these transitions occur, agents in a narrative may be in the same or a different place; this suggests the idea of tracking the spatial trajectory taken by the agent over time. Trajectories can crisscross one another; these are the points where interesting things can happen.

7   Tracking Narrative Progression

In chapter 6 ("Characters in Time") narrative progression was modeled in terms of the reader's evaluations of agents in the narrative, and the way these evaluations evolve over time, in terms of specific transitions and particular types of endings. These evaluations may coincide with agents being in places that are particularly significant for the narrative. The model accordingly included the representation of the spatiotemporal trajectories of agents in the narrative.

Now let us turn to how such a model can be computed. A system to track narrative progression must, first of all, be capable of constructing timelines. We saw earlier that all that was required for timelines was an ability to flag the events and the time expressions and to understand the temporal relations among them. This was achieved by marking up examples using a set of standard tags and training a program to faithfully reproduce these tags, based on statistical techniques. These techniques are relatively easily extended to encompass aspects of spatial language (using annotation schemes like SpatialML), to provide spatiotemporal trajectories for characters that can cross each other at points where the characters' fates collide.

What is needed further at this point is the computational ability to link agents to events in which they participate and then to determine the actual reader's evaluation of the character with respect to the outcomes of these events. This requires that the computer identify the agents in each sentence, link them to events in which they are said to participate, and then evaluate the character-event relations. It does not require understanding in any deep way what those events really mean to the character.

BACKGROUND

Let us consider a crucial sentence from Hemingway's "Short Happy Life of Francis Macomber," from the standpoint of automatic processing:

At the end of that time, his wife <u>came</u> into the tent, <u>lifted</u> her mosquito bar and <u>crawled</u> cozily into bed.

The computer will need to establish whether there is any evaluation by the reader of the event outcomes (coming in, lifting the mosquito bar, and crawling into bed) with respect to Margaret, on one hand, and Francis, on the other. Note that by statistically training the computer from a set of examples of character evaluations (namely, characters, events, and their evaluations), the computer can get around the need to understand that Margaret has been unfaithful to Francis. However, as a prerequisite the computer must recognize which events the agent (Margaret) was literally described as being involved in. To do so the computer will need to carry out, in addition to timelining, an analysis of the syntactic, semantic, and pragmatic features of the sentence. This section provides some brief background on computing such an analysis, leaving out the technical details of computational linguistics methods.[1]

As a symbol system language has many layers of structure through which meaning is packaged. One key form of packaging is the way information in sentences is structured syntactically. The automatic analysis of sentences into their syntactic structures, based on a grammar for the language, is called parsing.[2] Since the mid-1990s researchers have adopted statistical parsing instead of hand-developed grammars. Here a large collection of sentences is marked up by a human with grammatical analysis, with the help of a parsing program. This collection of documents is called a treebank, for example, the Penn Treebank of Mitchell Marcus, Beatrice Santorini, and Mary Ann Marcinkiewicz (1993). Given a treebank of sufficient size (a million words is a bare minimum), the parser then induces a grammar rule for each construction it sees.[3]

Statistical parsers tend to perform at above 90 percent accuracy when trained and tested on data from a similar genre. This level of performance, exhibited by high-performing parsers including a widely used one from Michael Collins (2003), has been observed on newspaper texts, transcribed telephone speech, and so on and is far better than that of any handcrafted grammar.

These parsing programs are assisted by tools that can help disambiguate words for their parts of speech. Given the ambiguous sentence "I can fish in my pajamas," a part-of-speech tagger will disambiguate "fish" as a noun or a verb based on statistics in the corpus. Such statistics will take into account the relative frequency of "fish" as a noun versus a verb, as well as the likelihood of "fish" as a noun following "can" as a verb versus a modal versus a noun, and so forth. (Thus some fish workers eat what they can and can what they can't!) Part-of-speech taggers score well above 95 percent, as indicated by Thorsten Brants (2000). The crucial limitation on accuracy for all these tools is finding adequate quantities of training data in the particular genre and language.

Successes in these areas have encouraged a tremendous fervor for the use of corpora and statistical modeling in other areas of computational linguistics.[4] This surge of activity in statistical modeling of corpora is good news for narratology. Even though statistical parsers haven't been trained on large treebanks of literary texts, it is possible to reuse one trained on some other data set, while allowing for poorer performance. My informal finding is that the performance doesn't drop drastically when a parser trained on news is run on a variety of literary texts. A parser called Apple Pie (from Sekine and Grishman 1995, trained on a million words of news articles) produces a syntactic analysis of the Macomber sentence as in figure 26.

The parsing performance on this sentence, and on related sentences discussed in this book, is, I believe, accurate enough to jump-start an effort at creating a treebank for a wide variety of English literary texts. Given that there are already several literary corpora that have been analyzed for parts of speech and so forth, treebanking them should be relatively easier. In fact, as we shall see, we could go well beyond treebanking and get at meaning as well.

Of course there will be sentences that will fool even a statistical parser trained on long-winded literary texts. I am thinking particularly of those apparently perverse run-on sentences that teachers and editors love to strike out. The ultralong, 24,194-word sentence at the end of *Ulysses*, Molly Bloom's soliloquy, will vex the human linguistic annotator as well as every parser on earth. Long sentences will have many possible syntactic ambiguities, but even short sentences such as "You can fish?" can exhibit these. For some constructions, especially in dialogue and in the informal and historical registers found in fiction, it may be unclear what the correct parse should look like, so annotation guidelines need to be developed for these.

With research on treebanks proving so successful for parsing, it is

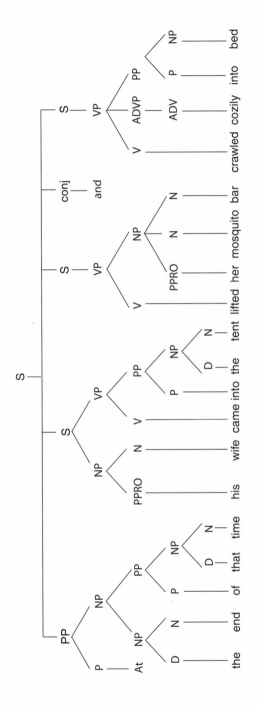

FIG. 26. Parse of "Francis Macomber" sentence.

natural to wonder whether the same success can be replicated for analyses of aspects of meaning. This has given rise to "proposition" banks, or propbanks (e.g., Palmer, Kingsbury, and Gildea 2005), which are treebanks augmented with semantic information. Essentially, the proposition level of representation captures the same meaning irrespective of how it may be expressed in different syntactic ways.

So if we have "Margaret got together with Wilson in the middle of the night," "Margaret and Wilson got together in the middle of the night," "Margaret and Wilson had a get-together in the middle of the night," and so forth, they would all have the same propbank representation. The relation between a verb (or even a noun) and its arguments (e.g., participants and properties of the event to which a verb corresponds, as stated in the text) is captured by means of argument roles, also called thematic roles or case roles, that correspond to Agent, Patient, and so on. Thus we have Margaret as the Agent (called ARG0) of the get-together and Wilson as the Patient (called ARG1), and the middle of the night as the time (called ARGM-TMP) of the get-together.

The single propbank representation for the Macomber sentence is shown in table 2. The bracketed arguments correspond to constituents in the parse tree in figure 26.

Given the propbank as training data, the challenge for a statistical classifier is to label the argument roles of constituents in the parse trees of test sentences. Thus, given the verb "lifted" in the parse tree in figure 26, the labeler has to classify the relation between "lifted" and the constituent "his wife," where the classes are the possible argument role labels, and likewise for the relation between "lifted" and the other constituent "her mosquito bar." (Once these character-event pairs are identified, character evaluation can be applied to them.)

Systems today have been evaluated in international competitions on propbank data at about 80 percent accuracy, when sufficient training data are made available, as shown in the work of Xavier Carreras and Luis Arquez (2005). Other propbank-like representations can also be used, such as FrameNet (of Johnson and Fillmore 2000).

However, we are not done yet: several other component technologies are also needed at a semantic level.

One key problem is coreference: figuring out, say in the Macomber sentence "At the end of that time his wife came into the tent, lifted her

TABLE 2. *Propbank representation for "Francis Macomber" sentence*

Propbank
[ARGM-TMP At the end of that time] [ARG0 his wife] <u>came</u> [ARGM-LOC into the tent],
[ARG0 his wife] <u>lifted</u> [ARG1 her mosquito bar] and
[ARG0 his wife] <u>crawled</u> [ARGM-ADV cosily] [ARGM-LOC into bed].

mosquito bar and crawled cozily into bed," what "his" and "his wife" refer to. Performance on coreference in general (including resolving pronouns and definite references) is only about 60 percent. An accuracy of 60 percent is poor, especially since the coreference component can propagate errors in other components.[5] Disambiguating word senses is also something a system that computes meaning must do. International competitions for word-sense disambiguation in different languages have shown that the best systems operate at about 65–75 percent accuracy (as discussed in Mihalcea and Pedersen 2005), though the results vary widely by task and language.

One more component technology is needed for understanding dialogue, involving the pragmatic dimension of meaning. Consider the subsequent scene in "The Short Happy Life of Francis Macomber." Francis lies awake in his tent at three in the morning, his wife, Margaret, having been out for the last two hours. She comes in, and Francis confronts her, demanding to know where she has been. She makes a lame excuse, which only confirms Francis's and the reader's suspicion.

1. "Where have you been?"
2. "I just went out to get a breath of air."
3. "You did, like hell."
4. "What do you want me to say, darling?"
5. "Where have you been?"
6. "Out to get a breath of air."
7. "That's a new name for it. You *are* a bitch."
8. "Well, you're a coward."

We will represent each step in the dialogue by means of dialogue acts, which are related to the speech acts proposed by the philosopher John

Searle. Francis is faced with a problem, the (extremely) negative effect of her absence, and he wants an explanation. In such cases the explanation can involve confirming one's worst fears or hoping for disconfirming evidence. His need to know can only be resolved by rudely asking her, by means of a DEMAND dialogue act (1). Margaret has been caught, and faced with the problem, wants to avoid further confrontation, so she offers (2) an utterly evasive explanation, by means of an EXCUSE dialogue act. Francis does not accept such a lame excuse, and his worse fears are confirmed. This makes him even more upset. He wants her to confess, so he can come to terms with where he stands with her. He (3) ACCUSES her of lying, and she responds (4) with a RHETORICAL question that ironically also suggests guilt. He DEMANDS yet again (5), only to have her respond (6) with her original EXCUSE, indicating to him that it's a stalemate; she's not going to cow before him. Notice that she never offers an APOLOGY; rather she's defiant right through. He then ACCUSES her with an epithet (7), in effect, of adultery, and she ACCUSES him (8) of being a coward, the counteraccusation in this case also being a further admission and reminder for his benefit of her motive. In short adultery is used here to exact revenge.

Accuracy for statistically trained dialogue-act tagging is about 65 percent for the Dialogue Act Markup in Several Layers (DAMSL) tagging scheme, as shown by Andreas Stolcke and his colleagues (2000), which is remarkable given the disfluencies in naturally occurring dialogue. Accommodating the kinds of dialogue acts one comes across in any sample of literature will of course require an annotation scheme and annotated data for training.

Figure 27 shows a meaning engine that puts all these components together. Note that the system architecture is somewhat simplistic; in practice some of these components might be interleaved. All together these tools can generate what we call a basic meaning representation. For the opening sentence of Serena's story, we can see the basic meaning representation in table 3, where the timeline has been computed (with respect to the speech time t0), the argument roles have been labeled, and coreference applied (indicated by subscripts F and S). Notice that the basic meaning representation leaves the marriage time t4 underspecified with respect to the speech time t0.

While statistical parsing technology is more or less ready for "prime time" in terms of application to literary texts, these other components

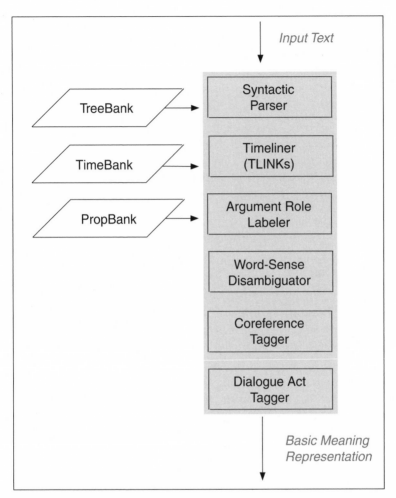

FIG. 27. Meaning engine.

need further improvements. Some of these improvements are likely to happen in due course, given the need for and profits from practical applications, along with the rapid pace of corpus creation and experimentation with learning algorithms. At the present time I have automatically parsed all the narratives quoted in this book through to their meaning representations (these are available on the book Web site). I feel confident in making the following claim:

TABLE 3. *Basic meaning representation for Serena opening sentence*

[ARGO Francisco$_F$] felt thrilled $_{t1}$ (ARGM-TMP when [ARGO Serena $_s$] agreed $_{t2}$
[ARG2 to [ARGO his$_F$] proposal $_{t3}$ [ARG1 of marriage $_{t4}$]])
t3 ‹ t2 ‹ t1 ‹ t0
t1 ‹ t4

Computing relatively accurate basic meaning representations for sentences in literary fiction is entirely feasible in the medium term and dependent mainly on research investments and the creation of annotated corpora.

THE SIGNIFICANCE OF ACCURACY

At this point the reader may find all this talk of accuracy figures rather tiresome. What, she may wonder, does a 90 percent accurate parser or an 80 percent argument-role labeler, or for that matter, an 85 percent accurate meaning engine have to do with enhancing our understanding of fiction? Well, accuracy is important because it tells us how much artificial intelligence we can expect. If a computer agrees well with humans in building meaning (say 90 percent of the time), we will have created at the very least a silicon Frankenstein's monster that, for any language on which it is trained, can substitute for the human in certain situations, making decisions about what to do next based on this (somewhat shallow) level of meaning. Now, we don't have such an accuracy figure as yet for literary fiction, but any such development would be entirely revolutionary from the standpoint of the history of ideas.

Still, the skeptical reader might be forgiven for wondering how this will make her life, as a lover of fiction, more insightful. Let me try to answer this question.

First, it will allow us, in passing, to do what corpus linguistics often has done, but this time at the semantic level, counting how often female characters in Victorian fiction speak in the first person, how often order within the sentence is nonchronological (as in the Francisco sentence), and so on. This will in turn provide grist for the mill for theorists of all stripes.

Second, and far more importantly, it also suggests the sort of know-how that goes into the linguistic hopper of an agent that understands meaning. The modules in figure 27 are mainly statistical, involving "subsymbolic" representations, that is, mathematical formulas with lots of parameters, including the frequencies of particular words, their linguistic features, and so forth, just as we saw used in the statistical methods in chapter 3 ("Computing Timelines"). Sometimes, however, the formulas involve rules that a human might make sense of. For example, third-person personal pronouns are more likely to refer to people mentioned in the past three sentences, and conjoined verb phrases will sometimes indicate strict temporal precedence—"lifted her mosquito bar and crawled cosily into bed"—and sometimes a looser relation—"wrote poetry, collected obscene jokes, and gave chase to the occasional rhinoceros."

These rules aren't all-or-nothing laws; instead, they have weights, based on how frequently particular phenomena occur, and these weights are learned from experience. In other words the rule induction framework suggests a microstructure for understanding fiction, involving many thousands of rules that are constantly being weighted based on experience, that together work to construct the most likely interpretation.

COMPUTING TRAJECTORIES

The basic meaning representation illustrated in table 3 allows computers to track characters and time without much difficulty. Given that characters play particular argument roles with respect to events, it is fairly simple to isolate the argument roles and identify which ones correspond to mentions of people names. Systems for named-entity extraction in different languages, based mainly on statistical classifiers, are able to do so almost as well as humans, achieving 95 percent accuracy on the standard data sets used in various competitions. Coreference for personal pronouns, which is easier than the general coreference problem, can be leveraged effectively as well.

The temporal relations between the events with which people are associated can then be extracted by a TLINK tagger, as described in figure 15 (see chapter 3). This allows one to obtain the sequence (in chronological order, text order, or any other order desired) of all events involving a particular character or the sequence of all events where that character was the agent of the action.

Such trajectories can also include a spatial component. Spatial descriptions (such as "the Slavyansky Bazaar Hotel" as in "Gurov went on to the Slavyansky Bazaar Hotel") can be associated with events (as occupying an ARGM-LOC role, for example, in the basic meaning representation). They can also be grounded in terms of a geographical representation like SpatialML; in fact a variety of research and commercial tools are available to tag and disambiguate places mentioned in texts, mapping them to geographical representations based on geo-coordinates where possible.

More formally, computing spatiotemporal trajectories relies on representing both three-dimensional objects (like people and places, which exist their entirety in each moment in time) and four-dimensional ones (as in noninstantaneous events like traveling, whose existence is defined over a time interval).

The accuracy of such systems depends on the size of the gazetteer used (the gazetteer allows one to map from place names to particular geo-coordinates), since a larger gazetteer will result in more ambiguity. For example, there are 1,037 places named "La Esperanza" in the GeoNames gazetteer produced by the U.S. Board on Geographic Names. Incorporating this spatial-inferencing capability allows the system to overlay the temporal trajectory on a map. Research systems to compute such spatiotemporal trajectories, addressing texts in the large (i.e., not focusing on fiction), have been developed. Figure 28 shows an example of a trajectory computing engine. It uses a preannotated SpatialML corpus (available from the Linguistic Data Consortium) that contains disambiguated place information.

One of the challenges for trajectories is interpolation. We don't quite know what route Gurov took to return to Moscow from Yalta, nor whether he was in Moscow throughout the time between his return from the encounter with Anna at S—— and their tryst at the Slavyansky Bazaar Hotel. In such cases elision can be used (e.g., by way of "dotted" lines) to indicate a path that is likely but not part of a conservative interpretation.

Another challenge comes from places that don't exist. This is not strictly a problem except when nonexistent places have to be integrated with existent ones. Macondo, the fictitious town of *One Hundred Years of Solitude*, also happens to be a town in Angola; the computer will

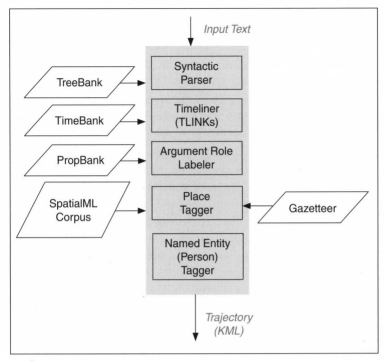

FIG. 28. Trajectory engine.

have to figure out that they are different places. Of course as those au courant with literary matters are aware, Macondo is based in part on Aracataca, the birthplace of Gabriel Garcia Marquez. In 2006 the mayor of Aracataca proposed renaming the town Macondo, in the hope of attracting tourists; however, not enough townsfolk turned up to vote. Had they succeeded, we would have a choice of whether to map the intended fictional place of Macondo to the real Macondo or not.

We took some obvious liberties when we mapped Anna's residence at S——. As for Marini's Xiros:

> The island was small and solitary, and the Aegean Sea surrounded it with an intense blue that exalted the curl of a dazzling and kind of petrified white, which down below would be foam breaking against the reefs and coves. (Cortázar 1973, 90–91)

We might place Xiros in the North Aegean, closer to Lesbos, as this might make for a shorter flight path. The name itself might also be taken as a hint; perhaps Cortázar wanted the reader to think of it as being near the island of Siros, in the Cyclades. Such choices involve more than a conservative interpretation, of course.

The problem is somewhat simpler when an entire area is fictional, as in the case of Thomas Hardy's Wessex, which was derived from the name of an ancient Saxon kingdom. While Hardy's Casterbridge is generally acknowledged to map to Dorchester, in West Dorset, it is an entirely fictional spot, even if it harbors memories of numerous tragic events, beginning with the barbaric sale by Michael Henchard—who eventually becomes mayor of Casterbridge—of his wife and child for five guineas. (There has been no proposal, as far as I know, to rename Dorchester to Casterbridge.) As McHale (1987) has argued, the emphasis on fictional places that can be fragmented, disordered, and inconsistent, but which are at the same time more or less loosely associated with real places, is another characteristic of postmodernist fiction. His examples include Borges's country of Uqbar, Calvino's Empire of the Great Khan, and Pynchon's Zone, among others.

For trajectories we will promiscuously propose such deliberately fictional places as distinct from real ones, using our system of correspondences (the double-equal sign) to map from one to the other. For places that aren't intended to be fictional but are merely used as a prop for a fictional work, such as London in Dickens's or Wodehouse's fiction, we can, as a matter of convention, use the actual location in the trajectory. Such locations may not be precise, as in the case of fictional addresses on real streets—a case in point being Sherlock Holmes's London address of 221B Baker Street, where the nonexistent 221B could be mapped at best to the actual Baker Street.

While we are on the subject of trajectories, it is worth noting that research is currently under way aimed at constructing rich spatiotemporal trajectories for motion events involving particular types of entities (such as people), from a variety of nonfictional text genres, including travel blogs of the kind examined earlier in chapter 4 ("Calendar Times"). These trajectories involve interpolation, for example, figuring out where a person might have been in between places mentioned in the text. This research is confined to explicitly stated relationships between the agents of events and the times and places of those events.

Let us return to the biking blog we examined briefly in chapter 4.

MARCH 7, 2006

<u>Leaving</u> San Cristobal de las Casas, I <u>biked</u> with Gregg and Brooks for one more day. We <u>climbed</u> over the mountains, and then <u>descended</u> to the east, where a thick green rainforest <u>grew up</u> around the road. We <u>arrived</u> in the town of Ocosingo and we were <u>advised</u> the road ahead was <u>unsafe</u> in the afternoon or night. I did not <u>ask</u> if there was a fire station and <u>went</u> straight to a cheap hotel that I <u>split</u> with Gregg and Brooks.

The following morning, as I was <u>planning</u> to <u>ride</u> farther that day, I <u>left</u> at dawn while Gregg and Brooks were still <u>asleep</u>. I <u>biked</u> 30 miles to the town of Agua Azul where I <u>played</u> for 4 hours in waterfalls and clean cool pools.

The ability to mark up events and times in TimeML, along with the places in SpatialML, forms a basis for annotating motion in such blogs. Figure 29 shows a snapshot from a Google Earth demonstration (from Plotnick 2008), where the human annotation of the biking trajectory of the blog's author is visualized in Google Earth. The detailed time stamps are left out for reasons of space.

I would now like to make another claim, which relies on some of the outcomes of this research:

> Computing relatively dense trajectories for characters in literary fiction is feasible based on analysis of explicitly stated spatiotemporal relationships within sentences.

COMPUTING CHARACTER EVALUATIONS

Now the basic meaning representation needs to be augmented with what we will call ψ-Evals, that is, the positive or negative or null evaluations by the actual reader for each character involved in an event. Note that once one knows the ψ-Evals, the characterization of narrative progression in terms of transitions, monotonic and otherwise, is easily computed.

The character-evaluation tagger takes each event on the timeline and

FIG. 29. Trajectory from a travel blog.

provides a ψ-Evals label. The basis for ψ-Evals tagging will be a statistical classifier, very similar to the one described in figure 13 (see chapter 3). Here the input to the tagger are pairs of agent-event pairs, and the output, the ψ-Evals classes, are positive, negative, or nil. One issue is whether humans can annotate ψ-Evals reliably: will one annotator be moved by Anna's (and Gurov's) situation at the Slavyansky Bazaar Hotel, while another turns a cold eye to it? Once this issue is addressed, the main challenge for automating ψ-Evals tagging is sufficient annotated data. As a statistical language processing researcher, Robert Mercer, once observed, "There is no data like more data."

LESSONS FOR NARRATOLOGISTS FROM CORPORA

We have come a long way: it is one thing to advocate the use of corpora for studying vocabulary, or parsing, or for tagging dialog acts, but now we have argued our way into creating and exploiting corpora for entire timelines and character evaluations across stories and novels! The narratologist reading this, if unaccustomed to corpus-based approaches, may simply throw up his hands. At this point it is worth articulating and addressing various lingering objections such a reader might have to the use of narrative corpora.

The most common objection to the use of corpora is "Why bother?"

One version of this argument was put forward over a half century ago by Chomsky (1957). His argument was that introspection is more than sufficient for generating linguistic data to answer questions about what sorts of syntactic structures might or might not be uttered. As he noted: "If you sit and think for a few minutes, you're just flooded with relevant data" (1984, 44).

However, introspection is notoriously unreliable. It also reflects the views of a particular speaker and her community. While Bostonians, for example, speak of a bubbla, a spukie, or a chowderhead, few other people have a clue what they are talking about. Finally, I, for one, am hardly conversant with the typical speech patterns of three-year-olds in my community.

Of course an even stronger argument for bothering about corpora is the proof of the pudding: It works! It works for literary and humanities computing, where fiction from different periods has been compared quite extensively to address questions of vocabulary and style, as well as the use of spatialization applied to literary narrative.[6] It works for parsing, aspects of meaning, and timelining, as we have just seen.

Chomsky also argued, more persuasively, that corpora offered at best only a biased sample of language use. Natural language is in principle infinite, whereas corpora are finite, because so many examples will be missed. Frequencies of linguistic items found in the corpus will reflect the peculiarities of the sample, not language use in general; for example, because New York City has a larger population than Dayton, Ohio, one would expect the frequency of "I live in New York" to be higher than "I live in Dayton."

Chomsky's point about sampling is a valid one, and the particular example he chose is instructive. In a corpus of news articles, for example, even one that spans a long time period, people, places and institutions deemed important will be mentioned more frequently than other places. Such is the biased nature of news, and similar problems arise with other "genres." Corpora are further bedeviled by the fact that even in very large collections, most of the words in them occur relatively infrequently. Words that might occur in one collection may not be seen at all in another. Things that are rare or unseen will not be picked up in training, so if they are seen in a test example, they may not be interpreted correctly.

Also, the idiosyncrasies of a particular genre will also "bias" the sample. Actually, staring at data long enough will reveal all kinds of fascinating idiosyncrasies. While developing the Time Tagger, described in figure 12 (see chapter 3), to tag and normalize time expressions, my colleague George Wilson (at Georgetown University) and I found various kinds of nonuniformities in the training data. In comparison with *New York Times* articles, broadcast news (transcribed Voice of America radio broadcasts) had a greater proportion of expressions referring to time of day, primarily due to repeated announcements of the current time and incessant reminders about the time of upcoming shows. Further, in print news not all days of the week were treated equal; Mondays were the most frequent, followed by Tuesdays and then Fridays.

A subsequent investigation by Wilson revealed (figure 30) that the named day of the week most mentioned in news articles was the next day (marked as 1 in figure 30), with the current day (i.e., the day the article was published) and two days later being the next most popular references. The hypothesis supported by such data is that what is going to happen in the future is the most interesting, actionable news.

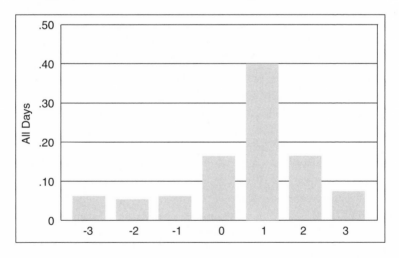

FIG. 30. Day of week offsets in news.

Fortunately, although this sort of skewed distribution can cause a problem for certain learning methods, it did not cause a problem for the Time Tagger. All in all, a wonderful benefit of using corpora is that they generate lots of fascinating anomalies and puzzles, as well as discovering new phenomena for further investigation.

Chomsky's objections (reiterated in interviews as late as 2004) hindered the development of corpus-based techniques in linguistics and consequently in computational linguistics as well. Progress in automatic speech recognition, now familiar to anyone who uses a telephone, was based on statistical methods and succeeded without the help of linguists. This development, along with the growing availability of cheap computer storage and very fast processing, resulted in a reawakening of practical interest in corpus-based methods for language understanding in the large. As far back as 1988, Fred Jelinek, a leading speech-recognition researcher, then at IBM, who was applying some of these statistical methods to parsing sentences, was quoted as saying, "Whenever I fire a linguist, our system performance improves."

Nevertheless, the debate about what it is that the human language faculty really uses, for example, statistical distributions or highly parameterized rules that are adjusted by the speaker in each language community, is by no means settled. Research on how children acquire language suggests that both are involved in some fashion, but the complete picture is still elusive, as shown by Michael Tomasello (2006).

One lesson, therefore, is not to dismiss empirically based methods out of hand, out of suspicion or other a priori biases. The temptation in narratology to spin theories out of thin air, supported as needed by a few carefully chosen examples, is a very great one, given that it keeps books in print and provides opportunities for endless commentary on those theories. There is in fact an incredible variety of forms of narrative to be found in actual data, with a rich vein of linguistic information relating to time and narrative, all of which can be discovered from corpora and used as evidence for or against particular theoretical claims.

The fact that progress in computational linguistics has occurred mostly in the 1990s onward, and not earlier, may be blamed on theoretical fashion and computer technology. Theoretical linguistics, particularly Chomskyan theories, were the driving force behind computational linguistics, and as we have seen, somewhat specious arguments against the use of corpora persuaded many (though not all) researchers not to consider the use of corpora.

However, this criticism should not be seen as detracting from Chomsky's focus on the expressiveness of representations and his many path-breaking and original contributions to linguistics, computer science, and philosophy. His arguments should, in any case, be taken with a historical grain of salt. They were a rejection of the structuralist linguists' focus on the surface form of patterns found in data, patterns that were unable to deal with underlying forms. Thus, the now celebrated sentences "John is eager to please" and "John is easy to please" have the same surface structure, but they mean very different things. What Chomsky was after was a science of mind, one that would be opposed to the truly reductionist behaviorist stimulus-response-reinforcement psychology of the time.[7]

Fortunately, the evolution of technology triumphed over the theoretical biases of the Chomskyan era. The availability of computers with vast amounts of storage capability and fast processing speeds made statistical analyses of corpora much more feasible. But lack of technology has never hampered the truly intrepid. As early as 1897, Friedrich Wilhelm Kaeding built tables of frequency distributions of letters and letter sequences in 11 million words of German text, going through them by hand with the help, it is said, of an army of five thousand Prussian analysts. The Brown corpus (a million words of written American English, covering many genres) was developed at Brown University in 1967.

These trends have a substantial bearing on the field of narratology. Derived as it is from structural linguistics, narratology has yet to see an expressive, generative account rivaling that of Chomskyan linguistics. The advent of large-scale corpora and corpus-derived methods for inducing linguistic rules has further changed the way we see linguistic rules, with many researchers viewing them as probabilistic in some form. Narratology needs to make a similar transition, moving to corpus-based analyses of time and narrative progression. It is also distressing to notice that narratology as practiced today apparently doesn't make much use of software or corpora.

To summarize, computational linguistics provides a variety of tools for computing form and meaning. These can be used to produce a basic level of meaning for sentences in a narrative. Treebanks and propbanks need to be created for fictional narratives, since training on other, nonfictional treebanks and propbanks and then running on fictional narratives is likely to lead to errors.

When combined with the timelining capabilities discussed in chapter 3 ("Computing Timelines"), a system can easily be assembled to construct trajectories for characters in a narrative. These trajectories can be augmented with spatial disambiguation tools that attempt to pinpoint locations mentioned in the text. Research systems have been developed to compute such trajectories on nonfictional texts. These trajectories require a degree of interpolation in order to provide a tightly connected path. Once constructed, the trajectories taken by fictional characters through a work can be made explicit along with the points at which they cross. These provide a map of the characters' perambulations through the space and time of the story world.

With the basic level of meaning computed, the character evaluations for each event in the timeline are recorded. These evaluations can be solicited with existing annotation editors like Callisto, and once acquired, they can then be used to train a statistical classifier to reproduce them. However, so far, character-evaluation taggers have not yet been implemented.

With the evaluations at hand, the character transitions, monotonic and nonmonotonic, are easily computed. Doing so allows the reader to see, for any work, the highlights and transitions in a character's passage through a story, in a way that reflects the moral emphasis we place on particular ways of behaving. These evaluations, sympathetic or antipathetic to a character's situation, allow us to express empathy in ways that reinforce our own sense of who we are and have become.

Alas, these statistical approaches do not in themselves provide a theory of fiction of the kind narratologists are used to constructing. But given any theory that a narratologist or other person may posit, the representations built by these tools will provide empirical evidence for or against the theory, assuming the theory is precise enough to be tested by observations.

8 Time Management

The reader should by now be intrigued by the role computation can and could play in terms of tracking how characters evolve over a narrative. The computational approach can plot the trajectories of character's lives in spatial and temporal terms, and it can compute the changes they effect on readers' emotions. Since we are concerned with time, however, we need to say something more precise about how much time these trajectories and transitions take.

Time doesn't push onward at the same tempo throughout a story. Our experience of time in everyday life is hardly one of its creeping on at a petty pace, unless we are very bored. Likewise, fiction thrives on variations in tempo. There may be long passages of dialogue and descriptions of scenes where the narrative doesn't seem to advance very much. A text may zoom in, paying microscopic attention to details occupying small time intervals, or it may zoom out and briskly cover, in a few sentences, entire decades of delight or desolation.

Tempo is based on rhythm, and rhythm involves recurrences. (As we saw earlier in chapter 4 ["Calendar Times"], recurrences of particular types of events that are significant to an individual, group, or culture are important in determining which times are expressed in fiction.) Rhythms of growth and decay are intrinsic to the life cycle of events experienced in the world. The tempo of a narrative reflects an authorial decision to tie textual descriptions to different stretches of these cycles. Certain segments, like the nightly routine of sleep, are often highly compressed or elided as nothing interesting happens then (except for the often fascinating turns of events in dreams). Bodily functions such as excretion are also typically excluded for their lack of significance (though notable exceptions abound in literature, including some of the best passages of Boccaccio, Rabelais, and Joyce). Birth, love, marriage, and death of principal characters are usually deemed significant, as are confrontations between those characters, and so a reader may expect an author to devote some space to them. An author is of course free to violate such an expectation. In fact fictional narratives exhibit an amazing variety of tempos, as Ken Ireland (2001) has documented for a variety of novels in different languages. In this chapter I will show that computational models of time in language allow one to characterize the tempo of a narrative in a more precise way than various proposals advanced by literary theorists.

Related to tempo is the topic of time span. There are numerous novels, including Joyce's *Ulysses*, Woolf's *Mrs. Dalloway*, and Lowry's *Under the Volcano*, that are said to occur on a single day, but the events that matter to the characters stretch well beyond the day in question. In these works it is the main story that lasts a day, while there are flashbacks and flash forwards that take longer. Faulkner's *The Sound and the Fury* covers four days (one per chapter), with three of those days being contiguous; yet the characters are all caught up in the past, which extends far behind. Faulkner's allegorical novel *A Fable* covers a week of the First World War in May 1918 (a week ended by a fictional armistice, though the historical armistice with Germany only occurred at 11:00 a.m. on November 11, 1918). However, the events spill over to 1925, when one of the characters, the Old Marshal, dies. Mann's *Magic Mountain* spans seven years at a sanatorium in Davos, where time is almost suspended in an eternal present.[1] And Garcia Marquez's *One Hundred Years of Solitude* doesn't quite span a hundred years. The framework laid for tempo can be extended to address the question of the span of time in a narrative.

TEMPO: A NARRATOLOGICAL PERSPECTIVE

At what speed is time covered in a narrative?

A "fast-paced" thriller may be expected to feature short sentences and plenty of action happening over a short span of time. This suggests that one might measure tempo in terms of the proportion of actions in a text: the number of distinct actions, or mentions of actions, divided by the number of words, that is, actions per word. But this crude measure is woefully inadequate. An extensive description of my actions while sleeping (one thinks of Andy Warhol's five-hour film *Sleep*) would not be of interest.

A more appropriate notion may involve fast-paced plot development. We might measure tempo in terms of how much the plot evolves over time. But again such a measure requires a model of plot and is far too crude, because it ignores the relationship between events in the narrative and their temporal experience by the reader.

A more substantial proposal that attempts to take the reading experience into account comes from Genette (1980), who compares story times for events with their discourse times. The story time of an event is, in our framework, the time an event occupies on the timeline; its discourse time is the amount of time devoted to the event in the narrative, that is, how long it takes to recount the event.

Genette provides a classification of different relationships between story and discourse times. An isochronous narrative is one in which both times are equal or almost so; it is exemplified by dialogue, though as pointed out by Michael J. Toolan (1988) and others, fictional dialogue need not run at the same pace as real dialogue. Acceleration involves a much shorter discourse time than story time, as in this highly accelerated example from James Michener's *Hawaii*:

> The years passed. The sun swept through its majestic cycles. The moon waxed and waned, and tides rushed back and forth across the surface of the world. Ice crept down from the north, and for ten thousand years covered the islands, its weight and power breaking down rocks and forming earth. (cited by Jahn 2007, N 5.2.2)

Deceleration of tempo can rely on devices such as repetition and elaboration. The disturbing descriptions of minutiae in Robbe-Grillet's *Jealousy* certainly involve an unhealthy elaboration on particulars, conveying the impression of a relentless voyeurism (very much in keeping with subsequent developments in our surveillance-oriented and Barnumism-prone society). As Ireland points out, deceleration is also seen in the closing chapters of Jane Austen's *Persuasion*.

Incidentally, Ireland (2001) states that the last six of *Persuasion*'s twenty-four chapters uses 73 pages to cover a story time of 1.5 weeks, implying much more discourse time for these than is devoted to any of the other three groups of chapters. The positing of a discourse time in terms of the time taken to read poses difficult problems of measurement.

Certainly, if we measure the length of a description, we can convert it to reading time assuming a particular reading speed. Assuming 350 words per page and a reading rate of 300 words per minute, this yields a reading time of 1.41 hours, which gives us a compression of 1:178 in terms of discourse time to story time.

However, the assumption of a particular number of words per page is highly dependent on the edition, the font size, page margins, and so on. Those six chapters of *Persuasion* span 26,904 words in the Project Gutenberg edition, yielding a slightly longer reading time of 1.49 hours, which gives a lower compression of 1:169. The assumption of an average reading rate is also problematic as it doesn't take individual variation into account. The measurement of discourse time as a function of text length is therefore not satisfactory.

Ireland cites the following passage from *Candide* (2006, 64, from Voltaire 2006) to illustrate some interesting variations in tempo (this passage occurs immediately after one where the sages of Portugal decide, when most of Lisbon is destroyed by the 1755 earthquake, that giving the people a beautiful auto-da-fé will prevent further tremors):

> They were <u>conducted</u> to separate apartments, extremely cold, as they were never <u>incommoded</u> by the sun. Eight days after, they were <u>dressed</u> in san-benitos and their heads <u>ornamented</u> with paper mitres. The mitre and san-benito belonging to Candide were <u>painted</u> with reversed flames and with devils that had neither tails nor claws; but Pangloss's devils had claws and tails and the flames were upright. They <u>marched</u> in procession thus <u>habited</u> and <u>heard</u> a very pathetic <u>sermon</u>, followed by fine church <u>music</u>. Candide was <u>whipped</u> in cadence while they were <u>singing</u>; the Biscayner, and the two men who had <u>refused</u> to <u>eat</u> bacon, were <u>burnt</u>; and Pangloss was <u>hanged</u>, though that was not the custom. The same day the earth <u>sustained</u> a most violent <u>concussion</u>.

Ireland notes that the story time of this passage far exceeds the discourse time, and that there is a great deal of change of tempo. The speed is quick until the description of Candide's and Pangloss's costumes, with the pace picking up considerably in the last two sentences. The quick and offhand account of the hanging of a principal character (Pangloss) only enhances Voltaire's characteristic satirical treatment.

The varieties of tempo have been tied to four underlying "narrative modes" by Helmut Bonheim (1982): description (involving actions and times), speech (direct as well as indirect, and including interior monologues), report (scene setting), and comment (metanarrative, including evaluations and generalizations). Bonheim's theory is drawn from a study of a collection of six hundred short stories and three hundred novels. Although the methodology is not based on an annotated corpus, it is empirically motivated and includes generalizations about the modes based on quantitative analyses. Comment and description result in a relatively slower tempo, whereas speech and report make for a faster one. However, these narrative modes may at times be hard to distinguish, particularly descriptions versus reports, as Bonheim acknowledges. And descriptions could involve agitated thoughts that might seem to go faster. Although the theory is certainly interesting in terms of accounting for pace by means of narrative modes, Bonheim does not extend his quantitative analyses to pace. For that a corpus-based approach would be required, one that marks up texts with perceived durations.

TEMPO AND DISCRETE-EVENT SIMULATION

These proposals for measuring tempo all seem to miss the point. They fail to get at the subjective experience of time in the reader's mind.

Tempo in fiction, as various scholars have emphasized, is inherently subjective. Bonheim points out that when a character fires a pistol shot while talking, the simultaneity (or overlap) of the two events on the timeline is presented sequentially in the narrative. Further, a character may speak for three minutes, and the reader, taking half that time to read the passage, may have the impression that three minutes has elapsed.

As discussed in chapter 5 ("Time in Mind"), humans simulate the events of a story as they read it, rather like running a movie in their minds. The text description of an event will give rise to a mental simulation of it. The simulated event duration (the time the event is construed as lasting) is inferred from clues in the text or else is filled in from commonsense knowledge of such events. The simulated event will usually take much less time for a human to experience vicariously while reading than its simulated duration. Otherwise, nobody would ever finish reading stories with long-span events.

If we take seriously the idea of the reader running a mental simulation of the events in the story, it is not hard to analyze the factors that come into play. Simulations are a standard feature of many design and engineering activities, and built into them are particular analogues of the world. Discrete-event simulation is used widely in everyday life; activities include the design of integrated circuits, the improvement of manufacturing processes such as food packaging and automobile assembly, the modeling of baggage handling for airports and teller services for banks, and the development of computer-game environments for training military personnel.

During a simulation thousands of events can be processed, all in a few seconds of computer run time. When running a computer simulation of discrete events, a master process manages the time of the simulation. This process either advances the time into the future by a fixed time step, irrespective of whether anything is happening at that next time, or else it advances to the next event, no matter how close or far away in time that next event is. Each time there is an advance, the clock time of the simulation is updated and moved forward through seconds, minutes, hours, days, and so forth, depending on the type of activity being simulated. We will refer to the represented time of an event (minutes, hours, years, etc.) as the simulation time, to be distinguished from actual run time.

We can think of the mental simulation of a narrative as involving a similar process (with some qualifications, to be discussed later). The reading of a text sets the reels spinning in the mind, and the simulation unfolds. The mind, before reading of an event like the imprisonment of Candide and Dr. Pangloss, starts the simulation time off at a reference time, RT. After processing the conducting event, the master process in the simulation advances the clock to the next event time, $t_1 = RT + t\text{-}conduct$. Another eight days (in simulation time) later, at time $t_2 = t_1 + P8D$, the pair are taken to be dressed in san-benitos (the sleeveless tunics worn by victims en route to their auto-da-fé). The dressing scene itself takes some simulated time, t-dress. So, after the dressing, the hapless pair are at simulation time $t_3 = t_2 + t\text{-}dress$. The marching takes some specified time, as does the sermon, followed by the whipping. Then comes the burning of the Biscayner and the non-Christian bacon-despisers and the hanging of Pangloss—two events whose relative order isn't precisely specified. We might summarize these time steps, all of which together take some particular "run time" to read, as follows:

$$t_1 = \text{RT} + t\text{-conduct}$$
$$t_2 = t_1 + \text{P8D}$$
$$t_3 = t_2 + t\text{-dress}$$
$$t_4 = t_3 + t\text{-march}$$
$$t_5 = t_4 + t\text{-sermon}$$
$$t_6 = t_5 + t\text{-whip}$$
$$t_7 = t_6 + t\text{-hang}$$
$$t_8 = t_6 + t\text{-burn}$$

Voltaire chose chronological order to relay the events of interest. A different order of narration could require buffering the input until a chronology could be built or else resetting the start time for the clock when an earlier event is encountered and readjusting all previous times accordingly. Perhaps this is why nonlinear narratives take longer to process, as pointed out in chapter 5 ("Time in Mind").

How long is t-hang, the simulation time of the hanging? If an execution or suicide is carried out "properly," the victim should be dead within ten minutes, according to experts and those in charge of carrying out death penalties (in those nations that still implement such barbaric punishment). This time doesn't include the preparatory and cleanup phases, which may or may not be viewed as part of the spectacle of hanging. A person who doesn't know such reference information might still have a rough idea that the time for a hanging runs from less than a minute (roughly the maximum time of a fall) to an hour at most. As for t-sermon, it might last from half an hour to several hours, depending on the enthusiasm of the preacher, but it should not, in the normal course of events, last for an entire day.

In short, as a result of experience humans have at their disposal commonsense intuitions about event durations and their time scales, allowing them to infer implicit durations for events when these aren't mentioned. The simulation of story events may therefore involve some of these intuitions.

One might wonder how accurate humans—or machines—are in their intuitions about durations. The answer, fortunately, is at hand. The AI researcher Jerry Hobbs and his colleagues have developed an annotation scheme for humans to mark up event durations in documents (described in Pan, Mulkar, and Hobbs 2006). They have annotated nearly five dozen documents from the TimeBank, augmenting the timeline annotation of TimeML events with minimal and maximal bounds on their durations. The annotators marked their durations based on a set of probable scenarios given the context (for example, watching a movie takes more time than watching a plane take off); they annotated the minimum and maximum bounds on the durations so as to cover roughly 80 percent of the possible cases.

Here is an example annotation, which records a saying event as taking between five seconds and five minutes and the single event of visiting a site as taking between ten minutes and one day:

The official <EVENT min="PT5S" max="PT5M">said</EVENT> the site could only be <EVENT min="PT10M" max="P1D">visited </EVENT> by a special team of U.N. monitors and diplomats.

An automatic tagger trained on the TimeBank subcorpus (containing 2,330 events thus annotated) scored 76 percent accuracy in determining whether an event lasted a day or longer (Pan, Mulkar, and Hobbs 2006). Such systems still have some way to go, as human agreement on this task is about 87 percent.

However, there is still some delicacy involved in the judgments for the more complex task of setting more fine-grained bounds than simply a day or longer; agreement was around 75 percent for these. More fine-grained durations may be learned by a program once more annotated data are made available.

We already saw that psychological experiments indicated that when reading a story, we carry out simulations of the events in the story when we represent how far apart events are in time, which of course requires some estimate of event durations. The fact that we are able to annotate bounds on durations for thousands of events in news stories suggests strongly that when mentally simulating the events in such stories, we can reason about temporal bounds if needed.

TIME SCALES IN COMMONSENSE ESTIMATES

Hobbs (2000) has argued that the scale we use in everyday reasoning about objects is based on how we interact with them. Objects of the same size are interacted with similarly, but an object (such as a basketball) three times the size of another (such as an orange) requires a very different type of handling. These human-centered scales for estimating quantities are more natural than estimating based on the decimal system (once, twice, thrice, four times, etc.). He points out that when making estimates of quantities for dimensions such as time, distance, size, and so forth, people are most comfortable when choosing between alternatives that differ by a half order of magnitude (HOM).

For example, estimating the size of an antiwar demonstration in terms of whether it is closer to 100, 300, or 1,000 people is easier and more meaningful for people to do than distinguishing between whether there are 300 versus 350 people. Increasing the size of an object by three to four times (or more precisely, $\sqrt{10}$ times) changes our interactions with it. The HOMs for times that would be more natural to distinguish (using a logarithmic scale with base $\sqrt{10}$) would be 1, 5, and 15 seconds; 1, 5, and 15 minutes; 1, 3, and 12 hours; 1 day, 3 days, 1 week, 1 month, 3 months, 1 year, and so on. As Hobbs observes: "We know for various types of events which HOM categories they fall into. Thus, a cough lasts one second, a lecture lasts one hour, and a course lasts three months. We know that if we are told that John missed a course because he coughed, this requires elaborate explanation" (2000, 9).

The study by Feng Pan, Rutu Mulkar, and Jerry Hobbs (2006) analyzed their annotated duration data in terms of a distribution of duration widths. The duration width of an event is the difference between maximum and minimum duration for each event. The distribution is shown in figure 31, where it is plotted on a natural log scale. It can be seen that the widths peak at a HOM.

The importance of HOMs for reasoning about temporal durations is further underlined in my research with Ben Wellner (Mani and Wellner 2006) on acquiring event durations from a raw (i.e., unannotated corpus). That study conducted searches on "lasted" in British National Corpus, or BNC, (containing 100 million words) and then automatically tagged the events and times using the TARSQI toolkit. Such a tagged example is shown below.

The <EVENT>storm</EVENT> lasted <TIMEX3 VAL="P5D">five days</TIMEX3>.

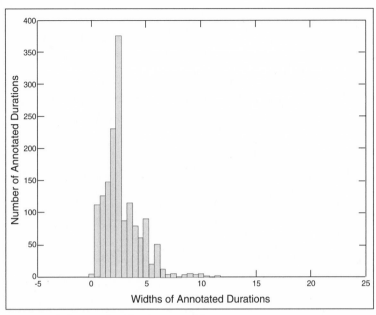

FIG. 31. Distribution of widths of annotated durations.

The result for the event "to lose" (covering "lose," "lost," "losses," "losing," etc.) is shown in figure 32. Here the durations in days are plotted on the horizontal axis in a natural log scale, and frequencies are plotted on the vertical axis.

Note that these durations reflect the financial sense of "loss" of value of stocks, rather than say the losses in sports matches, as the BNC is dominated by financial articles with specific information pinpointing the durations of financial events. It can be seen that the frequencies peak at three months (the financial quarter) and one year, which are natural HOMs for time.

Despite its apparent prevalence I suspect that even HOM reasoning is likely to be too precise for our mental simulations of narrated events. Coarse-grained differences in simulation time, such as a battle lasting much longer than a sneeze, are more the kind of difference that we may be consciously aware of. Our duration estimates during reading are likely to be far more qualitative than quantitative.

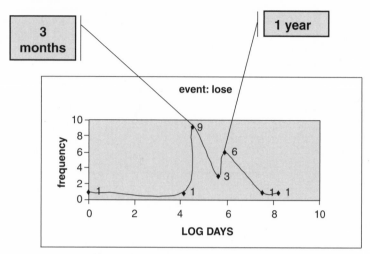

FIG. 32. Durations of "to lose" events in British National Corpus.

STORY TIME AND DISCOURSE TIME REVISITED

The argument so far suggests we need to distinguish the time of events in the written story from the time of simulated events in the mind and from the eventual time taken to read the story. This means we have a three-way distinction instead of just one based on story time and discourse time. The annotation of the *Candide* fragment, with durations based on the Hobbs group's guidelines, is shown in figure 33.

The burning at the stake, which I reckoned as taking five minutes to one hour, is left out of the diagram for reasons of space rather than squeamishness. It took me fifty-five seconds to read and understand the resulting passage; this reading time includes comprehension time. The timeline for the reading time (cumulative) is also shown. It can be seen that while the sermon might take the longest (maximum three hours) in terms of simulation time, the dressing (forty-five words) takes the longest in terms of reading length as well as reading time (thirteen seconds).

Given the subtlety of judgments of duration, which depend on the occurrence context and the estimation of the most probable scenario in 80 percent of the cases, the reader would be expected to agree with my judgments no more than three out of four times. It is instructive to compare my times for "conduct" (five to fifteen minutes), "march" (five minutes to one hour), and "burn" (five minutes to one hour) in

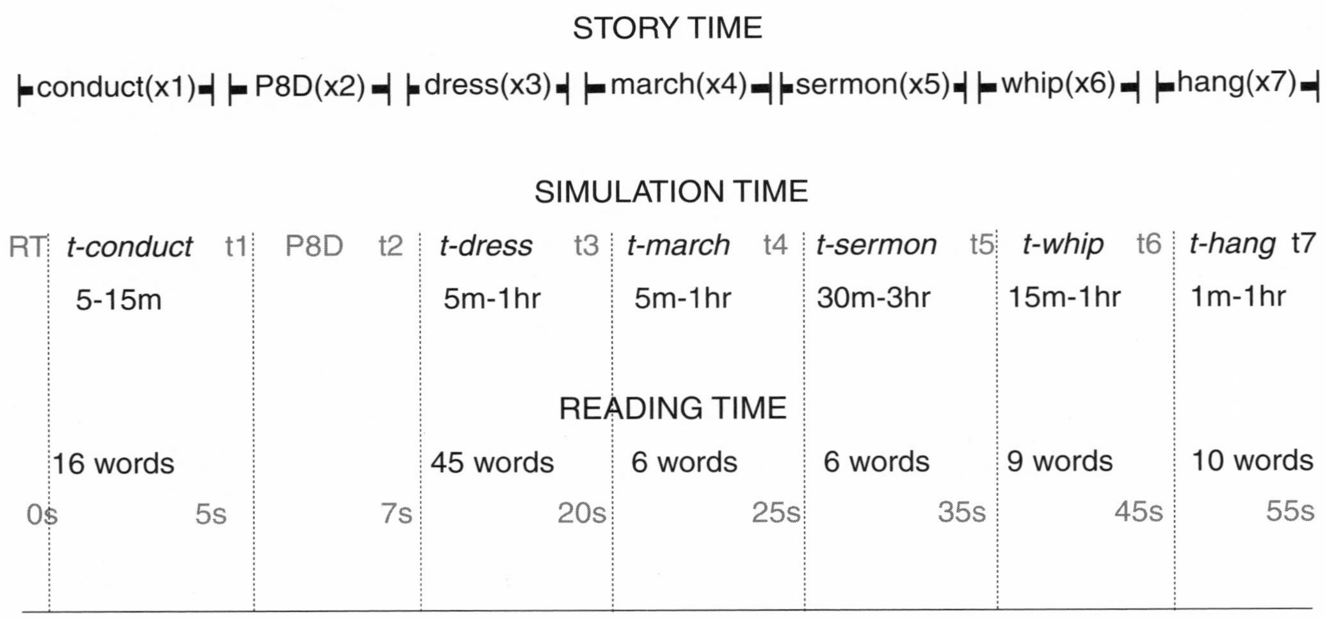

STORY TIME

conduct(x1) P8D(x2) dress(x3) march(x4) sermon(x5) whip(x6) hang(x7)

SIMULATION TIME

RT	t-conduct t1	P8D t2	t-dress	t-march t3	t-sermon t4	t-whip t5	t-hang t6 t7

t-conduct 5-15m

P8D

t-dress 5m-1hr

t-march 5m-1hr

t-sermon 30m-3hr

t-whip 15m-1hr

t-hang 1m-1hr

READING TIME

16 words — 0s 5s
45 words — 7s
6 words — 20s
6 words — 25s
6 words — 35s
9 words — 45s
10 words — 55s

FIG. 33. Story time, simulation time, and reading time in *Candide*.

this passage from *Candide* to the times for those events in the Hobbs group's annotated TimeBank. There we find the much longer one to two months for the Khmer Rouge conducting a search for a body, one to two years for conducting auction business, both of which involve the rather different sense of carrying out an activity rather than leading someone somewhere; the somewhat longer one to three hours for a march (in the related sense of a demonstration) by Catholics in Belfast, and thirty minutes to six hours for one by ethnic Albanians in Turkey, and the shorter time of thirty seconds to five minutes for those marching Albanians to burn a Serbian flag. The latter act of disrespect involves a time interval comparable to a subinterval of the incineration of Candide's cohorts, as this, after all, might be the time it would take to burn a corresponding size of cloth on the Biscayner's body. Obviously, judgments of duration can only be compared for the same type of event (i.e., a disambiguated and similar word sense) in a similar occurrence context.

Our sense of pace needs to be sensitized to this three-way distinction. I am convinced that the sense of narrative pace, which is a subjective notion, has more to do with the relation between simulation time and discourse time, rather than that between story time (i.e., event time derived from explicit predications in the text) and discourse time. After all, the *Candide* extract only provides two time expressions, both intervals—the eight-day gap and the interval before the earthquake (before the day's end). The other events certainly take time, as construed by the reader's estimates.

To facilitate comparison of simulation time and discourse time, let us normalize the measurements. We can calculate the average lengths of the simulated durations for each of the events as a percentage of the sum of those lengths. We can do the same for the lengths in words of each of the descriptions of the events, as a percentage of the sum of those lengths. These percentages can then be juxtaposed in a plot, as shown in figure 34, where the X-axis shows the events, and the Y-axis the percentages. Since nothing much happened during the eight-day period, we focus on the passage beginning at the dressing.

Comparing the two peaks, we see that while 44 percent of the simulated time is occupied by the sermon (a mere 8 percent of the description length), almost 60 percent of the description is spent on the dressing (which is no more than 14 percent of the simulation time). The reading length is also out of phase with the simulated time.

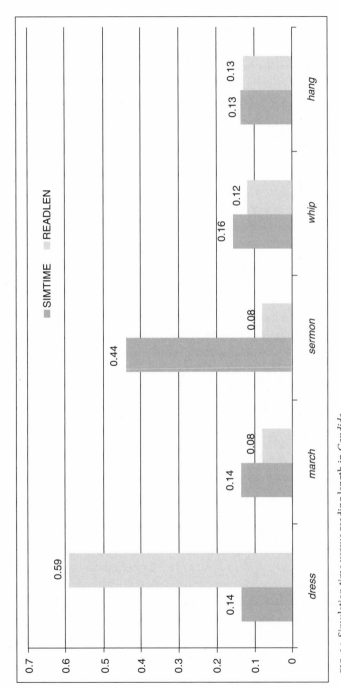

FIG. 34. Simulation time versus reading length in *Candide*.

Why is so much of the reading length devoted to the dressing? It is presented as a ritual preparation for death, the tarring of free men by the brush of religious intolerance, and thus something to which the reader reacts sympathetically (++ in character evaluations). The hanging of Pangloss, involving as it does a principal character, is also something that merits a sympathetic (++) character evaluation.

In any discrete-event simulation, the simulation times are only indirectly related to the computer run time. The latter is dependent on the number of steps (i.e., events). The duration of a simulation time should therefore have no impact on reading time. However, in narratives various factors enter in to influence the overall processing (and therefore, reading) time. Nonchronological order in the text description, as we saw in chapter 5 ("Time in Mind"), is one possible source of delay.

For tempo a sense of proportion is also required. Events that are simple time-fillers or of no use other than being required for purposes of moving the narrative along or providing information, what Barthes calls "indicial actions," can be compressed in various ways in the text. However, nonindicial events, which take up a high proportion of simulation time but which are allocated little reading length, and vice versa, are likely to cause a delay. That is what happens, for example, when there is a substantial temporal gap, as in the case of novels that catch up with events after a lapse of several decades (usually, these are broken out as separate parts of the novel). This lapse requires that the reader try to imagine what might have happened to characters in the intervening simulation time, populating it with some default events.

Finally, the significance of the event is also a factor in the delay. A significant event that is allocated a small proportion of reading length compared to insignificant ones, or an insignificant event that is overrepresented in its share of reading length, will also be a source of delay. And delays will increase reading time.

When all is said and done, texts that violate expectations about the relation between simulation time and description length are ubiquitous and make for more interesting reading. However, there are limits; the jettisoning of expected order and proportion based on a commonsense construal of reality comes with cognitive costs.

We are now ready to make an obvious claim:

> The reader expects significant events to be allocated a greater proportion of the total reading length in words than nonsignificant events, and vice versa. Violations of this expectation will result in longer reading times.

This prediction can only be tested by psychological experimentation, provided one defines what one means by "significant." Nevertheless, it is an intuitively satisfying claim. Indicial actions should not be expected to be dwelt on at great length. A text can of course do so, and skilled writing can do so to great literary effect, but this will result in a violation of expectations and more reading time.

This claim, however, suggests yet another, one that is specific to the theory in this book:

> Events whose outcomes lead to nonneutral character evaluations by the reader are more significant.

Given these two claims the reader of *Candide* should expect the dressing and the hanging to each be allocated a higher percentage of the reading length than the other events. The dressing meets this expectation, the hanging does not; the short shrift given to the hanging should make one pause, resulting in a delay. (For a comparison experiment to measure the processing delay, a variant of the above text with a longer hanging event might be compared with another with a shorter one, with both texts padded to be of the same length.)

Similarly, the reader of "The Short Happy Life of Francis Macomber," discussed earlier in the "Literary Examples" section in chapter 6 ("Characters in Time"), should expect that Margaret's slipping into Robert's bed (segment 2) and her later shooting of Francis (segment 3) will be allocated a higher proportion of the reading length than other events. The boudoir segment is not described directly, as a less skilled writer might, but dealt with obliquely, in terms of the focalized reactions of Francis and Robert and in dialogue between Margaret and the others replete with savage repartee and double entendre. The bed segment is allocated a substantial proportion of the reading length. The killing of Francis, coming as it does near the end, is allocated less reading length. This is characteristic of endings, and the abbreviated description gives the reader pause to reflect; a more extended description of death, as in a slow-motion melodrama, makes it less effective.

To pick another example from that section, the reader of "The Lady with the Pet Dog" should expect that Anna's feeling debased (segment 2) should be delved into relatively more, as should the confrontation with Anna (segment 4) and her confession (segment 5), along with the meeting in the Slavyansky Bazaar Hotel (segment 6). (Chekhov, as we noted earlier, has a style prone to a high density of reader evaluations.) These events are allocated substantial portions of the narrative.[2]

Interestingly, the construal of commonsense durations from reading literary narratives has been implicated as a factor in the discovery of Troy by Heinrich Schliemann. Schliemann (1875) narrowed the choice of Troy's location between two Turkish sites: Hisarlik versus Bunarbashi. In the *Iliad*, the Greeks were described as traveling on foot back and forth several times a day between their ships and Troy; Schliemann inferred from this that Troy could be no more than four miles from the sea. Bunarbashi is around eight miles from the coast, while Hisarlik met the bill.

TIME SPAN

How much time can a story be said to cover?

The answer is not as simple as it may seem. *One Hundred Years of Solitude*, which recounts the rise and fall of the Buendia family in a small, fictional town in Colombia, manages, in a fairly compact way, to cover seven generations, offering not only a comic and sympathetic chronicle of family life but also the history of the town from its founding to its end, and a history, in a sense, of civilization, with recurring human failures that seem to fit a pattern. And yet only a few years of the period are sampled.

There are numerous works that are said to span a day. Malcolm Lowry's *Under the Volcano* is set in Mexico in 1938, centered on the Mexican festival of the Day of the Dead (November 1). However, its first chapter begins a year later, on the Day of the Dead in 1939, after the death of the lead character, Geoffrey Firmin. The narrative is punctuated by numerous shots of *mezcal* imbibed by Firmin and (as documented extensively by his biographer Gordon Bowker, by Lowry while writing it). The fuel of alcohol notwithstanding, the book includes a great deal of reverie, back story, flashback, and speculation, making it seem to have spanned a much longer time.

Another example is James Joyce's *Ulysses*, said to take place on a single day (the eponymous Bloomsday, June 16, 1904). Like many other novels, *Ulysses* also has references and flashbacks to hundreds of earlier events, including the death of Stephen Dedalus's mother, the time of Molly's honeymoon with Bloom, historical events, mythological events, and so forth, as well as negated and hypothetical events. There are also events that are purely incidental, part of the bread-and-butter of scene description: lifting up a glass, drinking, walking, and the like. And all of these take time, but the amount of time varies greatly.

With such a large variation in temporal granularities of events, one approach to the question of time spans would involve picking some key initial event and some final event of what one deems the main story and viewing the span as the temporal distance between the two.

To compute the spans between events, it is first worth bearing in mind that the timelines we have been discussing, which involve qualitative temporal relations like BEFORE, DURING, and so on, are easily converted to a representation that uses inequalities. A time or event X can be viewed (as the TARSQI tool SputLink in fact does) as an interval starting at time point x_{start} and ending at time point x_{end}. For any interval X that is BEFORE another interval Y, $(y_{start} - x_{end})$ is positive. The inverse transformation, from inequalities to qualitative representations, is also easily achieved (algorithms to convert from one to the other are described in Kautz and Ladkin 1991 and Meiri 1996). In general a variety of algorithms similar to SputLink are available to infer temporal relations between any pair of events related by either inequalities (some of which may have numerical values), or qualitative relations, or both.

Turning to the *Candide* fragment analyzed in figure 23, the conducting has the simulated duration of five to fifteen minutes (i.e., $x_{end} < 5m$, or $x_{end} < 15m$). Then there is a gap of eight days, followed by a sequence of events culminating in the hanging that collectively lasts from fifty-six minutes to seven hours in simulation time. All three spans together have the simulated duration lasting from eight days, one hour, and one minute to eight days, seven and a quarter hours.

Now, the question remains as to how we pick the bounding events. In the case of the fragment, there was no back story or subordinated narrative, but of course in *Candide* itself as well as most fiction there will be many such. The bounding events must be picked from the supernarrative. To choose an earlier example, consider the text for figure 6, from chapter 2 ("Stories within Stories"):

> John <u>went</u> into the florist shop. He had <u>promised</u> Mary some flowers. She <u>said</u> she wouldn't <u>forgive</u> him if he <u>forgot</u>. So he <u>picked out</u> three red roses.

Here we will compute just the simulated spans for going into the florist shop and picking out three red roses, a total amount of time that might be estimated as lasting from five minutes to one hour. These kinds of computations can tell us various other measures, such as the mean length of events in a narrative. Narratives that dwell on longer events will have longer computed time spans.

In this chapter I examined two highly subjective temporal characteristics of narrative: tempo (the sense of how fast-paced a narrative is) and span (how much time a narrative covers).

Previous proposals for measuring tempo have relied on page lengths and reading times, which are subject to many confounding factors. Those measures also fail to get at the subjective experience of time in the reader's mind. The psychological evidence to date suggests that humans simulate the events of a story as they read it; and simulation is a well-understood computational process, found in many everyday software applications. I suggested that the simulated time of event is based on whatever cues are present in the text, falling back in other cases on the reader's commonsense knowledge of how long particular events might last.

Researchers have developed an annotation scheme for marking such commonsense durations of events, with interannotator agreement being around 75 percent. Computers have also been trained to compute durations for events on such annotated data, as to whether they occur within a day or longer, achieving a similar score. These results are for the TimeBank, which is newswire data. Once substantial fiction corpora are annotated using TimeML, annotating such durations would of course be an appropriate next step.

I hypothesized several factors that could influence the reading length for a narrative. Nonchronological text order has already been shown in psychological experiments to be one source of delay in reading time, which presumably slows the tempo as well. Readers also expect, along with a variation in pace, a sense of proportion to that variation: nonindicial events, which take up a high proportion of simulation time, should be allocated relatively more reading length. I offered a way of automatically computing such proportions, illustrating them with respect to a fragment from *Candide*. The reader also expects significant events to be allocated a greater proportion of the total reading length in words than nonsignificant events, and vice versa. I claimed, with a few illustrative examples, that events whose outcomes lead to nonneutral character evaluations ($^{++}$ or -) by the reader are more significant.

Violations of these expectations should result in longer reading times. Psychological experiments could test such predictions. However, the numerous and willful violations are often what make fiction especially engaging, since they contribute to a variety of literary effects, including satire and suspense.

Finally, I showed how the temporal framework with both qualitative temporal relations as well as commonsense durations can be used to address the question of the temporal span of a narrative, addressing both the "main story" and subordinated information.

Pace and extent together contribute to the elusive sense of "duration" (what Henri Bergson called "durée") for events in a narrative. It is this sense of subjective passage of time that we experience when reading *One Hundred Years of Solitude*, which can leave the reader, at the end of the reel, dazed and breathless, with a sense of having been a witness (in simulation time) to centuries.

9 | Digital Storytelling

We tend to think that we are living in times of immense change, but people seem to have always believed so. The nostalgia for a golden age, a remembrance of a time when everything was apparently so much simpler and less expensive—this sort of wishful thinking seems to have gone on since the habit of complaining first appeared among Homo sapiens. When it comes to literature, what really has changed?

The genres of fiction, it is true, have branched in many ways to express various slants on reality. The popular genres have also been refined into various categories (science fiction, historical romances, "chick lit," graphic novels, etc.) based on the economics of the marketplace. Most of today's printed novels and short-story collections are carefully packaged and targeted at today's consumer society, often backed by the marketing muscle of various corporations. Nevertheless, fictional creations are as lively as ever. And creative inspiration remains mysterious, still as prone as always to the whims of the Muses.

What has changed, of course, is technology. Since time immemorial, technology has long acted as an intermediary between producers and consumers of fiction, first with the advent of writing by the Sumerians on stone tablets (around 3100 BC), and later by means of reproduction, through copying by scribes and printing (with wood-block printing being used in China from around 550 AD). As this technological intermediary has grown over the centuries in sophistication and scope, live, impromptu performances have, of course, continued to coexist.

Computers began to be used in the editing and dissemination of fiction starting in the 1970s. Today's word-processing and desktop publishing platforms provide an entire suite of tools that authors can tap into to create polished works, including dictionaries and thesauri of all varieties; spelling, style, rhyme, and grammar checkers; encyclopedias and search tools; layout and graphics editors; and so on. Stories can now easily embed multimedia information, allowing a mix of writing, audio, images, and video, which can be presented and animated to create works like never before.

In fact the full scope of such tools has yet to be fully exploited by creators of literary fiction. I suspect this is due less to Luddite tendencies than to the sense of there already being one, rather different, creative medium that encompasses multiple modalities so well, namely, film. If one wanted to go beyond text, the writer might argue, why not simply write a play or a screenplay? Live performance and cinema both provide a richer set of cues for simulating the events in a story than text alone provides.

Still, the written word has its own subtle pleasures, much of it centered around the celebration of the texture and patter of syllables as they trip silently off the tongue, and the pictures they can vividly paint in the imagination without requiring any external visual cues. More crucially, however, when rendered well text brings with it the gift of creating heightened emotional states, a kind of reverberating joy, with a simple turn of phrase. There is hardly a passage in the *Iliad* that doesn't result in heightened reader responses, many of them sympathetic.

In recent years computer programmers have bravely taken the plunge into the uncertain waters of interactive fiction and drama. Many of them have come at it as game designers with experience in filmmaking or fiction writing, while at the same time thirsting for a much richer interactive experience than games can offer.

We are at an interesting inflection point in terms of the technologies that can be leveraged to tell stories. While we have so far considered how computer models and tools can enhance the understanding of time in narrative, it is time to consider what bearing these tools have on the production of narrative in our technology-drenched culture.

When considering narrative production, it's best to begin at the beginning.

ORAL NARRATIVES

The oldest stories were spoken. As discussed earlier, there is plenty of evidence, beginning with the Parry-Lord body of research (described in Lord 1960), that a high degree of improvisation is used in oral performances of epic narratives. The singer or poet, usually illiterate, expresses himself in short segments, approximated by a poetic line, that are then grouped into verses. Pauses are required for breathing, but also, one expects, for sneezing, the taking of applause, the sipping of tea or wine, and the like. Errors, hesitations, and corrections can occur, but they all take place in time, their traces indelible and ephemeral unless captured by a recording instrument.

For millennia the only such instrument was the memory of the listener, aided by a considerable number of mnemonic devices and considerable repetition. Most of this kind of skilled memorization is now lost to us as a side effect of literacy, though we still have musicians who can perform several hour-long concertos without a score, not to mention the hundreds of millions of Chinese readers who have memorized three to five thousand Chinese written characters. There are also lots of ordinary folks who remember vast bodies of scripture. For example, the Rig Veda, the four-thousand-year-old body of hymns in Vedic Sanskrit, is still recited across India. Its more than ten thousand verses were first redacted in the Iron Age and thence transmitted from one generation to the next by oral recitation, aided by a variety of indexes and guides that were themselves orally transmitted, as Rangaswamy Narasimhan (1991) observes. (Unlike traditional oral narratives, the variants recited across India are, as a result, very similar.)

Oral narratives are extremely versatile in the way they use time. In addition to a variety of stock and nonstock time expressions and the use of repetition to slow the tempo of the story, they express a great deal of variety in the way events can be ordered. As Walter Ong (1982) has noted, the narrated order of events can vary substantially with each oral performance. Oral narratives can start in medias res or with previews or highlights of the main action. They can involve movements back to the speech time, especially in evaluation segments, as in the case of the fight stories that William Labov (1972) studied and as we saw in the Mayan narratives recorded by Charles Hofling (1993); these segments allow the narrator to reflect on the subject matter of the story or bring the hearer back to the real world. And of course the ending may sometimes be given away at the beginning.

The primary constraint on the use of time in oral storytelling is the fact that the hearer's attention span is limited by the current line or verse. The hearer has no time to go back and compare with what was said earlier. Nor can the hearer look ahead. The interaction between speaker and hearer is live, in real time.

A written narrative, on the other hand, whether short story, poem, or novel, is deliberately constructed and allows for (and usually requires) copious revisions by the author. Sentences can be long, running into thousands of words, as the famous sentence of Molly Bloom's soliloquy that ends *Ulysses* does, and as does Bohumil Hrabal's one-sentence monologue of a novel *Dancing Lessons for the Advanced in Age*.

Written narratives encourage linear reading but allow the reader to go back and check things and make comparisons, or to skip ahead, even right to the end, to relieve suspense. A reader might even choose to peruse some material in reverse order of the chapters. Such a strategy is useful, for example, in reading and understanding *Time's Arrow*, by Martin Amis.

For this reason we must distinguish between nonlinear narratives, where what is meant is an "out of sequence" narrative, versus nonlinear reading styles, which are always possible on the part of the reader. However, the term "nonlinear narrative" is itself something of a misnomer, since most narratives do not in fact order the entire work in a single ordered sequence. Even when they do, the sequence, as we have shown throughout this book, is less commonly chronological.

In managing time in a written narrative, writers can rely on the fact that the reader will have access to the earlier part of the book, so reminders are not needed of who a minor character really is or of when something referred to earlier actually happened. A lesser degree of explicitness and situating of events is called for, though of course the more that is left out, the greater the likelihood of incoherence.

The reader is also expected to return to the book repeatedly after intervals away from it and will therefore be expected to be able to find her place. Writers can often help this process by including, in addition to page numbers and a detailed table of contents, various supplements such as a list of the cast of characters, a map, a family tree (as *One Hundred Years of Solitude* does), or a chronology, for reference purposes, of key events (as *War and Peace* does). Written narratives also allow for more time for long descriptive passages, where scene and atmosphere—of an external or internal world—can be gradually built up.

Finally, written narratives, as we have seen in the case of Robbe-Grillet and Faulkner, can easily allow for phenomena like achrony. The timeline can still be pieced together in such cases by careful study of the entire narrative. Opportunities for the hearer to piece things together are lacking in the case of purely oral narrative. As Herman (2004) argues, oral narrative forms such as conversational storytelling exhibit a preference for a determinate temporal structure, in order to communicate and interpret temporal and causal information while coping with the conversational constraint of (typically) short turns. Thus conversational storytelling, at least, would be expected to exploit only a small subset of the ordering devices found in written narratives.

TIME IN STORY-GENERATION SYSTEMS

Let us move from "organic" narratives generated by humans to synthetic ones generated by artificially intelligent agents. As described in the introduction, AI research has produced several systems that can generate stories. The stories in question have included animal fables, fairy tales, murder mysteries, and Arthurian legends. These systems must be provided with large amounts of knowledge, in advance, for each task. They actually generate language and can decide what to say next, based on goals that the characters are provided with and plans for how to realize them.

A basic distinction can be drawn between a story-generation system and a narrative-prose generator. The former type of system attempts to construct new stories from scratch. A well-known example is the MINSTREL system of Scott Turner (1994), which uses a goal-based problem-solving reminiscent of TALE-SPIN, discussed in the introduction. The goals in MINSTREL include not just ones for a character, as in TALE-SPIN, but author-level goals as well, namely, goals that relate to dramatic structure, including suspense, foreshadowing, and so on, and also goals to realize the story in natural language. The system is tied to the domain of Arthurian fable and manifests its creativity by starting with existing schemas related to these goals and then modifying them as needed to solve the goals. For example, as discussed in a review of MINSTREL by Rafael Pérez y Pérez and Mike Sharples (2004), if the system is given a goal to create a scene where a knight kills himself, it may try to find a plan where the knight can kill himself by drinking a potion. In doing so it will search through memory for existing schemas, finding, in our example, only one where a princess deliberately drinks a potion to make herself ill. Instead of giving up, it tries to "imagine" some different scenario with a similar outcome. By reasoning that being killed is similar to being injured, and that injury can result in death, MINSTREL will change the goal to one where a knight does something to injure himself. As there is still no schema matching this goal, MINSTREL will try to generalize the goal to find anyone doing something to injure himself (or herself), rather than just a knight. This time the princess schema is matched, and MINSTREL chooses a scene where the knight kills himself by drinking a potion.

While MINSTREL emphasizes creativity, addressing temporal ordering is not its primary focus. The JOSEPH system of Raymond Lang (2003) is one that does pay attention to time and is based on the framework of story grammars.[1] This framework was proposed for use in AI by Rumelhart (1975), among others, and has been used quite extensively for story understanding.[2] In Rumelhart's scheme a story might be made up of a setting and an episode, the latter made up, say, of one or more events (which may in turn contain episodes) followed by an outcome. JOSEPH takes this at least several steps further. Each episode begins with an initiating event followed by an emotional reaction on the part of the protagonist, then an action by the protagonist, and finally an outcome at the end of the episode. The time interval for the initiating event BEGINS the time interval for the episode and is IMMEDIATELY BEFORE the reaction. The time interval for the outcome ENDS the time of the episode, and the reaction by the protagonist STARTS BEFORE the action. The relation STARTS BEFORE is not a primitive relation in the interval calculus. However, it can be expressed as a disjunction of other relations: A STARTS BEFORE B if and only if either A is BEFORE B or A is IMMEDIATELY BEFORE B or A OVERLAPS B or B is DURING A or B ENDS A. See table 4 for details. It should be obvious from these statements that the underlying temporal representation used is the same as the one in this book, namely, the interval calculus.

Story grammars inherit the weaknesses of scripts, discussed in the introduction, where brittleness and overfitting to a domain cause seri-

TABLE 4. *STARTS-BEFORE in the interval calculus*

A before B	AAA BBB
A immediately before B	AAABBB
A overlaps B	AAAA BBBB
B during A	AAAAAA BBB
B ends A	AAAAAA BBB
A before B	AAA BBB

ous problems.[3] They can also be criticized from the standpoint of time: such a grammar presupposes a timeline that is consistent with it, and in a retrospective story, the outcome may be provided in advance, in contrast to JOSEPH's rules. A story grammar, which prescribes the plot as well as the order of events in the grammar, that is, globally constraining the narrative, fails miserably when we try to address the real timelines seen in narratives in this book; such timelines are extremely varied and elaborate in their temporal structure.

In contrast to story generators a narrative-prose generator has a large part of the story content already preselected by the user (or programmer). This type of system is given the outline of a story at a fairly abstract level, which typically includes a chronological ordering of events. The most elaborate of the narrative-prose generation systems to date, called STORYBOOK (from Callaway 2000), takes a set of propositions (who did what to whom) in the story world; this input representation is assumed to be the Russian formalist notion of a "fabula," that is, the "raw materials of the story," as defined by Wallace Martin (1986, 107). STORYBOOK must be provided with the characters, the scenes and their settings, the events and their properties, and a temporal ordering (usually a partial ordering) of those events. STORYBOOK's narrative planner takes the fabula and converts it to a sequence of sentence meanings, laid out in intended text order. This sequence corresponds to the Russian formalist notion of the *suzjet*, or the ordering of what is presented by the author, which is captured to a large extent (in terms of times and events) by the timeline.

Unlike the problem of computing timelines for narrative understanding, time in narrative-prose generators is easier to compute, since the system can be provided with the time stamps of input events in the story world. In converting from fabula to *suzjet*, STORYBOOK has parameters to specify which characters and events to focus on and what roles they should play in the narrative (hero, villain, etc.). It also has parameters for the point of view (narrator as character or disembodied narrator), the voice (first, second, or third person), and details of the plot. The choice of which particular strategy will best realize a particular literary effect and authorial goal in relation to global narrative constraints, such as those from plot, is a challenging question for which we don't yet have the answer. STORYBOOK relies very heavily on built-in defaults and user specifications for the values of these parameters.

The plot includes goals of the characters, incidental objects that function like stage props, and also the sequence of events and scenes in the appropriate temporal order. In computing the order, STORYBOOK uses an inventory of temporal relations similar to those we discussed in chapter 3 ("Computing Timelines"). STORYBOOK will automatically select exactly one path through a set of hand-created possibilities for sequences of events and scenes in the microworld of the story. The program is careful to ensure consistency across scenes, pruning inconsistent paths and relying on "safe" scenes that don't clash with anything else. The program then produces a hierarchical structure for the narrative, deciding along the way what tense to use and when to shift tense. In doing so it reasons whether to generate dialogue or not—in dialogue, conversations may be in a different tense from the narrative around them (e.g., present versus past tense, respectively). The system then plans individual sentences and then realizes them using a sentence-generation component that avails of a grammar and lexicon of English.

The following fragment of STORYBOOK's output for "Little Red Riding Hood" shows shifts in tense (implicit in the event mentions) and the use of time expressions and connecting words.

> Little Red Riding Hood had not <u>gone</u> far when she <u>met</u> a wolf.
> "Hello," <u>greeted</u> the wolf, who was a cunning-looking creature.
> "Where are you <u>going</u>?"

"I am going to my grandmother's house," Little Red Riding Hood replied.

"Ah, well then, take care in the forest, for there are many dangers." And then the wolf left.

Little Red Riding Hood was not in a hurry. Indeed, she gathered wild flowers and chased the pretty butterflies.

Meanwhile the wolf ran ahead very quickly and soon arrived at grandmother's house. He knocked on the door gently. The old lady asked, "Who is there?"

The wolf replied, "It is Little Red Riding Hood, your granddaughter."

And so the old lady opened the cottage door. The wolf rushed in immediately and devoured the lady in one bite. Then he shut the door and climbed into the old lady's bed.

Much later Little Red Riding Hood arrived at grandmother's house. She knocked on the door and shouted, "Grandmother, it is Little Red Riding Hood."

"Pull the string. The door will open."

And so Little Red Riding Hood opened the door and walked in. "Grandmother, what big eyes you have."

"All the better to see with, dear."

The timeline involves the phase of the poor girl meeting the wolf, then her going off gathering wildflowers and chasing butterflies, while the wolf rushes ahead (these two events are more or less in parallel), and then his arriving at her grandmother's house before she does. Exactly the same timeline representation we use in analysis can easily be used in generation; however, STORYBOOK predated the development of our timelining technology.

STORYBOOK is a significant advance over the paragraph-sized monologues generated by systems that came before. The temporal coherence of its narrative derives from decisions made by the system at many different levels, albeit relying largely on user settings and system defaults.[4] The price of such linguistic dexterity, however, is that for each new story, a substantial quantity of knowledge must be encoded by hand and supplied to the system.

Narrative generation systems can also produce multimedia narratives, where temporal coherence across different modalities such as speech, text, and gesture can be critical. In the AUTOBRIEFER authoring system of Elisabeth Andre and her colleagues (2003), the author provides a high-level outline for a presentation, which the system then fleshes out, automatically generating an animated multimedia presentation in formats such as Microsoft PowerPoint. Although the system doesn't generate fiction, its goal of a temporally coherent narrative is relevant for fictional output as well. AUTOBRIEFER's presentation is narrated by an artificial agent, that is, a "talking head." The user may provide more or less detail in terms of the overall outline, and the system fills in the rest, using or creating media elements (e.g., a summary from a query to a search engine or a provided image or video with a caption), allocating the number of slides, introducing narrative segues (e.g., "Next, I'll go over . . ."), deciding which elements should be laid out on each slide, and what should be presented as text versus speech (shorter descriptions, of fewer than 250 characters, as well as figure captions, are preferred for speech synthesis). AUTOBRIEFER also synchronizes the gestures—lip movements and pointing to the slide content—with the rest of the animated presentation.

The latter feat of temporal coordination is a result of using a narrative planner as well as a layout generator that are each temporally aware. For example, a rule inside the planner specifies that a title should start displaying one time unit before a video on that slide starts and should end being displayed exactly one time unit after the video ends. All such discourse time constraints along with any specified by the user are input to a SputLink-like constraint solving program called Cassowary, which determines a consistent spatial and temporal layout. Although sophisticated in temporal synchronization, AUTOBRIEFER, unlike STORYBOOK, doesn't attempt to generate text using linguistic knowledge; instead it fills in a template-driven form that controls what text gets generated.

INTERACTIVE FICTION

Research in computer animation has been successful in creating lifelike characters with models of emotion and the ability to communicate with speech and gesture. This technology is highly immersive and almost irresistible to the young (and sometimes the old as well). It has had a great influence in the entertainment industry, including video gaming and animated cinema. Games, like animated films, are heavily scripted, and the characters have to be told what to say at each point (unlike STORYBOOK and other generation systems). Obviously, there is a substantial opportunity to couple game technology with story-generation systems.

A computer game is an unlikely environment for embedding a literary narrative. Many popular computer games are action games, which involve a character moving about in a virtual space, performing physical actions like running or flying, and striking at and decimating other living bodies (a feature that makes them attractive as a tool for training soldiers). This sort of target recognition and destruction is not what makes fiction appealing. Even when the synthetic characters in the virtual world are embellished with all kinds of physical attributes and made to look and feel and sound more like real people, they don't interact with players in ways that contribute to the development of narrative structures in terms of plots and character evaluations. In such games there is a severely limited inventory of possible actions. Further, the subject matter of these games is not the bread and butter of our struggles in daily life. The literary appeal of such adolescent fun-oriented games is therefore minimal.

In addressing the problem of aesthetic appeal, interactive fiction (and drama) systems have striven for a more open-ended literary experience for the player. The player who adventures into a microworld of fiction can discover and figure out the physics and laws of that world in a way that is hard to do in traditional fiction, where a puzzle may be deciphered or not by the end of a work. The user can also become a significant character in the game. The player can experience fictional processes at different speeds. And the writer of such fiction can become adept both at constructing stories from a fixed palette of particular elements and assembly tools and sometimes in anticipating how the reader (player) will interact with it.

The provision of autonomy to the player ("reader") in deciding where the narrative should head means that authorial control and intent is weakened. Imagine a game version of "The Lady with the Pet Dog" where Gurov doesn't return to S—— to visit Anna, or where he visits her and then the player decides that she should shun him. The reader's emotional evaluation of such an outcome is unlikely to be as sympathetic as it is in Chekhov's version. Yet there may be alternative versions that would lead to interesting character transitions, for example, one that extends the Chekhov story in a way that allows the scene at the Slavyansky Bazaar Hotel to culminate in a dramatic outcome, such as death, a revelation, or some extraordinary change in Gurov. Note that in our analysis of the ending of the story (figure 24, in chapter 6), the reader evaluations would have to involve a switch in polarity for there to be a major change in their transitions.

Whether the player will hit upon an aesthetically satisfying outcome may depend on chance and on her literary skills, in the latter case requiring her to remember the course of the narrative thus far, including her history of evaluations along the way. An appropriate treatment of narrative progression is therefore crucial in interactive fiction (and drama).

Interactive fiction incorporates a blend of characteristics of oral and written narrative. As in written narrative the user can pause or scroll through a history of what has happened earlier. As in oral narrative the reader cannot look ahead. And as in some oral narratives, audience participation is allowed (in oral narratives the participation often occurs as a variety of call-and-response game). Unlike with either written or oral narrative, the reader may be able to explore choice points and also completely change the story line and the perception of the characters. Clearly, there has to be some way of preserving authorial intent, while allowing for a high degree of interactivity and "player" autonomy. The author might feel robbed of his vision, rather like Chekhov might have felt about an ending that wasn't "blessed." Creativity is an extremely personal thing.

FAÇADE (from Mateas and Stern 2005) is the world's first full-fledged interactive drama game. It is a wonderfully engrossing game (even for a nongamer like me) that incorporates a number of innovative AI techniques. FAÇADE is deliberately focused on a small virtual space (an apartment) and offers only two characters to interact with: Trip and Grace, who are modeled on George and Martha in Edward Albee's *Who's Afraid of Virginia Woolf*. Like them Trip and Grace come with a lot of prior emotional baggage. The couple, equipped with full-body animation along with facial expressions and prerecorded bits of speech, welcome the player into their apartment for an evening together, which soon turns ugly as the player gets caught up in the turmoil of their marriage.

By the end of the game, the player will have contributed to particular airings of Trip's and Grace's discontent and to irrevocable decisions by the couple regarding their relationship. The player can say whatever he likes and can flirt with his hosts; sometimes his input will be understood, sometimes not, but Trip and Grace don't reveal that. The play unfolds even if the player doesn't interact. The outcome is of course uncertain when one starts, and each game results in a different outcome. (This lack of control on the part of the player is often off-putting to seasoned game players who find that their interactions can be ignored.)

FAÇADE models narrative sequence in terms of story beats, for example, a dialogue fragment between the couple that exposes a conflict about Grace's obsession with redecorating or a harking back to a disastrous honeymoon trip to Italy. The next remaining beat is chosen based on its preconditions, taking into account the player's moment-by-moment interaction, the beats so far, and the constraint of an overall dramatic arc, one that follows a Freytagian model.

FAÇADE is a short game—one can reach an end point in about twenty minutes. Computer games, however, tend to be obsessively long, lasting for days in some cases. FAÇADE can potentially attract game players who hunger for a "deeper" interaction with game characters. Unlike a short story, however, the interactive drama genre involves considerable interaction with the player, which doesn't really allow enough time for narrative progression to develop. The experience of playing FAÇADE, as it stands, leaves one in an emotionally somewhat dissonant state. The short game time, among other factors, works against the development of a more measured relationship of player with characters. To reiterate the point made earlier, narrative progression, as we have explored it in this book, is key to the future success of genres like interactive drama.

nn (from Montfort 2007) takes up where STORYBOOK leaves off in terms of being the world's first interactive fiction system that uses intelligent strategies to temporally order its output. The system takes a list of events and their participants in the story world and plans how to narrate them. It then uses text-generation methods to produce its output. At each cycle of the system's narration and the user's interaction, the subsequent list of events to be narrated can change.

nn considers seven ways of ordering information that Genette identified in his work: chronicle, retrograde, zigzag, analepsis, prolepsis, syllepsis, and achrony. We have already discussed chronicle, retrograde, zigzag, and achrony. Analepsis is a fancy term for flashback, whereas prolepsis is a flash-forward. Syllepsis involves an order that isn't primarily related to chronology. As Nick Montfort points out, syllepsis is instantiated in George Perec's *Life: A User's Manual*. In that book the chapters are ordered mainly in terms of different apartments in a building at 11, Rue Simon-Crubellier in the 17th arrondissement in Paris (the street, like Xiros and Wessex, is entirely fictitious). Of course chronology does enter into syllepsis, since the narratives within each segment (e.g., in Perec's *Life* in each spatially organized chapter) must be narrated in some order, and so some principled temporal ordering is used there as well. In fact, to help the reader better digest the "manual," Perec also provides a chronology in an appendix.

nn implements chronicle, retrograde, and achrony by sorting the input events in chronological, reverse chronological, and random order, respectively. Zigzag involves interleaving between the two time periods, while allowing for a refinement to this order that permits events in a single physical location to be narrated together. For analepsis the flashback is injected based on a criterion for selecting the past event, for example, by using one of the following rules:

Select the most salient event from the first occasion when the focalizer (i.e., particular character from whose viewpoint the world is experienced) encountered this character.
Select the most salient things that the focalizer has seen happen in this room in the past, up to three of them.

For syllepsis events are organized into categories, and the narrator can move through each of the categories in chronological or other order. Prolepsis is more of a challenge, because *nn* doesn't have access to future events that could result from subsequent interaction. For prolepsis *nn* typically resorts to picking "inevitable" events such as the sun going down or nuclear missiles arriving.

nn's generation component thinks pretty hard about selecting the tense to use for narration, along with connecting words to express temporal relations (such as "then" and "before that"). It varies the narrator's speech time (ST) and the reference time (RT) with respect to the event time stamp to decide on the particular tense to use. For example, a chronicle that *nn* generates includes the following:

> Your senses were humming as you viewed the broad, circular, encircling Plaza of the Americas. The morning had concluded. It was midday then.

Similarly, an achrony can be generated, where the connecting words are left out. Although *nn* has all these ordering capabilities at its disposal, it does not itself reason as to when it is best to use one of the seven orderings. The choice of which particular strategy will best realize a particular literary effect and authorial goal remains very much an open question. Annotated corpora for literary texts can help address this question, as they will allow one to track particular timeline patterns and examine their correlations with plots and character evaluations. (For more details on narratological concepts as used in interactive fiction, see Cavazza and Pizzi 2006.)

TIME MANAGEMENT IN STORY AUTHORING

To keep track of content for their literary works, writers have normally followed ad hoc procedures, such as outlines on index cards, maps and diagrams, scribbled notes, and such. A visitor to Rowan Oak, Faulkner's home in Oxford, Mississippi, cannot miss the outline for each day of his week-spanning novel *A Fable* that he scrawled on the walls of his study.

Today computer-literate authors can manually create timelines using standard business software such as Microsoft Word, Excel, or Project. All the reader needs to do is to associate chunks of text with specific times. Faulkner, writing today, might easily have spared his walls! Writers also have more-specialized time-aware visualization products available (such as MIT's SIMILE timeline visualizer, Inxight's TimeWall, GeoTime from Oculus, and Intelligent Software Solutions' WebTAS), though these latter tools tend to be less well known outside the intelligence and defense communities. Note that these visualization tools don't handle fuzzy dates and times nor the set of interval relations that TimeML allows.

The fact that these tools aren't specifically tailored to writers makes them more or less independent of the writer's method of producing text. A writer could update the spreadsheet before she starts, as she goes along, or at the end, and so on.

Tools aimed more specifically at writers allow the user to manually record and thereby keep track of what characters are up to at particular points in the narrative. Such tools (like Dramatica Pro and Power Structure) come with their own theories of how to organize information in a narrative. For example, Dramatica Pro asks questions like "Does your main character change or remain steadfast?" and it allows the user to track narrative progression in terms of what it calls "plot points." These tools require that the user answer lots of questions, which writers can find not only onerous but also distracting from a creative standpoint. The tools' main advantage is that they provide for a level of detailed book-keeping, thereby guarding against inconsistencies and loose ends.

Unlike generic tools this latter variety of tools runs the risk of confining rather than liberating the writer. A writer may have no idea how to answer many of the questions posed by the tool, and abstracting the literary task in a particular way may not be conducive in the first place to writing. Writers also make use of differing methodologies: some writers design or plan first and then write, others do the opposite, and still others, a majority, seem to interleave one with the other; some, like Laurence Sterne, boldly announce their plans as part of the writing; and finally, there are the blessed few who do not seem to need to plan at all. Writing also usually requires relentless revision; as Dr. Johnson soundly advised: "Read over your compositions, and where ever you meet with a passage which you think is particularly fine, strike it out." Revision can alter overall themes, plots, chronologies, and so on in radical ways. Any tool aimed at fiction writers must come to terms with the sheer multiplicity of ways in which writers arrive at their final product. A tool that imposes its particular methodology on the author is likely to be less useful, except to beginners.

In all these first-generation tools, the computer is not engaged at all in synthesizing text for the writer, nor can it understand any of the text the writer has produced. Manually recording everything, especially at a fine-grained level, can more than double the work of writing a novel. Once the trajectory engine (figure 28, in chapter 7) becomes available for widespread use with literary texts, these could form part of a new wave of second-generation tools. Writers could examine the trajectories of various characters, checking for consistency, characterizing points at which character evaluations by the reader are predicted to emerge, and so forth. They would have a mirror to see work as it might unfold in the reader's eye. Faulkner, working on Benjy's narrative with such tools, could hit a button to analyze and visualize the timeline of the work in progress. And Chekhov, newly awakened to the time phases and transitions in "The Lady with the Pet Dog" (figure 24, in chapter 6) and enjoying a neat animation of the action along the timeline, might modulate his effects a little, perhaps shortening the time span between the confrontation in the theater to the scene at the Slavyansky Bazaar Hotel to a few months rather than few years. However, given the 75 percent accuracy of systems like TARSQI on news, there is still more research needed before such tools can achieve the much higher accuracy levels needed for everyday writerly use on literary fiction. One does not trouble the shades of Faulkner or Chekhov lightly!

The word, despite often being written and involving abstract symbols rather than pictures, is all-powerful and can produce altered states of consciousness. In oral storytelling, where it all started, the connection between speaker and hearer is live, in real time. This requires that the writer be considerate of the hearer's memory limitations, in turn providing more explicit temporal cues. Now, several millennia later, interactive fiction (and drama) allows the player ("reader") freedom in deciding where the narrative should head, at the expense of challenging authorial control and intent. To allow characters to develop adequately while allowing for interactivity, interactive systems need to take reader evaluations and transitions into account.

In deciding what to talk about next, fiction-generation systems have an easier time computing timelines and establishing temporal coherence compared with fiction-understanding systems. However, generation systems are faced with too many challenges compared to the creativity that human authors can provide for the reader; they are best coupled with human generation of literary material. It may be more feasible to provide a paraphrase capability for use as an author's aid; such a tool would generate variants of phrases or sentences, offering a menu of choices.

Authoring environments for writers will increasingly provide sophisticated tools to record timelines. Current tools require that this be done manually, which is far too tedious and intrusive to be of general utility. One fatal flaw of these tools is their tendency to impose particular creative methodologies on the author. Once the systems based on capabilities described in this book have been made accurate enough with fictional corpora, a second generation of tools will automatically generate timelines and character evaluations for writers from their work.

Conclusion

The central claim of this book is that the timelines needed for understanding the temporal aspects of all human narratives can be represented based on the annotation scheme described here. In the many examples drawn from my favorite texts, including those discussed by narratological scholars, events and times in the narrative and their temporal and subordinating relations are captured, from the standpoint of a conservative interpretation, using the TimeML standard, with some extensions to handle subnarratives and correspondences across fictional worlds.

Hopefully, the reader who has gotten this far will be convinced by my a priori arguments of the truth of this claim. There are also grounds for qualified optimism in terms of substantiating this claim computationally. Timelines for fictional texts can be annotated by humans in TimeML. Machines trained on annotated corpora have been able to produce timelines at 75 percent accuracy for news texts and have been used for a variety of languages and text genres. However, these programs haven't been applied in the large to fiction because of the lack of annotated fiction corpora—in turn because fiction is not perceived as "important" by the funding powers that be. Once corpora of literary texts are created and marked up with timelines, using existing editing tools, the computer can mark up timelines for thousands of literary narratives, allowing for empirical studies of time in narrative to get off the ground. This can help generate new data, test hypotheses, and also enhance the reading experience.

The psychological evidence to date suggests that humans simulate the events of a story as they read it. Subjects appear to subconsciously reenact actions they read about, providing a basis for an emotional response to the text. A second, entirely novel claim is that narrative progression can be characterized in terms of changes in readers' evaluations of characters over the course of the narrative. These evaluations, sympathetic or antipathetic to a character's situation, are made in terms of a moral framework that is (to some extent) culturally provided, and they allow us to express empathy in ways that reinforce our own moral sense of who we are and have become. Transitions, monotonic and nonmonotonic, in evaluations provide insight into how characters are transformed. This claim involves qualitative judgments, and it can be verified by measuring interannotator agreement on character evaluations. These evaluations can be learned using a statistical classifier and can be superimposed on the spatiotemporal trajectories of characters in a narrative. Accuracies for automatic character evaluations also need to be established to back this second claim. I further argue that events whose outcomes lead to nonneutral character evaluations by the reader are more significant. This latter prediction can be tested by psychological and neurological experiments.

Given that subjects carry out simulations while reading narratives, a third claim is that the simulated time of an event in a work of fiction is based on whatever cues are present in the text, falling back in other cases on the reader's commonsense knowledge of how long particular events might last. Researchers have developed an annotation scheme for marking such commonsense durations of events, with interannotator agreement being around 75 percent. Computers have also been trained to compute durations for events on such annotated data, as to whether they occur within a day or longer, achieving a similar score. Once substantial fiction corpora are annotated using TimeML, high reliability in annotating such durations for fiction would of course be a further backing for this claim. In terms of tempo I claim that the reader expects significant events to be allocated more space than nonsignificant events, and vice versa. Violations of this expectation (and good writers revel in the violation of expectations!) will result in longer reading times. This subclaim can of course be tested by psychological experiments.

TWO OPEN ISSUES

There are two key issues raised by this book that I believe are fundamental to how we understand literature. The first issue is how we mentally represent the complex temporal material we find in fiction. We already know that readers are biased creatures, overeager to remove details inconsistent with experience and inserting, when they can, imagined details that are consonant with their life experience and expectations. How does this affect the timeline? It is also known that readers prefer simpler timelines and represent how far apart events are in time. What types of subnarratives are less complex to deal with? Of the seven types of ordering that Genette has identified, which ones are easiest for readers to handle? How are distances in time scaled? What kinds of differences in temporal distance can readers distinguish? Are half orders of magnitude used during reading to estimate durations? What sorts of temporal relations do subjects construe for a work of fiction? Is the interval calculus too expressive compared to what humans do? (That would actually be good news from a computing standpoint, as various temporal relations might be collapsed.) A related set of questions concerns subnarratives. How well are subnarratives understood? One would predict that more complex subnarratives would require more time to integrate into memory, with more likelihood of errors in inference. Finally, does instructing the reader about the timeline improve appreciation of other aspects of a work?

The second issue is the nature of our emotional reactions to the narrative arc of fiction. These reactions were characterized in bivalent terms, of the reader being sympathetic or antipathetic to a character's situation. Clearly, one needs to carry out experiments to measure interannotator reliability in character evaluations. A high degree of reliability across pairs of readers for collections of texts will provide an empirical basis for the conceptualization of the actual reader. Also, my model of emotion has been confined to opposite poles of a continuum built around empathy, where the notion of what is desirable or undesirable behavior is given by cultural norms. This treatment of empathy can be extended to a more fine-grained scale rather than simply a Boolean judgment.

Further, there are many feelings other than empathy that readers can experience through reading, such as joy, sorrow, irritation, and anger, to name a few frequent ones; these emotions may be triggered not only by character evaluations but also by assessments of the environment in which the characters live and move. In other words the simulated world that the reader constructs can have all the analogues of the real-world stimuli that the brain normally attends to and evaluates for emotional impact. According to the theory of emotion proposed by Antonio Damasio (2003), if a real-world stimulus—a snake, a shadow on a wall—passes muster, various trigger points in the brain are activated, resulting in a general upheaval in the body with associated changes in heart rate, facial expressions, and so on. These entirely behavioral manifestations of emotional change give rise collectively to a qualitative state of recognizing and feeling the emotion, that is, the "mental" experience of sorrow or joy, along with characteristic thought patterns and themes associated with that emotion.

Research is needed to discover not only whether empathy based specifically on character evaluations has neural correlates, but also how feelings are triggered by particular patterns of a character's behavior and by purely formal patterns found in a work, in the quality of its prose, for example, but also especially in the shape of its narrative arc. Such research could involve brain imaging using fMRI scans correlated with subjective reports of feelings. Once the emotions that readers actually experience are tracked by means of experimental work, one can relate these emotions to a theory of emotions experienced by characters in a narrative.

GAZING INTO THE CRYSTAL BALL

Haruspication is a notoriously unscientific and error-prone exercise, but I have gone out on a limb and offered suggestions based on the rather unsatisfactory warrant of "experience." I have stated that it is only a matter of time before authoring environments for writers will increasingly provide sophisticated tools to record timelines. Such tools will not make the fatal error of imposing particular creative methodologies on the author. Eventually there will be literary search engines that can take advantage not only of timelines and character evaluations but also of text categorization and sentiment analysis technologies that would allow one to retrieve text segments satisfying certain qualitative properties. There will also be a role for animation that brings to life the most memorable characters from the world of fiction.

LIMITS

The resonances created in our minds when we read fiction have been explored here in terms of one particular cognitive slice: time. The exploration has been in terms of purely computational constructs that allow for a formal representation of timeline and changes in character evaluations.

Computation, however, is only a means to an end. Ultimately, one purpose of art is communication, and art is most successful when it results in deep arousal of the reader or listener. This requires a much richer understanding of language, especially literary language, in all its nuances, as well as an appreciation for the culture of the literary arts.

Humans are pretty good at all that, especially those who have retained their sense of wonder and who have spent a lot of time attuning themselves to careful reading. Computers don't really have the right sort of biological and social makeup to acquire such understanding and appreciation. Nevertheless, this book has argued that computation can still be extremely useful in modeling, relatively precisely, how time, that sublime and often mysterious concept, structures the understanding and creation of fictional narratives.

NOTES

INTRODUCTION

1. There is a small but active subcommunity of narratology scholars working in corpus linguistics, in particular the work of David Herman (e.g., Herman [2001], Herman [2005], Salway and Herman [2008]), whose goals of formulating an empirical discipline of narratology are similar to mine. Although they have taken several key steps in advancing toward these goals, they are yet to avail of the kinds of advanced techniques for timeline and plot analysis that my account provides.

2. Rabinowitz distinguishes the actual audience from two other ever-present audiences: One is the authorial audience, which accepts "the author's invitation to read in a particular socially constituted way that is shared by the author and his or her accepted reader" (1988, 20). As Rabinowitz clarifies, the authorial audience of Ian Fleming's *Live and Let Die* is expected to be racist (as well as, of course, familiar with the cold war). This audience is further distinguished from the narrative audience, which pretends that the work of fiction is real. "The authorial audience knows it is reading a work of art, while the narrative audience believes what it is reading is real" (100). Thus, the narrator of *War and Peace* is "writing for an audience that not only knows (as does the authorial audience) that Moscow was burned in 1812, but that also believes that Natasha, Pierre, and Andrei 'really' existed, and that the events of their lives 'really' took place" (95). The actual/authorial/narrative audience distinction can be cast in terms of possible world semantics; for a brief account along these lines, see Ryan (1991, 72).

3. In chapter 6 ("Characters in Time"), I have more to say about the relation between the identities that a narrative constructs for agents in a narrative and about Ricoeur's ideas on character.

4. A scientific theory of how humans understand natural language must provide an account of how the brain understands language, starting from the audio signals in any heard utterance, tracking the brain areas activated, the computations carried out, all the way to the accompanying response. Such a theory must provide a neural basis for language understanding, as opposed to

a purely functional box diagram that isn't tied to brain functioning. Although "functionalist" models have resulted in working systems capable of syntactically analyzing sentences in the *Wall Street Journal* and extracting key bits of information from them, computer systems using artificial neural networks (the closest approximations to computing brains) have only the most rudimentary language-understanding capabilities. One might further require that such a scientific theory provide an explanation of how a child acquires language. Here the dominant paradigm (as articulated in popular works such as Steven Pinker's scintillating book *The Language Instinct*) is that of Chomskyan Universal Grammar, namely, an innate set of rules that covers all human languages. When the child acquires a particular language, this involves turning on a number of switches or "parameters" for that language. There has been considerable debate as to the validity of this paradigm; for a critical discussion leaning toward an alternative paradigm, see Tomasello (2006). Finally, the question of how a genetic blueprint such as Universal Grammar might have evolved with Homo sapiens, whether by natural selection or by other means, remains a mystery.

5. Intelligence, an overloaded term, can mean many different things. AI researchers have focused on capabilities deemed of intellectual value, such as game playing (chess, rather than rugby or boxing), language, vision, logical and probabilistic reasoning, robotics, and so forth, but they have not made much headway with modeling creativity, intuition, and emotions, and with a few exceptions, they have mostly ignored the modeling of social intelligence, business savvy, political leadership, mass manipulation, and other kinds of "intelligent" skills that are valued, rightly or wrongly, by society.

6. As an example, the Script Applier Mechanism (SAM) program of Cullingford (1978) was an early story-understanding system that came out of the Yale effort. It activated scripts based on the mentions, in the input story, of a script setting (e.g., a restaurant), precondition (e.g., a character being hungry), an event in the script, and so on. Consider the following example:

John went to a restaurant. He ordered a hot dog. The waiter said they didn't have any. He asked for a hamburger. When the hamburger came, it was burnt. He left the restaurant.

SAM was able to answer commonsense inference questions such as whether John sat down in the restaurant (probably), whether he ordered a hot dog (yes), what the waiters served him (a hamburger), and whether John paid for his food (no, because he was angry over his burnt hamburger). Scripts are also viewed as essential in resolving discourse-dependent references. Thus, given the sentence "The hamburger came," SAM would use the restaurant script along with information from the prior discourse to infer that the agent who brought the hamburger was the waiter.

7. There are also interesting aspects of scripts that are related to the notions of character discussed in this book. Schank and Abelson also discuss "personal scripts," which are scripts activated by agents with stereotypical roles. Their examples include characters like the Flatterer, the Good Samaritan, the Jealous Spouse, the Pickpocket, the Spy, and so on. These roles involve particular patterns of behavior. In my view primitive actions such as retaliation can be executed without being triggered by a script for, say, a Jealous Spouse. Rather than indexing (or cataloging) behavior by the characteristics of agents, one could index behavior by constellations of primitive plot moves that an agent experiences or carries out.

8. Schank and Abelson offer the following example, where it is unclear whether there is one script (taking a trip) or two (taking a trip and visiting a museum), or even three (bus trip, museum visit, and a train trip): "John took a bus to New York. In New York he went to a museum. Then he took a train home" (1977, 31).

9. In order to accommodate such variation, scripts can be organized into "tracks." Thus a restaurant script may have a fast-food track, a cafeteria track, and so forth. Of course, this strategy doesn't take one very far: the problem of a lack of specification for the set of scripts applies to tracks as well. Another strategy is to simplify scripts. De Jong (1982) introduced the notion of a "sketchy script," which focuses only on the crucial events in a script, ignoring the rest. When one is processing a story, the mention of one of these key events can trigger the script. Thus the word "apprehension," used in the sense of arrest of suspects rather than anxiety, could invoke an Arrest sketchy script. Once triggered, the other slots in the sketchy script, such as the crime, the culprit, and so on, would be skimmed for and, hopefully, found in the text. In other words by focusing on what is salient in a given situation, one can expect to find those salient items in the input. The use of sketchy scripts reduces the knowledge required in a script and allows for easier selection of a script. But the burden here is to determine what is salient. If salient information that isn't coded in the script is present in the input, the script won't be triggered directly.

10. In story understanding, Wilensky's Plan Applier Mechanism (PAM), from Wilensky (1978), was one of the first systems to use goals. Consider the following story input to PAM:

John wanted money. He got a gun and walked into a liquor store. He told the owner he wanted some money. The owner gave John the money and John left.

PAM was able to make commonsense inferences without the use of scripts. By construing every action in a story as instantiating some goal and a plan to realize that goal, it could infer that since stores have money and John wanted money, John's walking into the store could help achieve that goal. Likewise, since a gun could be used to threaten others, John's getting a gun could be used for threatening the store owner, who in turn has a goal of avoiding getting hurt, and so on. All these bits of commonsense knowledge were brought into play in linking the actions of characters to their goals and plans, by searching through a large space of possible goals and plans. As a result of such reasoning, PAM could answer questions such as why John obtained the gun (to rob the store), why the owner complied with the request for money (to avoid getting shot), and why John left (to avoid being apprehended).

11. To bring home the point about character-driven narrative, here is a fragment of a story generated by TALE-SPIN:

> George was very thirsty. George wanted to get near some water. George walked from his patch of ground across the meadow through the valley to a riverbank. George fell into the water. . . . Wilma wanted George to get near the meadow. Wilma wanted to get near George. Wilma grabbed George with her claw. Wilma took George from the river through the valley to the meadow.

Agents like George and Wilma know that water quenches thirst. So they have to make a plan to get to a source of water, given the geography of their physical environment. The characters are altruistic and must rescue those in danger of death; both of them know that George would drown if he stayed in the river.

1. TIMELINES

1. There are two formal views of tense in linguistics. The first view is that tense behaves rather like a pronoun (like "I" or "he"), which depends on who is speaking or who has been talked about earlier. The classic work of Reichenbach (1947) treats tenses as pronounlike referring expressions whose meaning is based on the speech time, the time of the event, and the reference time. Reference times include expressions such as "Tuesday" and "the next week," but can also be implicit in the text. In the sentence "By five o'clock, John had already left," the reference time is five o'clock, and the event of John's leaving precedes the reference time. Both these times precede the speech time. This ordering captures the semantics of the past perfect tense. In the simple past tense, the reference and event times coincide and precede the speech time. The second view is that tense is like a mathematical function, or "operator."

Thus "Margaret deceived Francis" means that there is a time prior to the speech time when the event of deception occurred. This sort of approach results in formal (modal) logics for representing tense, the best-known of which includes the work of Prior (1967).

2. This distinction between subjective time, with its tensed view of past, present, and future, and objective time, where time is viewed as a sequence extending across all time, is explored in the philosophy of McTaggart (1908), who distinguishes the former as what he called the "A-series" view of time and the latter as the "B-series." McTaggart goes on to argue that time is illusory because the A-series (which he claims was needed to represent change and motion) is contradictory. His argument, in essence, is that the A-series needs to express that an event has the property of being present and also being past (i.e., when the event becomes past). Since an event can't be present and past at the same time, the A-series will be contradictory without reference to the B-series, which provides the logic of succession; such a move is viewed (incorrectly) as inadmissible by McTaggart. For an interesting discussion of the philosophical issues this raises for fiction, see the two authors G. Currie (1999) and M. Currie (2007).

3. Thanks to Brent Spencer of Creighton University for pointing me to the following Web page with the quote: http://mockingbird.creighton.edu/NCW/chekwrit.htm.

4. The *Jean Santeuil* passage is from the translation by Jane Lewin in Genette (1980, 38).

5. See Ryan (1991) for a thorough discussion of the application of the logic of possible worlds to fiction. For a brilliantly concise introduction to possible worlds and why they matter to fiction, see Eco (1990).

6. The timeline shown is not the only one possible. In fact Rebecca Passonneau at Columbia University has suggested to me that "some day" refers to the narrator's speech time rather than the subordinated time in Jean's thoughts. I think this is less likely but certainly possible.

7. For examples such as "took a lively interest," the annotation guidelines (for TimeML, discussed later) call for marking the light verb "took" and the argument nominal "interest" as distinct event mentions, with a relation of identity between them. In the text for the example, I've simplified matters by marking "took a lively interest" as a single event mention. For reasons of space I've represented this mention in the diagram as "took (x11)." Similar considerations apply to "giving a courteous nod," "taking a sip," and so on. As for phrasal verbs like "set up," TimeML calls for just marking "set"; I chose to deviate slightly from the guidelines to make matters clearer to the reader.

8. The hunger artist goes on fasting, and people eventually forget that he's

there. As Zadie Smith (2003) has noted, his handlers (at the circus, where he ends up) eventually "neglect to continue the tally of days written on the front of the cage. No matter how long he starves, no time will appear to have passed in the world."

2. STORIES WITHIN STORIES

1. Sternberg points out that a statement expressed by one subject is fundamentally altered when it is cited by another; the former becomes an "inset" in the "frame" of the latter. The thing quoted "always subserves the global perspective of the quoter, who adapts it to his own goals and needs" (1982, 109).

2. From Hwang and Schubert (1992, 237), with the last sentence modified.

3. COMPUTING TIMELINES

1. Kamp and Reyle (1993) point out the weakness in the earlier notion of reference time used by Reichenbach (1947). In the passage quoted in the text, the Reichenbachian reference will stay at 10:00 a.m.

2. The underlying representation used by the computer is somewhat different, since the function computed by "+" (as in RT+P1M) is expressed in TimeML and TIMEX2 through multiple attributes, but those details are omitted here to keep the discussion simple and to avoid getting bogged down in the specifics of the attributes used.

3. See http://callisto.mitre.org.

4. So far what we have been calling "events" correspond to what linguists call "eventualities," which include both events and states. TimeML tags events as well as certain states, those which change during the narrative.

5. The underlying representation used by the computer is somewhat different, since the function computed by "=" as an assignment statement (as in RT=XXXX-XX-TAF) is expressed via multiple attributes.

6. The discussion references two markup standards: TIMEX2/TERN for time expressions, and TimeML for timelines. For a description of TIMEX2/ TERN, see Ferro et al. (2005); for TimeML, see Pustejovsky et al. (2005). Subordinating relations are part of TimeML; subnarrative relations are described in Mani and Pustejovsky (2004). For algorithms related to automatically generating TimeML mark-up, see Boguraev and Ando (2005) and Mani et al. (2006); for TIMEX2, see Mani and Wilson (2000) and Ahn, Rantwijk, and de Rijke (2007). For algorithms applied to accident reports, see Berglund, Johansson, and Nugues (2006); applications to medical narratives are described in Bramsen et al. (2006) and Zhou et al. (2006).

7. For general background on formal and computational work related to time and language, see the classic work of Reichenbach (1947) and the recent

edited volume by Mani, Pustejovsky, and Gaizauskas (2005). For representative work in computer science on the interval calculus and temporal constraint satisfaction problems, see J. Allen (1984) and Meiri (1996).

8. For a thorough linguistic approach to narrative ordering, see Kamp and Reyle (1993).

9. The statistical classifier I described (with its behavior shown in figures 13 and 14) is fairly standard, one of many off-the-shelf tools that are freely available on the Web. This particular one is called a Support Vector Machine.

10. The expression "recent" in "the world was so recent" should be annotated as a time expression with value PAST_REF, meaning somewhere in the past, but the annotator chose to leave it out. This is one sort of omission that results in variance across annotators.

11. An entirely different approach is found in the literary computing work on time of Jan Christoph Meister at the University of Hamburg. In his scheme (Meister 2005), times annotated by a human are sorted in terms of precedence as well as deictic relations (past, present, or future) with respect to the speech time. This is part of a broader project described in Meister's (2003) book on the semiotics of action in narrative, where a theory of action is developed. In that latter body of work, events annotated by a human based on different perspectives (social, cognitive, etc.) are grouped automatically into episodes that are then arranged into actions. Such an approach, while being an original and substantial contribution to narratology, isn't aimed at evaluating state-of-the-art tools for automatically building timelines; rather, it involves the use of computers in developing substantial theoretical extensions to particular (mainly structuralist-inspired) approaches to action in fiction.

4. CALENDAR TIMES

1. Proust's letters clearly mark him as a writer who was given to complaining about his various ailments, including insomnia. For example, in a letter to Maria Hahn, written from Dieppe in August 1889, he declares, "My nerves are frayed from insomnia" (from Kolb 1983, 98). In another letter, written to Georges de Lauris in May 1903, he says, "I am exhausted after two days not only without sleep but without going to bed. I can't make up my mind to lie down!" (from Kolb 1983, 326).

2. Our master biological clock, located in the hypothalamus, runs on a twenty-four-hour cycle. It is sensitive to light from the retina, communicating this information to the pineal gland, a pine-cone shaped organ that secretes the tranquilizing hormone melatonin in response to lack of light.

3. Despite military people emphasizing punctuality and the use of twenty-four-hour clocks, the clock doesn't really rescue one from imprecision. For

example, the time of day is often measured in terms of the solar day, based on successive positions of the sun at midnight at the prime meridian (in Greenwich, located a pleasant boat cruise down the Thames from London). However, the time stated in terms of GMT is subject to seasonal variation and the slow lengthening of the day due to the Earth's nonuniform motion. Sidereal day, based on the time it takes for the earth to rotate around its axis (roughly, 23 hours and 56 minutes), is more precise but also subject to day lengthening. Atomic time is the most precise of all but is subject to relativistic effects.

4. All calendars are based on integral numbers of days in a year, whereas the number of days it takes for the earth to orbit the sun, the solar year, is a fractional and varying number, roughly 365.2422 days; this discrepancy results in various corrections involving leap years and other mechanisms. The oldest solar calendar was developed by the Egyptians as early as 3100 BC; it had a 365-day year with twelve 30-month days followed by another 5 days at the end of each year.

5. The term "chronicle" is also used by Genette (1980), somewhat differently, to reflect narration of events in their order of occurrence.

6. The timeline is thus straightforward; for readability we skip the marking of events in this passage.

7. Pepys's diary, incidentally, uses the Julian calendar, at a time when the year was stipulated to begin on March 25th. The Gregorian calendar was adopted in 1582 by Catholic countries in Europe, but with the rise of Protestantism its adoption elsewhere was delayed. It was finally accepted by the British and their colonies only in 1752. Nevertheless, Pepys continued to refer to January 1 (of the previous year) as New Year's Day.

8. See http://www.rideforclimate.com/journals/?cat=3.

9. Calendars are often of such symbolic significance that they are wedded to particular religious schools; the Greek Old Calendarists, who have clung to the Julian calendar, have often faced persecution. For more on the Old Calendarists, see http://www.omologitis.org/index_1024x768.htm.

10. The Iranian version of the Persian calendar uses Farsi month names, while Afghani versions use either Arabic or Pashto month names.

11. For details on calendars and time as a system of reckoning, see the excellent book by Reingold and Dershowitz (2004), which includes software to convert between the major calendars, both current and historical.

12. The four yugas (or epochs) of the ancient Hindu scriptures cover 4,320,000 years in all, less than a fifteenth of an *alautun*. According to those scriptures, one thousand such event-type cycles (68.48 *alautuns*) constitute only one day in the life of Brahma, the creator of the universe. At the end of each day, Brahma falls asleep in a state of Yogic meditation, during which

time everything that he creates is annihilated, to be recreated when he wakes up. In this way the cycle of eternity is tied to the diurnal cycle. Brahma is obviously running late, since not just the universe but the earth itself has existed for longer than one of his days. But running late may not matter much to him, since he's immortal. For a stimulating discussion of Hindu calendars, see Sen (2000).

5. TIME IN MIND

1. Unlike time, space (and motion) is directly perceived. Lakoff and Johnson (1980) have argued that our ability to communicate about abstract domains like time relies on metaphorical mappings of spatial concepts that are directly experienced. Experiments by Casasanto and Boroditsky (2007) have shown that when people make judgments about the temporal duration of visually perceived nonverbal stimuli (dots or lines on a screen), irrelevant spatial information about the stimulis's spatial displacement influences their judgments. However, the duration of the stimuli doesn't influence judgments of their distance. This provides indirect evidence that spatial reasoning is implicated in our understanding of time. Further, as earlier experiments by Boroditsky (2001) have suggested, the type of spatial metaphors used in one's native language seems to influence the way one thinks about time. For example, while both Mandarin and English speakers talk about time using horizontal metaphors ("front"/"back"), Mandarin speakers also talk about time with vertical metaphors ("up"/"down"); the use of vertical metaphors in English is less frequent and systematic. Mandarin speakers were faster to confirm that, for example, March comes earlier than April if they had just seen a vertical array of objects (perhaps related to their background in vertical metaphors) than if they had just seen a horizontal array; for English speakers the reverse was the case.

2. I have sidestepped the deeper metaphysical questions as to whether times or events are primitive in terms of actually existing independent of the mind. The computational approach in this book, which is in the spirit of AI work that models "commonsense" views of the world, is (loosely) compatible with a Kantian position, where (roughly stated) time and space are mental concepts that provide shape and structure to our experience. The psychological literature I cite is also compatible with this latter position.

3. How does one construct a representation of time for use in timelines without appealing to instants? There are two ways of addressing this question. One is to assume that intervals are primitive, banishing instants from the representation. So far the presentation of our timeline representation has not made use of instants. Another option, however, is to assume a more granular

view: time intervals are delimited by instants internally (with each time interval made up of a start instant t1 and an end instant t2), but without making these instants relevant. In other words instants aren't directly represented, but one can formally drill down to them if needed. The latter strategy has the advantage of flexibility.

4. Russell (1956) provides a well-known axiomatization of time based on events. To get a sense of what this involves, let me explicate the formalization of Walker (1948); see also Nauze (2002). Consider a simple narrative about our favorite character, involving a scene that leaves something to the imagination:

'Twas brillig, and it was also sweltering at the beach. Serena removed her blouse.

Let us imagine Francisco observing the beach through binoculars. He first sees an empty beach with a few gulls and then witnesses Serena's innocent unburdening. In the gap between the two events, there is a metaphorical cut in time, the cut that divides time into past and future. This gap, empty since there is no gap in time between the events (it's still okay to have it be empty), is what we will call an instant, i1, say. Then, after he watches her (partial) undressing, Francisco will look out to sea and notice that the tide is coming in. In the (again empty) gap between the event of seeing Serena and the event of seeing the tide, there is another metaphorical cut in time, the instant i2. Thus every change of state, irrevocable and forever advancing, is marked by an instant. And each instant presents an Augustinian vantage point, from which the disappeared past and the nonexistent future may be contemplated. The actual duration of an event is given by the difference in time between the delimiting instants that bound the event.

5. Memory of when particular past events occurred seems to involve not confabulation but rather well-defined psychological processes for organizing and retrieving information. Friedman (2001) argues that these processes are location based and distance based. With location-based processes a subject remembers when a past event occurred based on contextual patterns related to time (e.g., parts of the day or year) or personal experience (e.g., when the subject was in college). Distance-based processes are used to remember how far back an event was from the time of remembering; the ability to do this accurately may be based in part on how vivid the memory is. Chronological organization of events in memory does not seem to be involved. Narratives involving reminiscence, such as Proust's magnum opus, provide ample illustrations of both these organizational characteristics.

6. See Zwaan (1996), Van der Meer et al. (2002), and Kelter, Kaup, and Claus (2004).

7. It is not surprising that all these situations are unfamiliar to the average reader. The relativistic world is completely counterintuitive and at odds with the treatment of time and events in language and reasoning, and consequently also with the treatment in our timeline model as well. As Einstein's special theory of relativity shows, the time interval between events will vary, dependent on the speed of the observer. Thus the same event seen from a very fast-moving galaxy or spaceship will take less time than one seen from a slower-moving frame of reference like our own. This can result in the well-known paradoxes where a twin travels into space at high speed and returns younger than the twin on earth. Also, as explained by Einstein's general theory of relativity, clocks slow down as they get deeper into a gravitational field, so the same event clocked at the top of the Empire State Building will transpire faster than when it's clocked at the ground-floor lobby, though the difference is miniscule. According to the astronomer Paul Davies (2002), the Global Positioning System (GPS) must take these relativistic effects into consideration if navigators are to stay on course.

8. These results are also supported by Berman and Slobin (1994) in their cross-linguistic study of children's narrative skills. They found that in narrating a frog story from a picture book, children begin by listing events, then acquire the ability to arrange them into sequences, after which they can causally link them, before finally reaching a level where they can integrate events into plots. However, in limiting the study to stories elicited from a single picture book as a source, this particular study doesn't establish that these trends are borne out across a variety of different narratives.

9. In related work Halpin, Moore, and Robertson (2004) compared children's rewritings of exemplar stories in terms of the common events, the participants in the events, and their temporal order, using a thesaurus to aid in the comparison. The comparison algorithms were then used to automatically grade the rewritings, based on training data from humans.

6. CHARACTERS IN TIME

1. Translated from the Babylonian original in the *Encyclopedia of the Orient* (2008), http://lexicorient.com/e.o/texts/religion/gilgamesh08.htm.

2. See also Booth (1983) for further discussion of this issue.

3. A typical measure of agreement used in such situations is the kappa metric of Cohen (1960). See also Siegel and Castellan (1988).

4. In the *Rhetoric*, Aristotle (1954, bk. 2, pt. 8) defines the emotion of pity as a particular feeling associated with a particular type of cognitive reasoning, where the person having pity feels pain for the pitied, who doesn't deserve the evil that has befallen him. The person experiencing pity, Aristotle argues,

is able to empathize by imagining the same experience happening to him. In that same section he goes on to show how an orator can arouse pity in his audience.

5. Murray Smith (1995) defines a notion of allegiance on the part of a spectator of a film, which is a level of engagement resulting in spectators responding with sympathy or antipathy toward characters. In film, actions as well as the physical attributes of actors and their star status contribute to stereotypical inferences regarding their moral character. Smith speaks of characters who are "alloys" of positive and negative cultural traits, aimed at creating more rounded and realistic characters. However, these observations are not developed further into a full-fledged theory.

6. A more refined scheme would mark evaluations using a more nuanced theory of emotion than the merely Boolean or null classification described here. Further, such a scheme could, instead of marking the evaluations directly on events, mark them on higher-level structures in the narrative, such as the plot units of Lehnert ([1981] 1999). For further discussion of plot units, see Ryan (1991), Allen and Acheson (2000), Salway and Xu (2002), and Salway et al. (2003).

7. The cultural constructs evoked by narratives have been explored in a variety of works in sociolinguistics. Polanyi (1985) analyzes several constructs found in everyday stories told by Americans, for example, that withstanding pain is praiseworthy, people shouldn't hurt others, people can manipulate others, and so forth.

8. In personal stories that are narrated orally, the "evaluative" segments offered by narrators can of course influence the recipients' evaluations of the story. Such segments can reflect the importance of information to the narrator (Labov and Gravetsky 1967). However, the attitudes reflected in hearers' responses need not accord with those found in the speaker's evaluations. "Exit talk" by recipients can provide an indication of the recipients' attitudes to the story (Polanyi 1985). However, even when such segments are absent in the speaker's narrative, the hearer is still able to construct evaluations.

9. In chapter 4 ("Calendar Times"), I noted that space appears to persist, despite decay and change, whereas time moves on. In this chapter I add that time is one way of viewing space: while the locus of a place stays more or less constant (except for geological changes), its properties can change over time. In philosophy, there is a distinction (see Grenon and Smith [2004]) between items that endure through time, existing in full at each moment in time, and items whose identity is constituted over an interval of time. The items that endure, usually objects (including people and places), are called endurants; a person, despite obvious changes over the years, is still the same person.

Endurants are viewed as occupying space and are three-dimensional. In contrast, the things that take time, usually (the noninstantaneous) events and processes, such as the landing of an aircraft, are called perdurants. Perdurants are inherently four-dimensional. Grenon and Smith develop, for spatiotemporal reasoning, a SNAP ontology that takes a snapshot of endurants at a particular instant (and is thus three-dimensionalist, rather like a synchronic view), integrated with a SPAN ontology that represents perdurants as they evolve over a time interval that is four-dimensional (rather like a diachronic view).

7. TRACKING NARRATIVE PROGRESSION

1. For a readable introduction to computational linguistics (for freshmen), see Mani (2005a). Mitkov (2003) provides a collection of introductions to different areas. The links at the end of the book provide browsable information about online corpora. For those daring to dive deeper, the standard textbook on computational linguistics is now the highly readable Jurafsky and Martin (2000). For a guide to some of the statistical approaches in use today, see the rewarding Manning and Schutze (1999) and also the engineering-oriented Duda, Hart, and Stork (2000).

2. This computer science sense of parsing is to be distinguished from the more popular usage of the term "parsing," meaning to examine in a minute way; analyze critically, as Merriam-Webster's defines it.

3. For example, a minicorpus containing "Bombard Baghdad," "Blockade Bombay," and "The troops despise the president" would result in two instances of S → VP and one instance of S → NP VP, two instances of NP → ProperName, and two instances of NP → Determiner Noun. This process results in a huge grammar, because there is no generalization—there is a grammar rule for every distinct syntactic construction. The net result is massive ambiguity. However, note that in our example, an S expands to a VP twice as often as it expands to an NP followed by a VP; thus commands are twice as likely as statements based on this tiny set of examples. By computing probabilities for alternative expansions across thousands of training sentences in the treebank, and taking into account the frequencies of the words involved (computing the conditional probability of the expansion given a particular word, e.g., the probability of S → VP given the word "attack"), the statistical parser can not only handle language in the large but also disambiguate the sentences. The disambiguation involves building a parse tree with the highest probability, that is, the joint probability of all the expansions in the parse tree.

4. Access to enormous computational resources has in fact spawned a movement toward the use of raw compute power over linguistic sophistica-

tion, most evidenced in the field of automatic machine translation between languages. I do not personally endorse such a trend, because I believe that for many problems, rich linguistic features can be combined with statistical methods to give better performance than either ingredient alone.

5. Research is under way on integrating propbanks with coreference and sense-disambiguated word meanings in the OntoNotes project, which is currently being developed jointly at BBN Technologies, the University of Pennsylvania, the University of Colorado, and the University of Southern California. The OntoNotes corpus, available from the Linguistic Data Consortium, has sense-tagged 40,000 or word-sense examples in the Penn Treebank (integrated with propbank annotations). The integrated "banks" of training data that result from this and related efforts can help considerably in augmenting system performance.

6. Herman (2005) has successfully used data-analysis methods from corpus linguistics to investigate the way motion events are encoded in narrative texts from different genres and historical periods.

7. Chomsky (1957) argued that as a methodological strategy, linguistics requires a degree of idealization. The actual utterances we produce are full of blips and bleeps, subject to errors and corrections, hesitations and distractions, and so, it was argued, this factor made it difficult to arrive at the right sorts of generalizations about the mental faculty of language. Instead of focusing on such insignificant "noise," which Chomsky called "performance" data (of the kind found in corpora), he argued that linguistics should be aimed at the explanation of "competence," the knowledge of language that each human, viewed as an ideal speaker or listener, possesses. The emphasis on competence was aimed at eliciting more-abstract principles that might govern the set of acceptable utterances (sentences) that native speakers of a language could produce, a set that is in principle infinite. To discover these principles a linguist was required to rely on introspection, making judgments as to whether particular sentences seem grammatical or not.

8. TIME MANAGEMENT

1. Mann himself made the following observation on tempo in relation to *The Magic Mountain*: "A piece of music called a 'Five-minute Waltz' lasts five minutes, and this is its sole relation to the time element. But a narrative concerned itself with the events of five minutes, might, by extraordinary conscientiousness in the telling, take up a thousand time five minutes, and even then seem very short, though long in relation to its imaginary time. On the other hand, the contentual time of a story can shrink its actual time out of all measure" (1969, 542).

2. In "The Lady with the Pet Dog" the seduction, the lead-up to it, and Gurov's pining for Anna also occupy significant portions of the narrative. To properly address this, significant events will have to include the lead-up to the event, namely, we will need to look at, in terms of, say, the theory of plot of Lehnert ([1981] 1999), the plot unit that dominates the event. This requires further investigation.

9. DIGITAL STORYTELLING

1. Story-grammar-like rule systems have been popular in linguistics, in the form of the discourse grammars of Longacre (1983), the Tagmemics of Pike and Pike (1983), the discourse threads of Grimes (1975), and the macrostructures of Kintsch and Dijk (1978) and Dijk (1988). In the theory of macrostructures, propositions corresponding to individual sentences in a story (i.e., basic meaning representations) are linked together by various relations to form an overall story. These relations can include causal and temporal ones, as well as thematic relations, as in the case of a scene-setting description. The network of linked propositions is then mapped to a hierarchical representation, corresponding, in the case of stories, to categories such as introduction, complication, and resolution.

2. BUILDTALE, from Correira (1980), integrates research on story grammars with earlier work on macrostructures, while also leveraging some script-like mechanisms. In BUILDTALE a story may be made up of a setting followed by an episode. An episode is defined recursively as either (1) an interlude that leads into an episode followed by a new episode, (2) a complication followed by a new episode, or (3) a complication and a resolution.

3. As an example consider a fragment of a story from Boccaccio's *Decameron*, used in story understanding by Correira (1980, 139):

> Rufolo made the usual calculations that merchants make. He purchased a ship and loaded it with a cargo of goods that he paid for out of his own pocket. He sailed to Cyprus. When he got there he discovered other ships docked carrying the same goods as he had. Therefore he had to sell his goods at bargain prices. He was thus brought to the verge of ruin.

Understanding this passage requires leveraging scripts for travel, trading, etc. A script for an abstract event such as a trading voyage (involving a sailing trip carrying goods to a destination for trading) is implemented in BUILDTALE as a rule. A ship will be purchased by the agent, subject to the precondition (a subgoal) of the agent possessing wealth, then loaded, then sailed to the destination; then goods will be traded. Likewise, there will be a rule for purchasing, for trading, for a pirate voyage, and so on. As a result of purchasing, the wealth used for the purchase is no longer in the possession of the purchaser. These rules can be fairly complex and are closely tied to the examples the system is run on. For example, the trading rule involves adversarial competition, where the adverse trading rule specifically assumes that there are other ships in the destination dock that have the same goods.

4. See Lönneker (2005) for a detailed critique of STORYBOOK, including its overreliance on parameters.

GLOSSARY

Achrony: Informally, a situation where the ordering of information is left unclear. Genette defines this term in passing: "an anachrony deprived of every temporal connection, which is an event we must ultimately take to be dateless and ageless: to be an achrony" (1980, 84).

Actual reader: A generalization about flesh-and-blood readers, members of what Rabinowitz calls the "actual audience," namely, the "flesh-and-blood people who read the book" (1988, 20). The actual reader is empirically constituted from judgments obtained from a sample of real readers. While there is certainly a level of subjectivity to interpretation, the focus here is on two aspects of readers' interpretation: the annotation of timelines and reader evaluations. The actual reader is a consensus annotation of these aspects, measured to be statistically reliable (reproducible) across readers.

Anachrony: Any situation where the events are not narrated in order of occurrence. In Genette's terms, "all forms of discordance between the two temporal orders of story and narrative" (1980, 40).

Analepsis: Informally, a flashback. More precisely, "any evocation after the fact of an event that took place earlier than the point in the story where we are at any given moment" (Genette 1980, 40).

Character: (1) An agent in a narrative, whose behavior can be tracked. (2) The set of personal characteristics, virtues and vices, and dispositions that agents have; it can be something static, assumed, constructed initially, or developed through the narrative. These characteristics include those that constitute Ricoeur's (1995) concept of idem identity.

Character evaluation: An annotation by the reader on a mention of an event, indicating sympathy or antipathy with the outcome of that event for a particular character C, marked ^{++}C or ^{--}C on that event mention. The character evaluations can of course change over the course of a narrative. Unlike the approach of Phelan (1989), my notion involves Boolean judgments, which are in addition strung along the timeline of events.

Chronicle: A narrative in which the events are organized in terms of a fixed chronology, usually derived from a calendar. Travelogues, diaries, histories, ship logs, and so on are all forms of a chronicle. The term "chronicle" is also used by Genette (1980), somewhat differently, to reflect narration of events in their order of occurrence.

Conservative interpretation: A minimal interpretation of a text carried out based on information from the text, the reader's knowledge of language, and her knowledge of the real world. The interpretation does not appeal to guesses or "unusual" circumstances not mentioned in the text, nor does it rely on specific circumstances related to the author of the work, its creation, or the reader's prior experience. The conservative interpretation further constrains Ryan's (1991) "Principle of Minimal Departure," which posits that readers fill in gaps in the text by assuming the similarity of the fictional world to their own experienced world: the only gaps filled in are those based on information mentioned in the text and the reader's knowledge of language and the world.

Correspondences: Entities in a narrative can have differing fictive status. Entities that are asserted by a given speaker or narrator to have occurred or existed (viewed in possible-world semantics as taking place in an actual world) are different from those that are hypothetical, by virtue of being imagined, anticipated, remembered, and so on (and thus viewed as taking place in some possible world accessible through acts of imagining, etc.). These different entities are in correspondence with one another but are not identical, even though natural language is loose enough to make them seem the same. Thus in Proust's passage from *Jean Santeuil*, the rainy days when Jean thought and the rainy days he remembered, treated roughly as the same by the temporal adverbial "then," are distinct entities, related by the correspondence relation (the double equal sign "=="). This notion is related to the formal "counterpart relation" in the possible-world semantics of David Lewis (1986). See also Ryan (1991).

Cycle: A circularity in time. While many an ancient culture has viewed time as circular, the use of cyclical temporal structures is common across a variety of narratives including present-day ones. In a real cycle there is a contradiction in terms of temporal ordering of events in the world; this can be used to create the impression of a world unfolding into itself. A cycle can instead be virtual, where the inconsistency exists only in the character's imagination, creating a sense of disorientation. Cycles can also involve the repeated occurrence of an event. In an all-event cycle, an entire past is repeated, event for event. In an event-type cycle, a particular type of event occurs, based on a cultural or cosmological regularity, for example, breakfast or spring.

Diegesis: The act of narration, or telling. Plato drew a distinction in the *Republic* between mimesis (representation, or showing) versus diegesis (simple narration, or telling), a distinction elaborated upon by Aristotle and numerous other scholars. Genette further distinguishes between a homodiegetic narrator (a narrator who is part of the story world, i.e., a narrator as a character) versus a heterodiegetic narrator (where the narrator isn't part of the story, roughly, a disembodied narrator). The act of telling a story assumes a world, of narrator, the narrator's setting, the narrator's audience, what Genette calls the extradiegetic level. This world can be differentiated from the diegetic level, namely, the world of the events in the story.

Discourse: The broader context (beyond the sentence) used for interpretation of utterances. This can include both the linguistic context, in terms of utterances that have come before, and the extralinguistic context, namely, information about the speakers and hearers and their situation in the world. This linguistic notion is different from Genette's (1980) notion of "discourse," which corresponds to Tomashevsky's ([1925] 1965) refinement of Shklovsky's notion of *suzjet*; see also Todorov (1981) and Martin (1986). In Chatman (1980) "discourse" is the narrative's (media-independent) expression.

Discourse time: The amount of time devoted to the event in the narrative, that is, how long it takes to recount the event. This is measured in terms of the length, in words, of the recounting of the event. It is a more precise measure of the "narrative time" discussed in Müller (1968) and Genette (1980).

Event: A mention of what linguists term an eventuality, namely, something that can happen (e.g., "waltzing") or a circumstance that holds (e.g., "being thrilled"). In linguistic terminology the former is often called an "event" and the latter a "state"; I use "event" to mean an "eventuality." Note that ISO-TimeML (the international standard for TimeML) has gravitated toward the term "eventuality" instead of "event." Event mentions include nominal forms, for example, "war," "picnic." Events are marked in TimeML along with various properties, such as whether they correspond to mental states, their tense and aspect if expressed in the text, and so on.

Fabula: The "raw materials of the story" (Martin 1986, 107), a notion derived originally from the Russian formalists. In temporal terms the fabula provides the order of occurrence of events in the narrative, which is entirely captured by my timeline representation. More generally, in my framework the fabula includes some level of abstraction of what I've called the "plot." Interpretations of the term "fabula" have varied considerably, which is natural given that all we have is the text rather than the underlying material (except for rough drafts and so forth). In AI systems, for example, STORYBOOK (Callaway 2000), the fabula is the sequence of propositions that underlie the story. In later structuralists such as Bal (1997), the notion of fabula is made much stricter; in her account all versions of a given story, say of "Cinderella," will share the same fabula.

Macro-event: An entity used to represent a subnarrative. By treating an entire subnarrative as an abstract, overarching macro-event, one can bound the embedded story temporally within the macro-event.

Metalepsis: A narrative strategy where "the narrator pretends to enter (with or without his reader) into the diegetic universe" (Genette 1980, 101). For example, a narrator can intrude into the diegetic world, as when she leads the reader on a tour of a bedroom in a house, temporarily suspending the actions of the characters. In the case of "The Continuity of Parks," the narrator's metalepsis allows the character and his actions to extrude into the extradiegetic world. Note that Genette diverges from the use of the term in classical rhetoric, where "metalepsis" commonly means, according to Arthur Quinn (1982), a metonymy involving a double substitution, for example, "ears of corn."

Narrative: Any work of fiction or nonfiction in any medium (writing, speech, signing, dance, music, etc.) or media (paper, electronic, etc.) that purports to tell a story. As Genette (1980, 25–27) observes, there are three predominant senses of the term "narrative": (1) the thing that is narrated (the *récit*, translated as "narrative")—this sense is close to my term "text"; (2) the representation of a succession of events (in Genette *histoire*, translated as "story")—I call this "story"; and (3) the act of narration (which he calls "narrating"). My definition of "narrative" is related to sense 1 but differs from it in that, first, texts can occur in almost any genre, including political speeches, correspondence, almanacs, scientific articles, and so on, whereas narratives are restricted to genres (fiction, history, etc.) that tell a story; and, second, narratives can occur in any medium, whereas texts are written.

Narrator: The agent (speaker) who utters the story. In the simplest stories the agent is extradiegetic, though in general the agent can exist at any diegetic level. This agent is not necessarily the author and is distinct from Wayne Booth's (1983) implied author, which corresponds to the impression of the author created by the work.

Pace: The subjective notion of how fast the text is traversing its subject matter. In this book it is approximated by comparison of normalizations of simulation time and discourse time.

Plot: Plot is used in the Aristotelian sense. In his *Poetics* (1932) Aristotle defines plot as "a sequence of events linked by necessity or probability." Plot crucially involves an explanation of the causes of characters' actions and their consequences. As Aristotle observes, "Character determines men's qualities, but it is by their actions that they are happy or the reverse." He distinguishes plot (as evidenced in the poetry and drama of his day) from other sequences of events such as biography (where incidents in a person's life may lack a necessary and probable connection) and history (where events are confined to what actually happened, rather than hypothetical happenings). Incidental events do not form part of a plot, "for a thing whose presence or absence makes no visible difference, is not an organic part of the whole." A narrative, as embodied in a given written fictional text such as a particular edition of a novel, has a plot derived from that particular instance. The plot that all versions of the story share is an abstraction or generalization across these instances and can be more fine-grained or coarse-grained (in terms of including or excluding particular events and scenes, for example). AI accounts of plot that can form the underpinning for such an approach include the work of Lehnert ([1981] 1999) and Salway and his colleagues (Salway et al. 2003); see also Ryan (1991). Note that this notion of plot is more specific than discussions of the Russian formalist notion, where the term "plot" is sometimes used interchangeably with *suzjet*.

Prolepsis: Informally, a flash forward. More precisely, "any narrative maneuver that consists of narrating or evoking in advance an event that will take place later" (Genette 1980, 40).

Pseudo-exemplar: An example drawn from a set of habitual events, chosen as if it were representative of such events. Such an example allows the narrative to flesh out details about the habit, often erring on the side of over-specificity, so much so that those specific details are unlikely to occur for other instances of that habit.

Récit: The narrative statement, constituted by the written words of the text (Genette 1980, 25–27). *Récit* is the French word for "account"; it is translated in Genette (1980) as "narrative." Its closest approximation in my scheme is "text." The time that pulses through the *récit* is the speech time.

Reference time (RT): The temporal point to which the narrative has progressed, recording where the narrative stands in time. Time expressions that are anaphoric, such as "then" or "a month later," depend for their temporal interpretation on a time or event introduced in the prior discourse. For example, the discourse "In January 2005 . . . a month later" allows for the anaphoric expression "a month later" to be resolved to February 2005, by virtue of RT being "January 2005." For more details, see Hans Kamp and Uwe Reyle (1993), who develop a notion of reference time beyond the fundamental one introduced by Reichenbach (1947).

Script: A structure that serves to organize experiences in memory, representing a sequence of stereotypical activities (such as eating at a restaurant), proposed by Roger Schank and Robert Abelson (1977). Scripts are used for carrying out commonsense inferences when understanding stories. However, specifying the precise content of a script and which scripts apply in a given situation have proven problematic.

Simulation time: The commonsense estimate of the duration of an event, computed as the reader simulates the events she is reading about in her mind.

Speech time (ST): The time of an utterance. Time expressions that are deictic, for example, "yesterday" and "next year," depend for their interpretation on when they are uttered. Speech time expresses the time of the narration and accommodates any level of swapping or nesting of narrators; it is the time that moves inexorably on through the narration.

Story: My notion of "story" is pretheoretic and informal, given that humans do not draw a hard line between what is and isn't a story. The most common sense of "story" in narratology is *histoire* (the French word that means both story and history) from Genette (1980), translated as "story." This sense is focused on narrative content, involving a succession of events and the relations that hold among them. In Chatman (1980) "story" is the content of a narrative, as opposed to the "discourse," the narrative's expression. In Bal (1997) story is a particular rendition or interpretation by the storyteller of an underlying fabula; a given "story" of Cinderella may differ in presentation from another (whereas the fabula, in Bal's sense, remains the same). In temporal terms Genette's sense of "story" is captured in my framework by the precedence ordering offered by the timeline. However, the temporal relations being considered in the timeline are more expressive than merely precedence and equality in *l'histoire*, since we allow for time intervals that can coincide, precede, be included, or overlap in various ways. This sense is also consistent with formal, nonstructuralist approaches, such as E. M. Forster's, where a story is a narrative of "events arranged in their time sequence" (1963, 27). Other information in a "story" could include who did what to (or what happened to) whom, the agents, events, and entities involved, all of which, together with the timeline, cover what Ricoeur (1984) calls the level of narrative "prefiguration." Although this book doesn't deal with plot per se, it might be considered an additional layer, providing an explanation for why things happen, addressing, in part, Ricoeur's narrative level of "imaginative configuration." One might also include in the "story" the reader's evaluation of the character's situation at particular points in the narrative; this addresses an aspect of Ricoeur's narrative "refiguration."

Story time: The time an event occupies on the timeline for a narrative (based on predications in the narrative as to how long an event has lasted) and assuming a conservative interpretation. Müller (1968) drew a distinction between *erzählte Zeit* (story time) and *Erzählzeit* (narrative time); see also Genette (1980, 33).

Subnarrative: An embedded story. The use of subnarratives is a fundamental device within storytelling, often tied to the existence of an extradiegetic "frame" story. In the terminology of Genette (1980), the events in a subnarrative are at an immediately higher diegetic level than the embedding story.

Subordinating relation (SLINK): A relation between two events, where one is subordinated to the other by virtue of a modal relation. Examples include remembering to call, forgetting to eat, telling a story, promising to write, where the calling is subordinated to the remembering, the eating to the forgetting, the story to the telling, the writing to the promising. Subordinated events are not necessarily actual occurrences. The annotations of subordinating relations are coded in TimeML as links between the mentions of those events, along with features such as "factive," "modal," and so on.

Suzjet: The "narrative as told or written—incorporates the procedures, emphases, and thematic devices of the literary text" (Martin 1986, 108). This notion derives originally from the Russian formalist Victor Shklovsky (1973). In temporal terms the *suzjet* amounts to the ordering presented by the narrator, which is captured by my timeline representation.

Syllepsis: A clustering of events in a narrative "governed by one or another kinship (spatial, temporal, or other)" (Genette 1980, 85). For example, events may be narrated based on an ordering of the places where they occurred, rather than their temporal order. Analepsis and prolepsis correspond to temporal syllepsis. Genette's use of "syllepsis" is more restricted than its usage in classical rhetoric, where it means (Quinn 1982) an ellipsis that results in a pun, for example, "stain her Honour or her new Brocade."

Temporal relation (TLINK): A relation between events and/or times, along with a label as to whether the events (times) precede one another, are simultaneous, included, and so on. Examples include calling at 3:00 p.m., flossing after waking up. Both events and times are treated as intervals rather than points (thus necessitating the need for the relation of inclusion, or DURING). The inventory of relations is drawn from the interval calculus of Allen (1984) and consists of the following seven relations: BEFORE, DURING, SIMULTANEOUS, IMMEDIATELY BEFORE, BEGINS, ENDS, and OVERLAPS. These annotations are coded in TimeML as links between the mentions of those events or times, along with features indicating tense, aspect, whether the event is expressed by a noun, and so forth. The mapping to the interval calculus is shown in table 1 (in chapter 3).

Text: I use this term in the way it is commonly used by computational linguists, where it means the sequence of characters in a written work. This usage is more or less in keeping with two senses of the term in Merriam-Webster's: "the original words and form of a written or printed work" and "matter chiefly in the form of words or symbols that is treated as data for processing by computerized equipment." The text is thus the complete artifact, including typesetting, that is treated as fodder for computer analysis. A "narrative text," according to Bal's (1997) structuralist definition, is a text in which an agent relates ("tells") a story in a particular medium (here a "text" is a particular embodiment of the work, e.g., from first word to last word). My notion of text might seem like a restricted form of Bal's "text," except that I consider any written work to constitute a text, thus correspondence, political speeches, and scientific articles all constitute texts.

Time expression: A mention of a time in a text. Time expressions can be absolute, for example, "June 2007," "summer 1968," "June–July 1970," or relative. The latter include deictic expressions, for example, "yesterday," "next year," "the fall," which depend on the speech time, and anaphoric expressions, which depend on a reference time, for example, "then" and "a month later," which depend on a time or event in the prior discourse. Time expressions are annotated in TimeML as tags along with codes to capture calendrical information, as well as whether the time expression is a period, for example, "two weeks." The annotation captures sets of recurring times, along with mechanisms to record vagueness, such as using abbreviations for fuzzy periods (e.g., "summer") and placeholders for missing information (e.g., "a Saturday afternoon").

Timeline: A data structure that represents a text in terms of its time expressions, events, and their temporal and subordinating relations. These elements are marked according to the TimeML specification and are represented internally by a computational data structure. The representation used for computation is an interval-based one known as a temporal constraint satisfaction problem (TCSP), in a restricted form (where the TCSP is compiled into a point-based representation) that allows for computer algorithms to efficiently query the model.

TimeML: An emerging international standard from the International Organization for Standardization (ISO) for marking up events and times and their relationships, in human languages.

Trajectory: The path an agent in a story takes in space and time. The position of the character at different times in the story can be mapped in terms of a geography (at some level of underspecification).

Underspecification: The lack of information as to which particular temporal or other semantic relations hold between events and/or times. In such a case the relations in a narrative form what computer scientists call a partial ordering, where the ordering (chronological, subordinating, or other) between a pair of elements may not be known. Many a narrative will leave the relations between particular events and/or times underspecified.

Zigzag: A narrative pattern where the narrator alternates between two times, for example, "now" and "once," iterating thereafter (discussed in Genette 1980, 38).

Zooming: A narrative pattern where the narrator, after first describing events taking place habitually over a set of times or else with a vague temporal location, then drills down to a specific day or time period, where the description is then elaborated.

TOOL AND RESOURCE LINKS

BOOK WEBSITE

http://sites.google.com/site/theimaginedmoment/

TIMEML AND TEMPEVAL COMPETITION

http://timeml.org

TIMEX2 AND TERN COMPETITION

http://timex2.mitre.org

ANNOTATION EDITORS

http://calisto.mitre.org/
http://timeml.org/site/tango/tool.html

TARSQI TOOLKIT

http://timeml.org/site/tarsqi/toolkit/index.html

SPATIAL ML

http://sourceforge.net/projects/spatialml

SPATIOTEMPORAL ONTOLOGY

http://www.ontologyportal.org/ (SUMO)
http://www.loa-cnr.it/DOLCE.html (DOLCE)
http://www.opencyc.org/ (CYC)
http://www.w3.org/TR/owl-time/ (OWL Time)

TEMPORAL CONSTRAINT SATISFACTION TOOLS

http://sourceforge.net/projects/cassowary/
http://timeml.org/site/tarsqi/toolkit/index.html

TEMPORAL VISUALIZATION

http://www.inxight.com/products/sdks/tw/
http://www.oculusinfo.com/SoftwareProducts/GeoTime.html
http://simile.mit.edu/timeline/

SPATIAL REASONING TOOLS

http://www.comp.leeds.ac.uk/brandon/

PROPBANK AND BEYOND

http://www.cs.rochester.edu/~gildea/PropBank/
http://framenet.icsi.berkeley.edu/
http://www.cs.brandeis.edu/~marc/ula/xbank-browser/
http://www.bbn.com/ontonotes/

LINGUISTIC DATA CONSORTIUM

http://ldc.upenn.edu

INTERACTIVE DRAMA/FICTION

http://www.interactivestory.net/

NATURAL LANGUAGE PROCESSING COMPONENTS

http://www-nlp.stanford.edu/links/statnlp.html
http://nlp.cs.nyu.edu/app (Apple Pie)
http://svn.ask.it.usyd.edu.au/trac/candc/wiki

FOR MORE INFORMATION

http://www.cs.brandeis.edu/~im5/

REFERENCES

Ahn, D., J. Rantwijk, and M. de Rijke. 2007. A cascaded machine learning approach to interpreting temporal expressions. In *Proceedings of Human Language Technologies: The annual conference of the North American chapter of the Association for Computational Linguistics (NAACL-HLT 2007)*, ed. C. L. Sidner, T. Schultz, M. Stone, and C. Zhai, 420–27. http://www.aclweb.org/anthology/N07/N07-1053.pdf.

Allen, James. 1984. Towards a general theory of action and time. *Artificial Intelligence* 23:123–54.

Allen, Robert B., and Jane Acheson. 2000. Browsing the structure of multimedia stories. In *Proceedings of ACM Digital Libraries Conference*, ed. P. J. Nurnberg, D. L. Hicks, and R. Furuta, 11–18. San Antonio: Association for Computing Machinery.

Andre, E., K. Concepcion, I. Mani, and L. Van Guilder. 2003. AutoBriefer: A system for authoring narrated briefings. In *Multimodal intelligent information presentation*, ed. O. Stock and M. Zancanaro, 143–58. Dordrecht: Springer.

Applebee, A. 1978. *The child's concept of story*. Chicago: University of Chicago Press.

Aristotle. 1932. *Poetics*. Trans. W. H. Butcher. Project Gutenberg, no. 1974. http://www.gutenberg.org.

———. 1954. *Rhetoric*. Trans. W. Rhys Roberts. Internet Classics Archive. http://classics.mit.edu/Aristotle/rhetoric.2.ii.html.

Augustine. 1974. *Confessions*. Trans. and intro. Edward Bouverie Pusey. Project Gutenberg, no. 3296. http://www.gutenberg.org.

Aziz-Zadeh, L., S. Wilson, G. Rizzolatti, and M. Iacoboni. 2006. A comparison of premotor areas activated by action observation and action phrases. *Current Biology* 16 (18): 1818–23.

Bachelard, Gaston. 1964. *The poetics of space*. Trans. Maria Jolas. Boston: Beacon Press.

Bakhtin, Mikhail. 1994. *The dialogic imagination: Four essays by M. M.*

Bakhtin. Trans. Caryl Emerson and Michael Holquist. Austin: University of Texas Press.

Bal, Mieke. 1997. *Narratology: Introduction to the theory of narrative.* Toronto: University of Toronto Press.

Barthes, Roland. 1977. *Image, music, text.* New York: Hill & Wang.

Bartlett, Frederic. 1995. *Remembering.* 2nd ed. Cambridge: Cambridge University Press.

Berglund, A., R. Johansson, and P. Nugues. 2006. A machine learning approach to extract temporal information from texts in Swedish and generate animated 3D scenes. In *Proceedings of Eleventh Conference of the European Chapter of the Association for Computational Linguistics (EACL-2006),* ed. D. McCarthy and S. Wintner, 385–92. http://www.aclweb.org/anthology/E/E06/E06-1049.pdf.

Berman, R. A., and D. A. Slobin, eds. 1994. *A crosslinguistics developmental study.* Vol. 1 of *Relating events in narrative.* Hillsdale NJ: Lawrence Erlbaum.

Black, J. A., G. Cunningham, E. Fluckiger-Hawker, E. Robson, and G. Zólyomi. 1998. The electronic text corpus of Sumerian literature. http://www-etcsl.orient.ox.ac.uk/.

Boguraev, Branimir, and Rie Kubota Ando. 2005. TimeML-compliant text analysis for temporal reasoning. In *Proceedings of the International Joint Conference on Artificial Intelligence (IJCAI-05),* ed. L. P. Kaelbling and A. Saffiotti, 997–1003. http://www.ijcai.org/papers/1202.pdf.

Bonheim, Helmut. 1982. *The narrative modes: Techniques of the short story.* Cambridge: Brewer.

Booth, W. 1983. *The rhetoric of fiction.* Chicago: University of Chicago Press.

Borges, Jorge Luis. 1963. *Ficciones.* New York: Grove.

Boroditsky, L. 2001. Does language shape thought? Mandarin and English speakers' conceptions of time. *Cognitive Psychology* 43:1–22. http://dx.doi.org/10.1006/cogp.2001.0748.

Bramsen, P., P. Deshpande, Y. K. Lee, and R. Barzilay. 2006. Inducing temporal graphs. In *Proceedings of Conference on Empirical Methods in Natural Language Processing (EMNLP-2006),* ed. D. Juratsky and E. Gaussier, 189–98. http://www.aclweb.org/anthology/w/w06/w06-1623.pdf.

Brants, Thorsten. 2000. TnT-A statistical part-of-speech tagger. In *Proceedings of the Sixth Applied Natural Language Processing Conference (ANLP-2000) Seattle,* 224–31. http://www.aclweb.org/anthology/A/A00/A00-1031/pdf.

Brontë, Charlotte. 1998. *Jane Eyre.* Project Gutenberg, no. 1260. http://www.gutenberg.org.

Brooks, Cleanth. 1990. *William Faulkner: The Yoknapatawpha country.* Baton Rouge: Louisiana State University Press.

Callaway, Charles. 2000. Narrative prose generation. PhD diss., Department of Computer Science, North Carolina State University, Raleigh.

Calvino, Italo. 1988. *Six memos for the next millennium*. Cambridge MA: Harvard University Press.

Carreras, X., and L. Arquez. 2005. Introduction to the CoNLL-2005 shared task: Semantic role labeling. In *Proceedings of CoNLL-2005*. http://citeseer .ist.psu.edu/carreras05introduction.html.

Casasanto, D., and L. Boroditsky. 2007. Time in the mind: Using space to think about time. *Cognition*. http://dx.doi.org/10.1016/j.cogni tion.2007.03.004.

Cavazza, Marc, and David Pizzi. 2006. Narratology for interactive storytelling: A critical introduction. In *Technologies for Interactive Digital Storytelling and Entertainment: Third international conference, Darmstadt, Germany, December 4–6, 2006; Proceedings*, ed. S. Gobel, R. Malkewitz, and I. Iurgel, Lecture Notes in Computer Science 4326, 72–83. Berlin: Springer.

Chatman, Seymour. 1980. *Story and discourse: Narrative structure in fiction and film*. Cornell Paperbacks. Ithaca NY: Cornell University Press.

Chekhov, Anton. 1979. Letter to Maxim Gorky, September 3, 1899. In *The stories of Anton Chekhov*, ed. Ralph E. Matlaw, 275. New York: W. W. Norton.

———. 1988. *A doctor's visit: Short stories*. Ed. and intro. Tobias Wolff. New York: Bantam Classics.

Chomsky, Noam. 1957. *Syntactic structures*. The Hague: Mouton.

———. 1984. *Modular approaches to the study of the mind*. San Diego: San Diego State University Press.

Cohen, Jacob. 1960. A coefficient of agreement for nominal scales. *Educational and Psychological Measurement* 20 (1): 37–46.

Collins, Michael. 2003. Head-driven statistical models for natural language parsing. *Computational Linguistics* 29:589–637.

Correira, A. 1980. Computing story trees. *American Journal of Computational Linguistics* 6:3–4, 135–49.

Cortázar, Julio. 1973. *All fires the fire and other stories*. New York: Random House.

———. 2006. The continuity of parks. Trans. David Page. http://www.continu ityofparks.com/by-cortazar/.

Cullingford, R. E. 1978. *Script application: Computer understanding of newspaper stories*. Research Report 116. New Haven CT: Computer Science Department, Yale University.

Currie, Gregory. 1999. Can there be a literary philosophy of time? In *The arguments of time*, ed. J. Butterfield, 204–20. Oxford: Oxford University Press.

Currie, Mark. 2007. *About time: Narrative, fiction, and the philosophy of time.* Edinburgh: Edinburgh University Press.

Damasio, Antonio. 2003. *Looking for Spinoza: Joy, sorrow and the feeling brain.* Orlando FL: Harcourt.

Davies, Paul. 2002. How to build a time machine. *Scientific American,* August 13.

De Jong, G. 1982. An overview of the FRUMP system. In *Strategies for natural language processing,* ed. W. G. Lehnert and M. H. Ringle, 149–76. Hillsdale NJ: Lawrence Erlbaum.

Dijk, Teun A. van. 1980. *Macrostructures: An interdisciplinary study of global structures in discourse, interaction, and cognition.* Hillsdale NJ: Lawrence Erlbaum.

Dijk, T. van, and W. Kintsch. 1977. Cognitive psychology and discourse: Recalling and summarizing stories. In *Current trends in textlinguistics,* ed. Wolfgang Dresser, 61–80. Berlin: W. de Gruyter.

Duda, Richard O., Peter E. Hart, and David G. Stork. 2000. *Pattern classification.* 2nd ed. New York: Wiley Interscience.

Eco, Umberto. 1990. Small worlds. In *The limits of interpretation,* 64–82. Bloomington: Indiana University Press.

Faulkner, William. [1929] 1994a. *The sound and the fury.* Ed. David Minter. 2nd ed. New York: Norton.

———. 1994b. Letter to Ben Wasson. In Faulkner [1929] 1994a, 220–21.

Ferro, L., L. Gerber, I. Mani, B. Sundheim, and G. Wilson. 2005. TIDES 2005 standard for the annotation of temporal expressions. April, updated September. http://timex2.mitre.org/annotation_guidelines/timex2_annota tion_guidelines.html.

Finnegan, Ruth. 1992. *Oral poetry: Its nature, significance and social context.* 2nd ed. Bloomington: Indiana University Press.

Forster, E. M. 1963. *Aspects of the novel.* Harmondsworth, England: Penguin.

Friedman, W. J. 2001. Memory processes underlying humans' chronological sense of the past. In *Time and memory: Issues in philosophy and psychology,* ed. C. Hoerl and T. McCormack, 139–67. Oxford: Oxford University Press.

Garcia Marquez, Gabriel. 1995. *One hundred years of solitude.* New York: Alfred A. Knopf.

Genette, Gérard. 1980. *Narrative discourse.* Trans. Jane Lewin. Ithaca NY: Cornell University Press.

Gentner, D. 2001. Spatial metaphors in temporal reasoning. In *Spatial schemas in abstract thought,* ed. M. Gattis, 203–22. Cambridge MA: MIT Press.

Ghosh, Amitav. 2005. The man behind the mosque. http://www.amitavghosh .com/.

Gibson, William. 2003. *Pattern recognition*. New York: G. P. Putnam.

Graesser, Arthur C., Brent Olde, and Bianca Klettke. 2003. How does the mind construct and represent stories? In *Narrative impact: Social and cognitive foundations*, ed. M. C. Green, J. J. Strange, and T. C. Brock, 231–63. Hillsdale NJ: Lawrence Erlbaum.

Graesser, Arthur C., M. A. Kassler, R. J. Kreuz, and B. McLain-Allen. 1998. Verification of statements about story worlds that deviate from normal conceptions of time: What is true about Einstein's dreams? *Cognitive Psychology* 35 (3) (April): 246–301.

Grenon, P. and B. Smith. 2004. SNAP and SPAN: Towards dynamic spatial ontology. *Spatial Cognition and Computation* 4 (1): 69–104.

Grice, Paul. 1975. Logic and conversation. In *Syntax and semantics*, ed. P. Cole and J. Morgan, 3:41–58. New York: Academic Press.

Grimes, J. E. 1975. *The thread of discourse*. The Hague: Mouton.

Grishman, R., and B. Sundheim. 1996. Message understanding conference-6: A brief history. In *Proceedings of the 16th International Conference on Computational Linguistics, New Brunswick, New Jersey, Association for Computational Linguistics*. http://www.muc.saic,com/muc_7_proceedings/ltg-muc7.ps.

Halpin, Harry, Johanna D. Moore, and Judy Robertson. 2004. Automatic analysis of plot for story rewriting. In *Proceedings of Empirical Methods in Natural Language Processing (EMNLP 2004), Barcelona, Spain*. http://www.aclweb.org/anthology/P/P06/P06-1108.pdf.

Hass, Robert. 1990. Misery and splendor. In *Human wishes*. New York: Ecco.

Hemingway, Ernest. 1954. *The first 49 stories*. London: Jonathan Cape.

Herman, David. 2001. Spatial reference in narrative domains. *TEXT: An Interdisciplinary Journal for the Study of Discourse* 21 (4): 515–41.

———. 2002. *Story logic: Problems and possibilities of narrative*. Lincoln: University of Nebraska Press.

———. 2004. Toward a transmedial narratology. In *Narrative across media: The languages of storytelling*, ed. Marie-Laure Ryan, 47–75. Lincoln: University of Nebraska Press.

———. 2005. Quantitative methods in narratology: A corpus-based study of motion events in stories. In *Narratology beyond literary criticism*, ed. Jan Christoph Meister, 125–49. Berlin: De Gruyter.

Herrnstein-Smith, Barbara. 1980. Narrative versions, narrative theories. *Critical Inquiry* 7:209–18.

Hickmann, M. 2003. *Children's discourse: Person, space and time across language*. Cambridge: Cambridge University Press.

Hobbs, Jerry. 2000. Half orders of magnitude. In *Proceedings of the workshop on semantic approximation, granularity, and vagueness: A workshop of the Seventh International Conference on Principles of Knowledge Representation and Reasoning KR2000, Breckenridge, Colorado, April 11, 2000*, ed. L. Obrst and I. Mani, 28–38. http://www.kr.org/KR2000/.

Hofling, Charles. 1993. Marking space and time in Itzaj Maya narrative. *Journal of Linguistic Anthropology* 3 (2): 164–84.

Hogan, Patrick. 2003. *The mind and its stories: Narrative universals and human emotion*. New York: Cambridge University Press.

Horace. 2004. *The works of Horace*. ("The art of poetry" and "An epistle to the Pisos.") Trans. C. Smart and T. A. Buckley. Project Gutenberg, no. 14020. http://www.gutenberg.org.

Hume, David. 2003. *A treatise of human nature*. Project Gutenberg, no. 4705. http://www.gutenberg.org.

Hwang, Chung Hee, and Lenhart K. Schubert. 1992. Tense trees as the "fine structure" of discourse. In *Proceedings of the Thirtieth Annual Meeting of the Association for Computational Linguistics*, 232–40. http://www.aclweb.org/anthology/P/P92/P92-1030.pdf.

Ireland, Ken. 2001. *The sequential dynamics of narrative*. Madison NJ: Fairleigh Dickinson University Press.

Jahn, Manfred. 2005. *Narratology: A guide to the theory of narrative*. English Department, University of Cologne. http://www.uni-koeln.de/~ame02/ppp.htm.

Johnson, Christopher R., and Charles J. Fillmore. 2000. The FrameNet tagset for frame-semantic and syntactic coding of predicate-argument structure. In *Proceedings of the 1st meeting of the North American chapter of the Association for Computational Linguistics (ANLP-NAACL 2000), Seattle*, 56–62. http://www.aclweb.org/anthology/A/A00/A00-2008.pdf.

Jurafsky, D., and J. H. Martin. 2000. *Speech and language processing: An introduction to natural language processing, computational linguistics, and speech recognition*. Saddle River NJ: Prentice Hall.

Kafka, Franz. 1975. A hunger artist. In *"The metamorphosis," "In the penal colony" and other stories*, trans. Will and Edwin Muir, 231–77. New York: Schocken Books.

Kamp, H., and U. Reyle. 1993. Tense and aspect. In *Discourse to logic*, pt. 2, chap. 5, 483–546. Dordrecht: Kluwer.

Kanabus, M., E. Szelag, and E. Pöppel. 2002. Temporal order judgement for auditory and visual stimuli. *Acta Neurobiologiae Experimentalis* 62:263–70.

Kautz, Henry A., and Peter B. Ladkin. 1991. Integrating metric and qualitative temporal reasoning. In *Proceedings of the Ninth National Conference on Artificial Intelligence (AAAI'91)*, ed. T. Dean and K. McKeown, 241–46. Menlo Park CA: AAAI Press.

Kelter, S., B. Kaup, and B. Claus. 2004. Representing a described sequence of events: A dynamic view of narrative comprehension. *Journal of Experimental Psychology: Learning, Memory, and Cognition* 30:451–64.

Kolb, Philip. 1983. *Marcel Proust: Selected letters, 1880–1903*. Trans. Ralph Manheim. New York: Doubleday.

Kundera, Milan. 1991. *The unbearable lightness of being*. New York: Harper Collins.

Labov, William, and Joshua Gravetsky. 1967. Narrative analysis. In *Essays on the verbal and visual arts*, ed. J. Helm, 12–44. Seattle: University of Washington Press.

Lakoff, G., and M. Johnson. 1980. *Metaphors we live by*. Chicago: University of Chicago Press.

Lang, Raymond. 2003. A declarative model for simple narratives. In *Narrative intelligence*, ed. M. Mateas and P. Sengers, 199–214. Amsterdam: John Benjamins.

Lebowitz, M. 1985. Story-telling as planning and learning. *Poetics* 14:483–502.

Lehnert, Wendy. [1981] 1999. Plot units: A narrative summarization strategy. In *Strategies for natural language processing*, ed. W. G. Lehnert and M. H. Ringle. Hillsdale NJ: Lawrence Erlbaum. Reprinted in *Advances in automatic text summarization*, ed. I. Mani and M. T. Maybury, 177–214. Cambridge MA: MIT Press.

Lewis, David. 1986. *On the plurality of worlds*. Malden MA: Blackwell.

Lightman, Alan. 1994. *Einstein's dreams*. New York: Warner Books.

Longacre, R. 1983. *The grammar of discourse: Notional and surface structures*. New York: Plenum Press.

Lönneker, Birte. 2005. Narratological knowledge for natural language generation. In *Proceedings of the 10th European Workshop on Natural Language Generation (ENLG-05), Aberdeen, Scotland, 8–10 August 2005*, 91–100. http://www.aclweb.org/anthology/w/w05/w05-1610.pdf.

Lord, Albert. 1960. *The singer of tales*. Cambridge MA: Harvard University Press.

Mani, Inderjeet. 2005a. Computational linguistics. In *Introduction to language and linguistics*, ed. R. Fasold and J. Connor-Linton, 465–92. Cambridge: Cambridge University Press.

———. 2005b. Narrative summarization. *Journal Traitement automatique des langues (TAL)*, Special issue on context: Automatic text summarization, 15–38.

Mani, I., and B. Schiffman. 2009. Temporally anchoring and ordering events in news. In *Time and event recognition in natural language*, ed. J. Pustejovsky and R. Gaizauskas. Amsterdam: John Benjamins.

Mani, I., and B. Wellner. 2006. A pilot study on acquiring metric and temporal constraints for events. In *Proceedings of the ACL 2006 Workshop on Annotating and Reasoning about Time and Events (ARTE 2006), Sydney, Australia*, 753–60. http://www.aclweb.org/anthology/w/w06/w06-0904.pdf.

Mani, I., B. Wellner, M. Verhagen, C. M. Lee, and J. Pustejovsky. 2006. Machine learning of temporal relations. In *Proceedings of the 44th Annual Meeting of the Association for Computational Linguistics (COLING-ACL), Sydney, Australia*, 753–60. http://www.aclweb.org/anthology/P/P07/P07-2044.pdf.

Mani, I., and G. Wilson. 2000. Robust temporal processing of news. In *Proceedings of the 44th Annual Meeting of the Association for Computational Linguistics (COLING-ACL), Sydney, Australia*, 69–76. http://www.aclweb.org/anthology/P/P00/P00-1010.pdf.

Mani, I., and J. Pustejovsky. 2004. Temporal discourse models for narrative structure. ACL Workshop on Discourse Annotation, Barcelona, Spain (2004). http://www.aclweb.org/anthology/w/w04/w04-0208.pdf.

Mani, I., J. Pustejovsky, and R. Gaizauskas, eds. 2005. *The language of time: A reader*. New York: Oxford University Press.

Mann, Thomas. 1969. *The magic mountain*. Trans. H. T. Lowe-Porter. New York: Vintage.

Manning, C., and H. Schutze. 1999. *Foundations of statistical natural language processing*. Cambridge MA: MIT Press.

Marcus, M., B. Santorini, and M. Marcinkiewicz. 1993. Building a large annotated corpus of English: The Penn Treebank. *Computational Linguistics* 19 (2): 313–30.

Margolin, Uri. 2007. Character. In *The Cambridge companion to narrative*, ed. D. Herman, 66–79. Cambridge: Cambridge University Press.

Martin, Wallace. 1986. *Recent theories of narrative*. Ithaca NY: Cornell University Press.

Mateas, M., and A. Stern. 2005. Structuring content in the facade interactive drama architecture. In *Proceedings of Artificial Intelligence and Interactive Digital Entertainment (AIIDE 2005), Marina del Rey, June 2005*, ed. R. M. Young and J. E. Laird, 93–98. Menlo Park CA: AAAI Press.

McHale, Brian. 1987. *Postmodernist fiction*. London: Routledge.

McTaggart, J. M. E. 1908. The unreality of time. *Mind* 17:457–74.

Meehan, James R. 1977. TALE-SPIN, an interactive program that writes stories. In *Proceedings of the Fifth International Joint Conference on Artificial Intelligence*, ed. R. Reddy, 91–98. San Francisco: William Kaufmann.

Meiri, I. 1996. Combining qualitative and quantitative constraints in temporal reasoning. *Artificial Intelligence* 87:343–85.

Meister, Jan Christof. 2003. *Computing action.* Berlin: Walter de Gruyter.

———. 2005. Tagging time in prolog: The temporality effect project. *Journal of Literary and Linguistic Computing* 20:107–24.

Mihalcea, R., and T. Pedersen. 2005. Advances in word sense disambiguation: Tutorial notes. In *Proceedings of AAAI-2005.* http://www.d.umn.edu/~tpederse/wsdTtorial.html.

Mitkov, Ruslan, ed. 2003. *The Oxford handbook of computational linguistics.* Oxford: Oxford University Press.

Montfort, Nick. 2007. Ordering events in interactive fiction narratives. In *Proceedings of the AAAI Fall Symposium on Intelligent Narrative Technologies,* Technical Report FS-07-05, ed. B. S. Magerko and M. O. Riedl, 87–94. Menlo Park CA AAAI Press.

Mueller, Erik T. 2002. Story understanding. In *Encyclopedia of cognitive science,* ed. Lynn Nadel, 4:238–46. London: Nature.

———. 2007. Modeling space and time in narratives about restaurants. *Literary and Linguistic Computing* 22 (1): 67–84.

Müller, Günther. 1968. Erzählzeit und erzählte zeit. In *Morphologische poetik,* 195–212. Tübingen: Niemeyer.

Nagel, Thomas. 1974. What is it like to be a bat? *Philosophical Review* 83 (4): 435–50. http://organizations.utep.edu/Portals/1475/nagel_bat.pdf.

Narasimhan, R. 1991. Literacy: Its characterization and implications. In *Literacy and orality,* ed. David R. Olson and Nancy Torrance, 177–97. Cambridge: Cambridge University Press.

Nauze, F. 2002. Scenarios for the passé simple and imparfait: An event calculus approach to French semantics. Master's thesis, ILLC, University of Amsterdam.

Oatley, Keith. 2006. Simulation of substance and shadow: Inner emotions and outer behavior in Shakespeare's psychology of character. *College Literature* 33 (1): 15–33.

Oatley, Keith, Dacher Keltner, and Jennifer M. Jenkins. 2006. *Understanding emotions.* 2nd ed. Malden MA: Blackwell.

Ong, Walter J. 1982. *Orality and literacy: The technologizing of the word.* London: Methuen.

Oriel, C. 1990. Narrative levels and the fictionality of Don Quijote, I: Cardenio's story. *Cervantes: Bulletin of the Cervantes Society of America* 10 (2): 55–72.

Orwell, G. 1982. *1984.* Harcourt Brace Jovanovich: New York.

Palmer, M., P. Kingsbury, and D. Gildea. 2005. The proposition bank: An annotated corpus of semantic roles. *Computational Linguistics* 31 (1): 71–106.

Pan, F., R. Mulkar, and J. Hobbs. 2006. Learning event durations from event descriptions. In *Proceedings of the 44th Annual Meeting of the Association for Computational Linguistics (COLING-ACL2006), Sydney, Australia,* 393–400. http://aclweb.org/anthology/P/P06/P06-1050.pdf.

Pepys, Samuel. 1893. *The diary of Samuel Pepys.* Ed. Henry Wheatley. Project Gutenberg, no. 4200. http://www.gutenberg.org.

Pérez y Pérez, R., and M. Sharples. 2004. Three computer-based models of storytelling: BRUTUS, MINSTREL and MEXICA. *Knowledge-Based Systems* 17 (1): 15–29.

Phelan, James. 1989. *Reading people, reading plots: Character, progression, and the interpretation of narrative.* Chicago: University of Chicago Press.

Pinker, Steven. 2007. *The language instinct.* New York: Harper Perennial.

Plato. 2008. *Republic.* Trans. B. Jowett. Project Gutenberg, no. 1497. http://www.gutenberg.org.

Plotnick, A. 2008. Space-time annotation. Paper delivered at the Workshop on Methodologies and Resources for Processing Spatial Language at the Sixth International Conference on Language Resources and Evaluation (LREC 2008), Marrakech, May 31, 2008. http://www.sfbtr8.uni-bremen.de/SpatialLREC/.

Polanyi, Livia. 1985. *Telling the American story: A structural and cultural analysis of conversational storytelling.* Norwood NJ: Ablex.

Pöppel, Ernst. 1994. Temporal mechanisms in perception. *International Review of Neurobiology* 37:185–202.

———. 1997. A hierarchical model of temporal perception. *Trends in Cognitive Sciences* 1 (2): 56–61.

Prior, Arthur N. 1967. *Past, present, and future.* Oxford: Oxford University Press.

Proust, Marcel. 1922. *Swann's way.* Trans. C. K. Scott-Montcrieff. Project Gutenberg, no. 7178. http://www.gutenberg.org.

Pustejovsky, J., B. Ingria, R. Sauri, J. Castano, J. Littman, R. Gaizauskas, A. Setzer, G. Katz, and I. Mani. 2005. The specification language TimeML. In Mani, Pustejovsky, and Gaizauskas 2005. http://timeml.org.

Quinn, Arthur. 1982. *Figures of speech.* Layton UT: Gibbs Smith.

Rabinowitz, Peter. 1988. *Before reading: Narrative conventions and the politics of interpretation.* Columbus: Ohio State University Press.

Reichenbach, Hans. 1947. The tenses of verbs. In *Elements of symbolic logic,* sec. 51, 287–98. New York: Macmillan.

Reingold, E., and N. Dershowitz. 2004. *Calendrical calculations: The millennium edition.* New York: Cambridge University Press.

Ricoeur, Paul. 1984. *Time and narrative.* Vol. 1. Trans. Kathleen McLaughlin and David Pellauer. Chicago: University of Chicago Press.

————. 1990. *Time and narrative*. Vol. 2. Trans. Kathleen McLaughlin and David Pellauer. Chicago: University of Chicago Press.

————. 1995. *Oneself as another*. Trans. Kathleen Blamey. Chicago: University of Chicago Press.

Robbe-Grillet, Alain. 1965. *Two novels by Robbe-Grillet: "Jealousy" and "In the labyrinth."* New York: Grove Press.

Rossetti, Dante Gabriel. 2006. Autumn song. In *The complete poetical works of Dante Gabriel Rossetti*, ed. William M. Rossetti, 288. Whitefish MT: Kessinger.

Rumelhart, D. E. 1975. Notes on a schema for stories. In *Representation and understanding: Studies in cognitive science*, ed. D. G. Bobrow and A. Collins, 211–36. New York: Academic Press.

Russell, B. 1956. On order in time. In *Logic and knowledge: Essays, 1901–1950*. London: Allen & Unwin.

Ryan, Marie-Laure. 1991. *Possible worlds, artificial intelligence, and narrative theory*. Bloomington: Indiana University Press.

Salway, Andrew, and David Herman. 2010. Digitized corpora as theory-building resource: New foundations for narrative inquiry. In *New narratives: Theory and practice*, ed. R. Page and B. Thomas. Lincoln: University of Nebraska Press.

Salway, Andrew, Mike Graham, Eleftheria Tomadaki, and Yan Xu. 2003. Linking video and text via representations of narrative. In *Proceedings of the AAAI Spring Symposium on Intelligent Multimedia Knowledge Management, Palo Alto, 24–26 March 2003*, 104–12. Menlo Park CA: AAAI Press.

Salway, Andrew, and Yan Xu. 2002. *Navigating stories in films*. Technical Report CS-05-04, Department of Computing, University of Surrey. http://epubs.surrey.ac.uk/publcomp/4/.

Sartre, Jean-Paul. 1966. On "The sound and the fury": Time in the work of Faulkner. In *Faulkner: A collection of critical essays*, ed. Robert Penn Warren, 89. Englewood Cliffs NJ: Prentice-Hall.

Sauri, Roser, Robert Knippen, Marc Verhagen, and James Pustejovsky. 2005. Evita: A robust event recognizer for QA systems. In *Proceedings of HLT/EMNLP 2005*, 700–707. http://www.aclweb.org/anthology/P/P06-1095.pdf.

Schacter, Daniel L., and Donna R. Addis. 2007. The cognitive neuroscience of constructive memory: Remembering the past and imagining the future. *Philosophical Transactions of the Royal Society* B (362): 773–86.

Schank, Roger C., and Robert P. Abelson. 1977. *Scripts, plans, goals, and understanding: An inquiry into human knowledge structures*. Hillsdale NJ: Lawrence Erlbaum.

Schliemann, Heinrich. 1875. *Troy and its remains: A narrative of researches and discoveries made on the site of Ilium, and in the Trojan plain.* London: John Methuen.

Sebald, W. G. 2001. *Austerlitz.* New York: Modern Library.

Sekine, S., and R. Grishman. 1995. A corpus-based probabilistic grammar with only two non-terminals. Paper presented at the Fourth International Workshop on Parsing Technologies, Prague. http://www.aclweb.org/anthology/P/P97/P97-1021.pdf.

Sen, Amartya. 2000. India through its calendars. *Little Magazine* 1 (1). http://www.littlemag.com/2000/sen.htm.

Shklovsky, V. 1972. On the connection between devices of syuzhet construction and general stylistic devices. *Twentieth Century Studies*, nos. 7–8:54–61.

Siegel, S., and N. J. Castellan. 1988. *Nonparametric statistics for the social sciences.* 2nd ed. New York: McGraw-Hill.

Smith, Murray. 1995. *Engaging characters: Fiction, emotion, and the cinema.* Oxford: Clarendon.

Smith, Zadie. 2003. The limited circle is pure. *New Republic*, November 3.

Sternberg, Meir. 1982. Proteus in quotation-land: Mimesis and the forms of reported discourse. *Poetics Today* 3:107–56.

Stoicheff, R. P., Alison Muri, Joel Deshaye, et al., eds. 2003. The sound and the fury: A hypertext edition. University of Saskatchewan. http://www.usask.ca/english/faulkner.

Stolcke, A., K. Ries, N. Coccaro, E. Shriberg, R. Bates, D. Jurafsky, P. Taylor, R. Martin, C. VanEss-Dykema, and M. Meteer. 2000. Dialogue act modeling for automatic tagging and recognition of conversational speech. *Computational Linguistics* 26 (3): 1–34.

Thucydides. 1903. *The history of the Peloponnesian War.* Trans. Richard Crawley. Project Gutenberg, no. 7142. http://www.gutenberg.org.

Todorov, Tzvetan. 1981. *Introduction to poetics.* Trans. R. Howard. Minneapolis: University of Minnesota Press.

Tomasello, M. 2006. Acquiring linguistic constructions. In *Social, emotional and personality development*, ed. W. Damon, N. Eisenberg, and R. M. Lerner, 255–98. New York: Wiley.

Tomashevsky, Boris. [1925] 1965. Thematics. In *Russian formalist criticism: Four essays*, ed. L. Lemon and M. Reis, 61–95. Lincoln: University of Nebraska Press.

Toolan, Michael J. 1988. *Narrative: A critical linguistic introduction.* Routledge: New York.

Turner, F., and E. Pöppel. 1980. The neural lyre: Poetic meter, the brain, and time. *Poetry*, April.

Turner, S. R. 1994. *The creative process: A computer model of storytelling and creativity*. Mahwah NJ: Lawrence Erlbaum.

Van der Meer, E., R. Beyer, B. Heinze, and I. Badel. 2002. Temporal order relations in language comprehension. *Journal of Experimental Psychology: Learning, Memory, and Cognition* 28 (4): 770–79.

Voltaire. 2006. *Candide*. Project Gutenberg, no. 19942. http://www.gutenberg.org.

Walker, A. G. 1948. *Foundations of relativity: Parts I and II*. In *Proceedings of the Royal Society of Edinburgh (section A)*, 62, 319–35. Cambridge: Cambridge University Press.

Webber, Bonnie. 1988. Tense as discourse anaphor. *Computational Linguistics* 14 (2): 61–73.

Wilensky, Robert W. 1978. *Understanding goal-based stories*. New York: Garland.

Woolf, Virginia. 1996. *Mrs. Dalloway*. Ware, England: Wordsworth Editions.

Zhou, L., G. B. Melton, S. Parsons, and G. Hripcsak. 2006. A temporal constraint structure for extracting temporal information from clinical narrative. *Journal of Biomedical Informatics* 29:424–39.

Zwaan, R. A. 1996. Processing narrative time shifts. *Journal of Experimental Psychology: Learning, Memory, and Cognition* 22:1196–1207.

INDEX

Bramsen, P., 204n6
Brants, Thorsten, 138
Brontë, Charlotte: *Jane Eyre*, 33
Brooks, Cleanth, 42
BUILDTALE, 213nn2–3
Burmese, 29

calendars, 92–93
Callaway, Charles, 182–84, 185, 218
Callisto, 58–59, *59*, 155
Calvino, Italo, 20
Candide (Voltaire), 159, 161–62, 166, 167, 168, *169*, 170–71, 173–74
Canterbury Tales (Chaucer), 10
Carreras, Xavier, 140
Casanto, D., 207n1
Cassowary, 185
Castellan, N. J., 209n3
Castellanos, Rosario: *The Book of Lamentations*, 90
Catalan, 28
Cavazza, Marc, 190
Cervantes, Miguel de: *Don Quixote*, 47
character: definition of, 22, 120, 215; development of, 127–31; empathy for, 105–6; evaluation of, 115–16, *117*, 118, 215; tagging evaluations of, 149–50; transitions in evaluations of, 126–31
Chatman, Seymour, 112, 124–25, 220
Chaucer, Geoffrey: *Canterbury Tales*, 10
Chekhov, Anton, 31; "The Lady with the Pet Dog," 125–26, 128–33, 146, 172, 186–87, 192, 213n2 (chap. 8)
Chibemba, 28
Chinese, 28–29, 58, 207n1
Chomsky, Noam, 13, 151–54, 212n7
Christie, Agatha: *The Murder of Roger Ackroyd*, 47
chronicle, 81–86, *86*, 189, 215–16
chronotope, 134
Cinderella, 11–12

claims, 30, 127, 144, 149, 171
Claus, B., 208n6
Cohen, Jacob, 209n3
Collins, Michael, 137
computable representation, 56
The Conference of Birds (Attār), 10
configuration, 5–6
"The Continuity of Parks" (Cortazar), 52–54
coreference, 141
corpora, 13–14, 18–19, 65–66, 73–76, 137–38, *143*, 144–45, *147*, 150–54, 162–63, 164–66
Correira, A., 213nn2–3
correspondences, 35, *36*, 37, 45, 76, 216
Cortazar, Julio: "The Continuity of Parks," 52–54; "The Island at Noon," 130–31
Cullingford, R. E., 200n6
Currie, G., 203n2
Currie, M., 203n2
cycle: all-event vs. event-type, 89–90, *91*, 92; definition of, 216; real, 52–53, *54*, 55; virtual, 48–49, *49*, 51–52, *51*, 55

Damasio, Antonio, 196
Davies, Paul, 209n7
De Jong, G., 201n9
Demeter, 10, 89–90
Dershowitz, N., 206n11
dialogue act, 141–42
Diary (Pepys), 83–84, 206n7
Dickens, Charles: *Oliver Twist*, 118
diegesis, 13, 217. *See also* narrator
Dijk, T. van, 213n1
discourse time, 158, 166–72, 217
Don Quixote (Cervantes), 47
Dreamtime, 94
Duda, Richard, 211n1
duration, 160–65, *165*, *166*, 175
Dyirbal, 28

Eco, Umberto, 203n5

narrative, 91; psychological question of, 110, 196; and real cycle, 52–54; in *The Sound and the Fury*, 42; timeline example of, 45, 46, *46* subordination relation (SLINK), 36–37, 60, 68, *69*, *71*, 74, 221. *See also* subnarrative

Sundheim, Beth, 74

supernarrative, 46

suzjet, 182–83, 221

Swann's Way (Proust), 49–50, 78, 81

Swedish, 58

syllepsis, 189, 221

Szelag, E., 100

TALE-SPIN, 17, 180, 202n11

TANGO, 61

Tanizaki, Junichiro: *The Makioka Sisters*, 93

TARSQI, 68–73, 173

tempo, 156–63, 166–72, 219

temporal constraint satisfaction problem (TCSP), 61–62. *See also* Cassowary; interval calculus; SputLink

temporal relation (TLINK): acquisition of, 107–8; coding of, 60–62, *62*; definition of, 221–22; table of, 62; tagging of, 64–68, *69*, 72; tagging accuracy of, 73–74; in timelines, 25–27. *See also* interval calculus

tense, 27–29

"The Terrible Vengeance" (Gogol), 133

text, 22, 222

Thai, 58

thematic roles. *See* argument roles

Thucydides, 82–83

time: absolute vs. relative, 57; and all-event vs. event-type cycle, 89–90, *91*, 92; coding of, 57–59; length of present, 100–101; and real cycle, 52–53, *54*, 55; scales of, 163–66, *165*, *166*; span of, 157, 172–74; in story generation, 180–85; subjective versus objective, 97–99; and virtual cycle, 48–49, *49*, 51–52, *51*, 55. *See also* calendars; simulation; tempo

TimeBank, *143*, *147*, 163, 168, 174. *See also* corpora; TimeML

time expressions, 25–27, 39–41, 62, *63*, 73–74, 152, *152*, 222. *See also* Callisto

timeline, 25–27, 30, 106–7, 109–10, 222. *See also* temporal constraint satisfaction problem (TCSP)

TimeML, 61, 163, 190, 194, 195, 203n7, 204n2 (chap. 3), 204n4, 204n6, 223

Time's Arrow (Amis), 42, 179

TLINK. *See* temporal relation (TLINK)

Todorov, Tzvetan, 217

Tolstoy, Leo: *War and Peace*, 83, 179, 199n2

Tomasello, Michael, 153, 200n4

Tomashevsky, Boris, 217

Toolan, Michael, 158

trajectory, 131–34, *132*, 145–49, *147*, 150, *150*, 191, 223

transitions, 126–31

treebank, 137–38, 211n3, 212n5. *See also* Penn Treebank

Turing Test, 20

Turner, Frederick, 101

Turner, S. R., 180–81

Ulysses (Joyce), 38, 173, 179

The Unbearable Lightness of Being (Kundera), 89

underspecification, 27, 41–42, 46, 48, 223

Under the Volcano (Lowry), 157, 172–73

unit of analysis, 54

Universal Grammar, 200n4

UNIVERSE, 17

Voltaire: *Candide*, 159, 161–62, 166, *167*, 168, *169*, 170–71, 173–74

Walker, A. G., 208n4

The imagined moment : time, narrative, and computation

PN3352.T5/M35/2010   jgsu